Dec. 2016

To Dad

Happy Birthday!
with love
from
Anna
xxx

# *just a simple seaman*

*An autobiography by no one famous*

ANDREW PARKS

*AuthorHouse™*
*1663 Liberty Drive*
*Bloomington, IN 47403*
*www.authorhouse.com*
*Phone: 1-800-839-8640*

© *2012 by Andrew Parks. All rights reserved.*

*No part of this book may be reproduced, stored in a retrieval system, or transmitted by any means without the written permission of the author.*

*Published by AuthorHouse 04/05/2012*

*ISBN: 978-1-4670-1394-9 (sc)*
*ISBN: 978-1-4670-1395-6 (e)*

*For Fiona*

*Fiona, you are the first of our grandchildren to reach the age of twenty-one and you asked me to write a book for you for your twenty-first birthday. You said wanted to read of mischief when I was a child and something of the adventures I have experienced since. Well, here it is—or the first part.*

*This book covers only the time until I met Granny but there is more to come. I hope you will enjoy reading it as I hope that your sister, cousins and others in the family will too.*

*As it is you, Fi, that finally spurred me on to write something I had only idly considered before, this is dedicated to you with love.*

# ACKNOWLEDGEMENTS

Whenever I have written reports and other longer items (and there have been a few over the years!) and then tried to proofread them, mistakes have passed un-noticed. I believe this is because I have only been reading only what I *think* I have written. It was therefore imperative that someone should cast an expert eye over these texts.

In this, I have been very fortunate. My friend Robina Bourne, retired from teaching English, kindly undertook the task.

Thank you, Robina. I hope my grammar 'n other errors ain't made you cringe too much!

My thanks go also to Joan Reed who was my English teacher at Frome Grammar School. Miss Reed read the manuscript and reminded me of some elements of grammar she had taught me which I had forgotten!

Finally, thanks to my wife Ruth. Without her encouragement and tolerance when I have absented myself for long periods to work at my computer, this project would not have been completed.

Andrew Parks
October 2011

# INTRODUCTION

I suppose that in most families the younger generation love to hear stories of their parents' childhood. They seem to particularly delight in hearing of misdeeds, mischief and misfortunes, and very likely empathise with being told off for being naughty themselves. Probably they enjoy hearing, too, of adventures and experiences later in their parents' lives.

My own family is no exception and when our girls were younger, there were always favourite stories that they wanted to hear time and again. Usually, they were those that told of me being in trouble for one or another reason, but often of just being mischievous. They also liked me to recount stories of my experiences at sea, which they regarded as adventures and now often ask me to tell these stories to their children.

'Dad, tell them about the time Uncle Steve broke down the garage doors.' Or, 'Has Granddad told you about the time they had a serious fire on board his ship?'

Indeed, the grandchildren themselves now sometimes ask for favourite stories to be repeated to the extent that I have been encouraged to try to compile some record, which will be easiest in the form of a biography.

Now some two years into my retirement, I can look back over the years and think how very fortunate I have been in so many ways, my wife, family, health and, importantly, in my occupation. It is well over fifty years ago that I, as an excited sixteen-year-old joined my first ship—but more of that later.

In our modern era, many employees work in jobs that they dislike. Sunday evening may be a time of wishing they did not have to return to work the next morning. There is often an underlying fear that they may be made redundant, 'Let go,' as our American cousins say, which always sounds to me rather more like some unfortunate being suspended over an abyss. Employees may feel dissatisfied with their remuneration and often have little or no loyalty towards their employer. After all, why should they? Many modern employers show little concern or loyalty toward the employee. Targets and profit margins drive everything. Even the employees themselves are now dehumanised and are but a 'resource'.

Seafaring is rapidly becoming like that too. It is changing, with cost cutting and crew reductions constantly eroding the conditions we used to enjoy while significantly increasing the workload of the modern seafarer.

Whenever I have met contemporaries in recent times, it has been natural to reminisce. 'Slopping salt water around,' we call it. My wife avers we are just gossiping, but whatever, we have invariably concluded that we 'Have seen the best of it.'

Just a few years ago, while sailing off the coast of Oman, I was stood on the bridge wing in the afternoon sun talking with the Second Officer, a man of similar age to myself who remembered the hey days of the Merchant Navies. Hermann's story, while it may be a tad apocryphal, does illustrate rather well the extent to which things have changed.

As a younger officer sailing on Dutch ships he had experienced similar standards to those I had seen in the

British Merchant Navy. Captains in those days always had their own personal steward or butler, often referred to as The Old Man's Tiger.

He recounted how one captain he had sailed with had decided that his life was too sedentary and that he needed to take more exercise. The solution, the captain decided, was to purchase a rowing machine. All went well for a few days until one lunchtime, Hermann had taken the captain's daily chit showing the ship's noon position and distance run down to the captain's cabin.

'I could hardly believe it,' Hermann told me. 'There was the Old Man relaxing in the rowing machine with a large pink gin in his hand. Sitting cross-legged between his knees in a lather and rowing like hell, was his tiger!'

Yes, we have seen the best of it.

Now, the younger generation of seafarers look on in disbelief when told of the standards of the past, some of which I will attempt to describe when recounting my early days at sea.

Although there have been occasions when I may have wished I was somewhere else—as when docking a ship in a force ten storm and worrying about the possibility of damage to the vessel and for passenger safety—generally I have enjoyed all the things I have done in my working life, and that has included some periods working ashore.

I qualified the statement with 'generally' as there was one exception. I had returned to working in London after a spell with a major civil engineering project in the Middle East. The shipping company I returned to London to work for had engaged me as their Marine Personnel Manager. I put up with the rudeness and tantrums of the Managing Director for only about one month before telling him that I was unhappy with the organisation and intended to leave. He started to rant and told me that it was not permitted for me to quit because I was still on a probationary status. I pointed out that as far as I was concerned, so was the company and so was he. I walked out leaving him shouting at a closed door.

I was lucky. I could return to seafaring and lost no time in doing so! Many are not so fortunate now as to have such an option.

During my working time at sea, I have had adventures and experiences so divers and so very different from many working ashore that I hope recounting a few of them may give some small enjoyment—at least to the family. I have been told so many times that a 'Seafarer always has stories to tell.'

I will strive to tell them well.

*Andrew Parks,*
*October 2010*

## CHAPTER 1
# EARLY MEMORIES

### *About the families, first the Parks*

My father, William Parks, was the eldest of five: William, Violet, Fred, Horace and Hilda. He was born in 1910 at Royston, near Barnsley.

My grandfather, also William, worked all his life in collieries in the Barnsley area. He was originally a joiner who specialised in constructing pit headstocks in days when they were primarily built of pitch pine. Later, he became a foreman ganger responsible for teams of Irish labourers when pit shafts were dug by hand. By all accounts, it was no mean task. The labourers worked hard and drank hard and disputes were often settled with the flat of a shovel. Very many years later, I was both surprised and privileged to be shown a display of leather-bound ledgers that recorded in detail the sinking of some of the Monckton shafts.

One of them related to a shaft that Granddad Parks had been responsible for and was written as diary recording the progress and the materials removed each day as the sinking progressed. It described in detail the type of material removed—stone, sand, shale, et cetera—with illustrations drawn in the margin. Each of the copperplate entries was signed: *W$^m$ Parks*.

He spent the last few years of his working life driving a steam winding engine, a much respected position as the safety of the face workers depended on the winder's skills and the speed at which he hoisted cages up and down the shafts. (Thirty feet per second for men, twice that when winding only tubs of coal.)

I remember the excitement when as a small child of around seven, Father took me to visit the colliery. When we went to the winding house I stood alongside Granddad as he sat in the winder's chair, throwing levers to control an enormous steam engine. There was a bell system, jangling, telegraphing information from the pit bottom, and a very large circular dial with a pointer showing the location of the cages. The noise and hissing of steam as the engine began to move at Granddad's behest was rather frightening but when the engine was at full speed it was awesome.

We also visited one of the huge fan rooms where I was shown how a special flashing light was used to inspect the fan blades. By changing the speed at which it flashed, it could also make the fan appear to go backwards. This really was magic to a small boy! It was my father's way of introducing me to simple processes. It is my earliest memory of becoming interested in technical matters and it gave me the glimmering of understanding stroboscopic effect and why the wagon wheels in cowboy films often seemed to go backwards.

Monckton Pit had its own steam-driven power generating plant and Granddad often told the story of when they had steeplejacks working at the top of the chimneys repairing the brickwork. When they were in the canteen, the steeplejacks were asking what it was like working at the coalface.

'I'll arrange to take you below, if you like,' offered Granddad.

'Not a chance!' was the unanimous and unequivocal response. Apparently, they were entirely at ease walking around the rim of a chimney two hundred feet in the air (and there was no Health and Safety Executive to insist on safety harnesses in those days), but the prospect of descending some fourteen hundred feet underground was most decidedly not on.

Granddad Parks was a smart man. When he was not working, he was always dressed in a suit, wore gleaming black ankle boots and would never venture out, except when working, without his Homburg hat. To the day he died, then well into his eighties, he had a fine head of wavy white hair and my father always maintained this was due to 'Young Horace and the Homburg.'

When the family were young, their summer holidays consisted of day outings to Bridlington or Scarborough. Even when they were on the beach Granddad would be fully attired in customary suit and hat. Father claimed that when infant Horace, the youngest brother, soiled his nappy, his mother would roll it up and pass it to his father. My father's story of Granddad Parks lifting his hat, placing the dirty napkin on his head, replacing the Homburg and walking from the beach to dispose of its contents always raised a tolerant smile from Uncle Horace.

My father had followed in Granddad Parks' footsteps and on leaving school served an apprenticeship as a joiner. He later went on to further studies, particularly mathematics which he taught for a short time before qualifying as a Municipal Engineer. He then left the colliery environment entirely, taking up a position as assistant to the Surveyor for the Urban District Council in Bridport, Dorset. Thence for his entire working life, he remained in Local Government.

I was aware of Father having lived and worked in Bridport, where he met my mother, but I did not find out about his having served a joinery apprenticeship until well after he had retired. He never talked of it. It was his younger brother who eventually told me the story.

Just about the time Dad was completing his apprenticeship at the colliery, Uncle Horace divulged, Father and a close pal from boyhood, also an apprentice joiner, were working from the roof of a cage near the top of the pit shaft. Horace was not quite clear of the exact circumstances but evidently there was a horrific accident and Father's boyhood mate tumbled from the cage. Father heard him shouting and screaming as he fell over a thousand feet to the pit bottom.

From that day, my father never returned to the colliery.

Many years later when taking one of my brothers to the cemetery in Royston to visit Granddad Parks' grave, we came across another headstone not too distant. It was engraved: *From all his mates at Monckton pit bottom.* The dates were about right for it to have been the resting place of Dad's pal.

I can empathise with Father who never talked of the accident. When I was only sixteen and on my first voyage to sea, under rather similarly tragic circumstances, one of my cabin mates lost his life as a consequence of falling into one the cargo holds. Like myself, he was an apprentice navigator—but more of this later.

My father was always clever with his hands and had a comprehensive kit of woodworking tools. Later, my brother Stephen and I often wondered that he had a locked chest in the garage with so many tools. None of our pal's dads did. Even as a very small child in Ledbury, I remember his trying to teach me to use a wooden smoothing plane. I remember it well because I dropped the accursed thing on my foot!

My grandma Parks' parents kept a public house in Royston and, I was told, Grandfather Dickinson also ran something of a bare-knuckle boxing academy.

## *As to the Balson family*

Another large family for Mother, Aileen, too, who was one of five but in her case all sisters: Olive, Kathleen, Doris, Aileen and Joan. She was born at New Close farm, Dottery, on the outskirts of Bridport in 1913. Her father, farmer William Balson, died long before I was born but I was seven years old when Granny Balson passed away in 1948. At that time, she was living with us and we had moved from Ledbury to Warminster.

As a child, I was often told I was a favourite with Granny Balson (even though Father had disagreed with her over the choice of my Christian names—of which more later!). My Prayer Book and Bible were given to me not long before she died and inscribed:

*To Andrew Parks March 21$^{st}$ 1947, given to him by his Gran. A B Balson.*

(Most of my generation had their own Bible and Prayer Book, often given at baptism. The practice started to die when the Church of England decided the Book of Common Prayer was no longer acceptable and had to be revised, with the consequence that now no two churches seem to use the same order of service—or even the same wording for the Lord's Prayer or the Apostles Creed.)

On my first birthday, Granny Balson gave me an antique child's rocking chair. Well over sixty years later, I still have it and it has been the model for at least a dozen copies I have made for Godchildren and others. Shortly before the family moved from Ledbury, she also gave me my first two-wheeled bicycle.

It replaced a tricycle that Father had made which I had outgrown. The tricycle was made primarily of wood and had black garden hosepipe nailed around the rim of the wheels to serve as tyres. The crank pedals on the front wheel and the steering bracket had been forged by the local blacksmith. He had a son of a similar age and two such trikes were made, father doing the woodwork, the blacksmith fabricating the steel parts. A co-operative.

The acquisition of the two-wheeler was quite an achievement, given the shortage of such items in the years following the war! The bike, a dark red BSA with curved, twin-tube crossbars, was subsequently also used by brother Stephen, cousin Chester Jefferies and was only scrapped after use by my youngest brother, William. I very much doubt that a bicycle made today could withstand the successive and hard use of four young boys!

## *Wartime Ledbury*

My birth town of Ledbury is a small market town in Herefordshire, quaintly picturesque with a number of black and white, half-timbered buildings dotted around the town centre. The summer of nineteen forty-one, when I was born, was a time of considerable national austerity.

The country was in the grips of World War Two and many things were in short supply—or not available at all. The population had been issued with ration books and gas masks and food and clothing could only be purchased in exchange for coupons. It was a time of make-do and mend when nothing was discarded if it could possibly be re-used or in some way re-cycled especially clothing and fabrics. Even the material from an airman's parachute was considered a prize and much sought after.

Everyone was encouraged to 'do their bit' for Britain and be as self-sufficient as possible. 'Dig for victory.' Flowerbeds and lawns were dug up in favour of cultivating fruit and vegetables and my parents, as did many other families in those times, kept a few chicken.

One bird from the small flock of chicken, a red hen, had been adopted as my pet and named Marmalade. Supposedly many of the boiled eggs I enjoyed dipping with 'soldiers' as a toddler were courtesy of Marmalade—until the day my father came into the house carrying a very limp hen. He told me that the bird was so stupid it had strangled itself. He went on to explain that he thought poor Marmalade had reached through the chicken wire of her run for a nearby tasty worm but instead of then withdrawing back, had put her head through an adjacent hole and in the ensuing struggle to free herself, broken her neck. As I said, nothing was wasted and the bird ended up on the table. It was many years later that I realised Father had told me this tale rather than upset me by admitting to pulling the bird's neck when it was no longer an egg producer and of value only for the pot.

For a while, we also had a pet dog, a black Labrador named Mickey. In those days, the butcher and other tradesmen would deliver their wares to customers' houses. Usually this was by a junior member of staff—the 'butcher's boy'—riding a specially constructed bicycle. It had a small front wheel with a large frame mounted above wherein a wicker basket for goods was carried.

Mickey, who it would seem, had evidently sussed the delivery routines, planned an ambush. He lay in waiting near the corner of the house until he saw the butcher's delivery boy riding down the road. As the bike approached, Mickey bounded down the path, leapt the gate and crashed into the bike. The collision caused the delivery boy to wobble, then fall from the cycle with the contents of the basket being scattered across the road. It had been carefully planned and this was Mickey's chance. He seized the largest piece of meat he could carry and made off down the road to consume it in some safe hideaway.

He got away with stealing someone's meat ration once. The second time was once too often. He had to leave home and I never saw him again.

## *Birth Certificate, Baptism and In-laws*

It was several years later when I needed access to my birth certificate to apply for my seaman's papers that I found out how, shortly after my birth, my father had been caught in the crossfire between his mother and his mother-in-law.

In Mother's family, the Balsons, Simon had become a favoured family name and in Father's, the family name was William. Indeed, it was both his and my grandfather's given name. Not surprisingly, my registered names were both these family names, Simon William, but a little later, I had been baptised—christened—as Graham Andrew. Both sets of names are clearly recorded on my birth certificate.

When I asked how this could be, Father explained that when he and Mother had planned to used the family names, William and Simon, he had really wanted to use his family name as the first name because I was the first male grandchild of my generation in his family. When this was suggested, he hadn't foreseen the bickering that ensued between my two grandmothers. The matriarchs were unable to agree which name should be first. It was typical of Dad that he put a stop to it by using neither.

But this still didn't explain why I have always been called Andrew, never Graham. I had left home and been at sea for two or three years before this was resolved.

Dad was always interested in my literary education and would usually ask me when I came on leave, what books I had read while away at sea. On one occasion, I told him of one I had particularly enjoyed reading: *The Citadel*, by A J Cronin.

He started to smile before divulging, 'Your mother was reading it when you were an infant.' She had, Dad said, been particularly taken by the name Andrew, after the hero of the book, Doctor Andrew Manson.

## *The Aussies thought they discovered going walkabout...*

It wasn't exactly that I ran away; I went out on explorations.

Of course, there was very little traffic indeed on the roads in the nineteen forties—and many of the few who owned a car, had very little fuel to use—so a three or four year old child was relatively safe and parents were not unduly concerned if one went out exploring for a while.

My first recollection of being somewhere where I shouldn't have been was when I became involved in a funeral party, although I had no idea what it was at the time.

On the opposite side of the road and not too far from home, was a cemetery that also had a small chapel. I had been wandering among the gravestones minding my own business, when many people began arriving. Naturally curious and wanting some of the action that may be going, I followed them into the chapel. I was causing some commotion dodging among a forest of black trouser legs to avoid be caught when an angry lady, also dressed in black, managed to grab me. I was extricated from the chapel, by the ear I think. As she dragged me back home, I thought she was probably a witch anyway. Mother was more embarrassed than angry at what I had done.

On another occasion, I ventured much further afield. Mother and Dad had some friends, Mr and Mrs James, who had a farm two miles or so down the road.

I knew where it was because I remembered being there before and having my photograph taken sitting atop the head of their bull and holding on to his horns. I thought it would be nice to go and visit on my own so off I went.

I don't remember whether or not they were surprised to see me, but I do remember being later scolded and told off by Mother.

It wasn't because I had run away. I hadn't. Not really. It was for something I had said to Mrs James. Evidently, when I turned up, she had telephoned Mother to tell her where I was and to reassure her that I was safe.

While waiting for me to be collected, Mrs James kindly asked if I would like a nice boiled egg for tea. I remembered that I had had one of their lovely brown eggs with crusty soldiers smothered in farm butter when I visited before.

'Yea, please' I replied. 'I'll have two.'

It was the latter bit which got me into trouble. I thought this was unfair because Mrs James couldn't stop laughing when she told Mother.

But I did enjoy the two eggs.

Some way up New Street, towards Ledbury, there was Taylor's Garage. I quite often went there because I knew the mechanics really needed and valued my help.

On one occasion, I was present when they were receiving their pay packets. As a regular spanner-passer, I thought it was time I had some wages too and asked for my pay packet. I was given two shiny washers.

When I arrived home, I proffered them to Mother, priding myself on using grown-up language like the men at the garage.

'Two bloody bob for a whole bloody afternoon bloody working!'

And I got into trouble for that, too—but it was as nothing compared to the event that finally put paid to me visiting the garage.

Petrol was in short supply and strictly rationed. So, on a subsequent visit to Taylor's Garage when wages were mentioned I said I would take some petrol instead.

One of the mechanics took an empty pop bottle and as I watched him filling it from the hand pump over the sink in the yard, he reassured me, 'This is far better stuff than that we sell out the front.'

Naturally, he was telling the truth and I later proudly presented the bottle of 'petrol' to Dad. He realised that it wasn't fuel but went along with the charade by telling me I had better go and put it in the car, although he evidently had some doubts.

'... but I don't suppose you can get the petrol cap off.'

"Course I can,' I had replied.

Apparently, he was so certain that I would not succeed that when I returned to the house with the empty bottle he was convinced I had poured the contents away rather than admit Dad was right and the fuel cap had defeated me.

The following day, we were well on the way to Hereford when the car stuttered a few times and then lurched to a standstill. I had never seen my father so angry—and his ire was made no less when Granny Balson who was in the car with us, stood up for me.

'William, it's your own silly fault,' she pointed out. 'You told him to do it.'

I think I said before that I was considered Granny Balson's 'favourite'. Mother, I realize now, wisely kept her own council.

Father was so angry at losing some of the precious fuel ration. He blamed the garage for behaving irresponsibly and insisted that problem should be resolved and the car refilled at their cost. The incident put paid to me being allowed to visit the garage again.

The petrol incident took place around the time of my brother Stephen's birth and both Granny Balson and Mother's eldest sister were staying with us. Although I can't remember the details of the petrol incident, it was Aunt Olive who, with evident enjoyment, recounted the story many times over the years; hence my knowing what was said.

The story became well known through the family and as a child, I would cringe when anyone said 'Do you remember the time when Andrew put waster in the petrol in Bill's car?' I somehow knew that it would put Dad into a bad mood.

## *An addition to the family*

I was so busy being fussed over by Granny B and Aunt Olive that I don't recall being aware that Mother had been absent for a while until she turned up again.

She and Dad arrived back home from Hereford in the car, getting out carefully carrying what I thought was a large package with handles.

'Come and meet your brother,' they invited, 'he'll be somebody for you to play with'

Evidently, I did the grown-up thing and went and vigorously shook his hand—until they told me to stop and to calm down. I thought it was all a con as he wasn't big enough to go and play with anyway.

Steve's birth date is memorable. June 6$^{th}$, 1944. D Day and I was very nearly three years old.

## *Your Country Needs You*

This was a time of conscription and able-bodied men were called into military service to fight for their country. The womenfolk did their bit too as in the case of some of my older cousins who, having been brought up on a farm became Land Army Girls. Mother, I learned later, did some ambulance driving.

Certain occupations and professions were essential for maintaining and running the country and men so employed were exempt from military call-up. Surveyor to the Urban District Council in Ledbury, Father's position, was such a 'reserved' occupation.

Feeling that he should do more for the community, Dad trained as a part-time fireman, eventually becoming the Station Officer for Ledbury.

When Bristol was being heavily bombed, fire services from other towns and cities were summoned to help and I have vague memories of this happening with assistance being sought from even as far away as Ledbury. Certainly,

I remember standing, shivering in the darkness, outside the house at night with Mother and Dad and listening to the low drone of bombers flying over. They may have been on their way too or from Hereford. My parents were clearly upset, but I did not then understand why.

On the landing of our house, there was an electric bell that was connected to the fire station. Father had devised a cunning means of knowing if there had been an alarm call should the house be empty for a period. When going out, he placed a cigarette card on top of the bell, which he immediately checked on his return. If it was still in place, all was well, but if it had fallen to the floor, there was likely a fire to fight.

## *Alarm bells and daffodils*

Much of the bombing, and hence the fires, occurred during darkness and Dad was frequently about at night. Aunt Olive, who was staying with us for a while, often pulled Dad's leg about his nocturnal movements, joking that he was going to the bathroom.

I remember her taking me into Woolworth's and buying a chamber pot. When we returned home, she and Mother carefully wrapped it, finishing the package with ribbon and a large bow. When Dad's birthday came soon after, the gift was presented to him with much laughter. Aunt Olive said that she thought it might save him having to get up so often during the night.

Dad smiled and said very little but a short while later took his revenge.

My mother, as most of her family, always enjoyed playing cards. Through some bridge-playing friends, she had been introduced to some other enthusiasts for whom she decided to have a small card party at home. She and Aunt Olive worked all afternoon eking out meagre food rations to prepare some appetising supper refreshments. Everything was carefully placed in the front room in readiness for entertaining. The grate was filled with burning logs and the room warming. A corner table had been nicely set with lace cloth and snacks and in the centre, a cut-glass vase displayed an attractive bouquet of spring flowers, mainly daffodils.

Everything was ready. Mother was set to impress the new acquaintances. When they arrived, Dad was hanging their coats in the hallway as Mother ushered them into the front room. To her extreme dismay, she quickly realised that her prized cut-glass vase was missing. The bouquet of spring flowers, though, was still in the middle of the table but now standing in a chamber pot.

Dad's description of my mother's face when she saw what he had done was, to her embarrassment, repeated many times at family gatherings. About as often as the water in the petrol tank story.

## *And so to first school*

I can remember starting school while we still lived in Ledbury but, not surprisingly, only a little of the detail.

We were, I recall, being taught to count and were starting to learn some of our tables. The teacher had drawn groups of circles on the blackboard, filled them in with different coloured chalks, and the class counted them, chanting the numbers as we went. The alphabet was taught in a similar way with large coloured letters.

But one memory remains firmly in my mind; the toilets, all two of them, standing in somewhat solitary splendour in a small outhouse in the grounds behind the school. They were, I later learned, of a type called earth closets, which does explain my rather unpleasant recollection of them.

## *Moving to Warminster*

I was five years old when the family moved from Ledbury to Warminster where Father had accepted a position as Urban District Surveyor, similar to the employment he had in Ledbury.

When we actually moved, the journey was broken with the short stop at The Cross in the centre of Gloucester. Dad parked in Southgate Street right outside a jewellers and watchmakers shop, Bakers, saying he wanted to show us something. I remember watching, enthralled, as the figures in an alcove above the shop window started to strike their bells to mark the hour. Many years later, when I was living in Gloucester, I came to know that the figures represented England, Ireland, Scotland and Wales with the fifth figure being Father Time. Gloucester was once an important manufacturer of church bells.

Our first dwelling in Warminster was a ground floor flat. Stoneleigh House, which was an imposing red brick building, had been converted into a number of apartments. It was on the same side of the road as the Church of England primary school I attended about half a mile away, St John's. Mostly, I went to and from school on my own.

At this time, I was aware that Dad was very ill and he was clutching a hot water bottle to his tummy all the time. He was eventually admitted to hospital in Bath where he underwent surgery for a duodenal ulcer and subsequently went to convalesce staying with his sister, my Aunt Vi, who had a guesthouse in Southbourne.

## *Neighbours*

Miss Stanbrook, an elderly lady, occupied one of the flats around the side of Stoneleigh House. Whenever I saw her and started to speak to her, Miss Stanbrook produced this long, shiny trumpet thing and stuck one end in her ear before bending down and thrusting the large end into my face. I couldn't understand why she didn't put it to her mouth and play it normally, the way I had seen the soldiers play bugles, but it didn't make any noise anyway.

When I asked Mother, she explained 'Miss Stanbrook is deaf. She can't hear very well and her ear-trumpet helps her. You should speak to her loudly.'

So I did—and then got told off by Mrs Anderson, a resident in one of the other flats.

'You shouldn't shout at people. It's rude.'

## *Demolition driving*

There was a corrugated iron garage at the side of Stoneleigh House where Dad used to keep the Vauxhall. Brother Stephen was not much more than a toddler when, during an inspection of the interior of the car he found a knob which when he tugged it, caused a funny noise. I told him it was the thing that made the engine start and it was the same noise the car made for Dad just before he started the engine. Of course, being nearly three years older, I naturally knew all about these things.

Cars in those days did not have complex electrics and the ignition key was literally that. It switched on the ignition system; the starter motor was completely independent.

Stephen had been telling his friend Carol Anderson—he used to call her Plumb Pudding—all about it and thought he would show her.

I was sitting on the steps outside the front door when the car appeared from around the side of the house. It was going backwards erratically but quite quickly and one of the garage doors was hanging from the back. I am not too sure whether it stopped before it hit the wall or not but Stephen and Carol climbed out just as Mother came rushing from the house.

Dad was summoned and Stephen claimed that I had told him the knob was the starter. I was beginning to find that life is not always fair and it was only one of many occasions when I was held to blame for Steve's misdeeds.

Many years later, though, Stephen had another incident with garage doors that had absolutely nothing to do with me. I was away at sea when it happened.

Steve, cousin Chester and another friend were all in their teens. Between them, they had acquired two wrecked Ford Prefect cars and were using the salvaged parts to rebuild one working banger. A garage belonging to their pal's dad was the project venue. It was one in number of lock-up garages built around three sides of a rectangle.

As soon as they had the car sufficiently assembled to give it a trial, the three lads did so, taking it in turns to race it around the enclosed space.

It is not clear who was driving when the car went out of control and walloped the front corner of one the garages. It was one in a row of about ten. The damage appeared to be insignificant—until one of the other garage users tried to open the doors. He was unable to do so and it was soon discovered, with much dismay, that his was not the only one. The entire block had been pushed from the perpendicular and none of the doors would open.

The garage complex was an amenity for some nearby council houses and thereby the property of the Local Authority. It was Father, as Surveyor, who had to mobilise labour and materials to make an emergency repair.

When I came on leave, Steve told me all about the incident. He said that Dad was not best pleased which I know was likely to have been a considerable understatement.

## *Pigs and tonsils*

Although the war was over, the country was still in the grips of shortages and many necessities remained subject to rationing. There was no possibility at Stoneleigh to supplement rationing by keeping a few hens so my father, the Chairman of The Council and some of the councillors formed a pig club.

The half a dozen or so pigs they purchased were kept at the town's sewage works. Sewage and water supply were the responsibility of the local Authority in those days and thus under Father's supervision and control. The council employee permanently stationed at the works—he was well known only by the name Stinky—had the task of feeding the pigs and looking after them. For these services, he enjoyed honorary membership of the club, participating in the benefits but without having to share in the cost of buying the animals.

About twice a year, as the pigs reached so-called bacon weight, they went for slaughter. The Ministry of Food commandeered a percentage of the outcome and the remainder was shared among the club members. Consequently, despite general food shortage, there was usually a flitch of home cured bacon hanging in our larder.

One morning, Mother was preparing breakfast and there was a wonderful aroma of frying bacon. Dad asked me to go with him while he went to buy a newspaper, which I did.

To my surprise, he took me to Warminster Hospital where I was admitted for a tonsillectomy. It took two nurses, assisted by Father, to drag me the length of the ward to my bed. I was yelling, screaming and kicking all the way.

It was not so much that I minded going into hospital. The fuss was all because I had been conned out of my breakfast and I couldn't forget the appetising smell of that home-cured bacon.

And that I found very hard to forgive!

My father's family, c 1925

Back row: Grandfather William, my father William, Fred, Violet, Grandma Edith

Front row: Horace and Hilda

Grandma Balson

My mother, Aileen Mary Balson

Granddad Parks preparing for inspection of pit shaft

Granddad used to erect pit headstocks

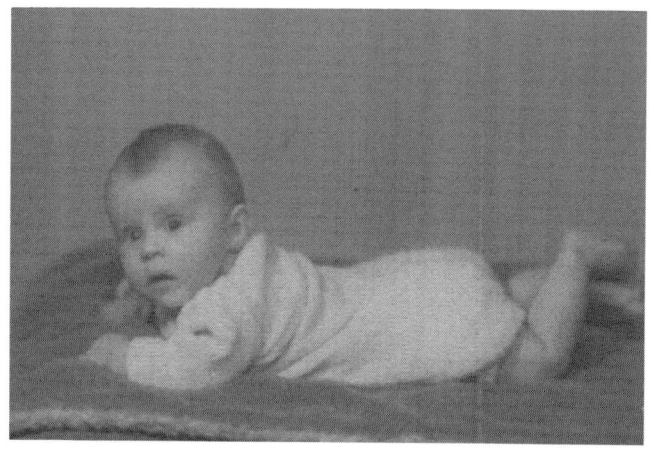

My proud parents included this with their 1941 Christmas cards!

My father made this table with the barley-twist legs

Dad with Mickey the meat thief

Paddling in the river at Toller Porcorum

My older cousins Esme and Peggy, who had been Land Army Girls, with Judith and me.

## CHAPTER 2
# PRIMARY SCHOOL DAYS

### *Moving home, gangs and holidays*

In late 1946, we moved from Stoneleigh House to a semi-detached house in an avenue off the main road and closer to the town centre. It was exciting to be moving to a house that actually had a sand pit in the garden!

There were several other children of similar age living in East End Avenue and I soon made many new friends. We formed a couple of 'gangs' but they were fun groups. Gangs were competitive but only to the extent of those really important things like who could ride his bike fastest, or climb the highest tree.

Christmas 1946 was the first Christmas I can actually remember. We spent it with mother's youngest sister, Aunt Joan and her family, who had a farm at Cranborne, near Wimborne, Dorset. My two cousins, Judith and Simon were of an age with Stephen and myself and we had great fun together. We seemed to spend most of our time either taking turns to slide down the staircase on a large tin tray or out in the granary swinging on a rope tail from the rafters. We could safely jump from the loft into the grain below, sinking almost to our waists—and the scuttling of rats bothered no one.

Granny Balson was also with us and I recall that she gave me a clockwork Hornby train set. I was the envy of many of my pals!

The days after Christmas were frosty and Uncle David fastened a sledge behind his motorbike and towed us around the lanes. I think he had as much fun as we did.

They still used horses on the farm then and his cob was Uncle David's primary means of transport. He even used his horse to go to the pub, which Aunt Joan said was good because the horse was always sober and knew the way home. This gave rise to a family saying and over the years whenever my father reversed the car into a parking space it was usually accompanied with, 'Always leave your horse facing home.'

January of 1947 saw the start of one of the worst winters recorded. Dad made toboggans for each of us—mine was bigger than Steve's of course! We were the envy of several of our friends whose Dads were not so skilled but we were all a 'gang' and shared anyway. We were supposed to confine our sledging activities to the grass hillside overlooking the park but the snow was so compacted, that roads and pavements were just as good. Also, there was the advantage that the road did not have obstacles like bramble bushes—nor was it dotted with hidden cowpats.

The bottom of the avenue, where it approached the junction onto the main road, was quite steeply sloped. One afternoon, some pals and I were taking turns to sledge down this slope and always at the last minute before reaching the main road, swerved to the right into the forecourt of Walls's Garage. At least I did—until a truck pulled from the garage forecourt just as I was approaching. Panicking and virtually losing control, I had little choice but to keep going and shot under one side of the lorry, out the other side and skittered straight across the main road, coming to a standstill in the yard of a removal company opposite. I frightened myself so much that I never told my parents. The telling off I received from the driver of the lorry was quite sufficient, I thought.

After the particularly hard winter, that summer was first of several I remember from childhood that seemed hot and long. To a small child they lasted for ever and I don't recall any time that we had to stay indoors because of rain. It seemed that from the moment school finished for the summer, we took out shirts off and didn't resume wearing them until we returned to school in the autumn. We spent the entire summer holidays in shorts and sandals—and that included some of the girls in our gangs too! There was no discrimination.

We were always cadging extra pennies to go and hire rowing boats in the park. We could all handle a skiff and the greatest fun was to see who could row the fastest. When we tired of racing the length of the lake, we devised a new game to see who the strongest rower was. This was gauged by rowing full speed at the bank or one of the islands in the lake and the champion was judged as the one who succeeded in ramming the most of his boat from the water.

We were often in trouble with the Park Keeper for these and other exploits but he and his reprimands were always respected—at least, until the next time he caught us in some or another mischief. For me, his threats 'I'll tell your father of you,' were always very real because I knew that Dad used to attend the park as part of his weekly routine. What we failed to realise at first was that as long as we were behaving, if there was little demand for the skiffs, the park keeper would often 'forget' to call us in when our time was up.

## Cubs and choristers

We were never bored. Three of us were accepted into St John's Church Choir as probationers. Several of us boys joined the Wolf Cubs and the girls went off to join the Brownies. We wore our Wolf Cub lapel badges proudly and when King George VIth died, someone suggested it would be appropriate to wear the badges upside down.

Choir practices were fun but when the choirmaster, Mr House, caught us with peashooters firing elderberries at each other across the chancel, he threatened to expel us. Fortunately, he did not, nor did he carry out his threat to tell our parents for had they seen the dark red stains on the oak choir stalls made by the ripe berries, there would have been serious repercussions. With hindsight, I realise this may have been because one of the boys involved was his elder son, Peter. To my certain knowledge, the stains were still visible some ten years later and possibly still are.

In due turn, brother Stephen joined the choir too. Although I cannot remember the occasion, Father liked to tell of meeting us as we came from the vestry one morning. It was after one of Steve's first attendances at Matins and Dad claimed to have overheard him ask one of the other boy choristers, 'When they came round with that pouch, I managed to get tuppence. How much did you get out?'

I was about ten when I was allocated one of the readings at the Christmas nine-lesson Carol Service. My reading was that telling of the Angel appearing to Mary. For some reason, Mother was not entirely happy about my reading that phrase about Mary conceiving and bearing a child. Nevertheless, she was in church when I stood nervously on the chancel steps and misread, 'Hail, thou that art highly flavoured in the eyes of the Lord . . .'

About this time Bobby Still and I, the third chorister who had joined at the same time as I, became head choirboys. We sat facing each other, one each side of the chancel.

In our youthful impatience, the sermons seemed interminable—and probably were. (Then as now, did someone say?) To alleviate our boredom we learned the deaf and dumb sign alphabet and passed time 'talking' to each other as we practised our newly acquired skill.

I know it irritated some of the others, who just had to sit in their customary silent inattentiveness, especially our first lady chorister. She was a large woman who sang alto and would glower at us with an expression of disapproval that could have stripped paint. Bobby and I didn't care. When she glowered at us, we just talked about her—but we had to be careful what we signalled to each other in case it should be the cause of an uncontrolled smile. Or worse, a snigger of laughter for she would surely have known who we were laughing at because we reckoned the hearing aid she wore didn't work very well, judging by the way she sang.

It was about that time that I heard Mother first tell a story about a deaf lady who had a huge family of ten or so children.

The story was always told in a broad Dorset dialect. When the deaf lady, so the story went, reached the milestone of her ninetieth birthday she was being interviewed by the local press. The reporter asked how she came to have so many children, to which she replied, 'Were in they days afore we 'ad these new-fangled yerin aids. When we went a bed, my ubbie used a say to I "Shall we go a sleep or what?" and I alles replied "Whaat?" as I cudn't yer 'n proper.'

So what, I thought, is funny in that? The story always produced gales of laughter and I concluded that the strangest things amused grown-ups. I also had the feeling it might have had something to do with a friend of Mother's. She was deaf and a mean spirited woman whose Scotty dog was equally mean spirited. Whenever I went near it, the dog would bare its teeth and snarl for no apparent reason—unless it was because it was aware of my thoughts. I would cheerfully have kicked the cur if I had thought I could get away with it.

Doris Hedges and I had an un-shakeable, mutual dislike of each other. As far as I was concerned, what had been a mild dislike had been irrevocably escalated on the occasion she took Mother, Stephen and me to fetch some dog meat from a slaughterhouse on the outskirts of town. It was bad enough visiting such a noxious place but, unheard by my Mum, she hissed a threat at me. She said she would like to put me out of her car and leave me with the blood-covered slaughter men to be turned into dog meat. I was about six years old and terrified. I never forgave her for it. She was, I recall, unmarried and would have been called a woman of independent means—at least I never heard that she worked, but that, I suppose could have been because there was no broomstick factory in Warminster.

## *Change of school*

In the interim, I had reached the age of changing from St. John's Infants' School to attending The Close Primary School, situated at almost the opposite end of town. Nevertheless, except on market days, I was usually permitted to cycle to school with some of my classmates even though this meant passing through the main part of the town. There is no doubt that we were all proficient cyclists—we rode for miles in the lanes and in the woods playing follow-my-leader—but it is more indicative of the lack of traffic. Also, which might surprise today's young people, wherever you left your bike, you could be sure of it still being there on your return. We had no need to lock our bikes; indeed, we had no means of doing so.

The main part of the Close school was a collection of older buildings along one side of a narrow one-way street. On the opposite side was Warminster's fire station and it was quite usual for lessons to be disrupted by the fire siren. The station was un-manned and volunteers (of which our choirmaster was one) provided the service. The siren would only be turned off when one of the firemen arrived at the station. In those days before political correctness, the designation of fire-fighter was un-necessary as the volunteers were all men. (I am only thankful that the daftness of modern PC has not required that they all be called fire fighting persons. Or not yet, anyway.)

At The Close, we were all being crammed in preparation for the dreaded Eleven Plus Examination and discipline was much stricter than that at the infants' school.

The headmaster, Mr Brody, would often walk around with a cane tucked down his trouser leg. When he opened his jacket to tuck his hands into his waistcoat pockets, the cane became conspicuous by the handle looped over the waistband of his trousers. The gesture usually spelled trouble for someone, although to be truthful, the cane was seldom used. Its ominous presence was sufficient.

One morning after we had all sung the daily hymn and said prayers, Mr Brody dismissed all the girls, instructing the boys to remain. Fingers in his waistcoat pockets, thumbs outside, the cane handle was threateningly visible and he was very evidently displeased about something.

He looked sternly at us assembled boys, pacing up and down for a few moments before beginning, 'I am aware that when in the toilets some of you boys have been playing a game which, for the want of a better name, we shall call higher and higher. You know what I am referring to, boys,' he stated, sternly. 'Consider the competition—if that it what it was—to have been finally won. This game *will* cease,' Mr Brody ordered

The boys' toilets at The Close were in a lean-to along the side of the main building and there was a gap between the top of the wall and the roof. Apparently, one of the teachers, Miss Petty, a rather plump and kindly teacher whom we all liked, had been passing when someone actually managed to reach the gap under the roof and cleared the wall, urinating into the playground outside.

The culprit was never publicly identified and no one received any punishment but looking back on the incident, I have to admire Mr Brody. That he was able to handle the admonition without even the least hint of a smile must have needed the most rigorous self-control. Perhaps when he spent those few moments pacing and glowering at us assembled boys, he was actually using the time to compose himself and muster that self-control.

## *The Maltings*

One of my closest pals, Malcolm, lived almost opposite our house. We thought his parents were just like mine. Strict. Of course, at that age we didn't understand the concept of *caring* parents. Whenever we were refused something that some of the other children we played with were permitted, I am sure we responded n the age-old way, 'It's not fair!' Children's cinema on a Saturday afternoon always required special permission but Malcolm and I thought we had developed a good ruse.

In the morning, the pair of us would go and see Malcolm's mother. 'Andrew is allowed to go to the cinema this afternoon,' Malcolm would say, 'but only if I can go with him.' Mrs Davies would then grant permission, usually with an admonition to come straight home afterwards. Safety in numbers, we thought.

Next stop, across the road to my house where we told my mother the same story. We thought we were really clever, playing one parent against the other. Now, though, I am quite certain they both knew what we were up to and probably assented with tolerant amusement.

Malcolm's Dad was employed by Arthur Guinness and Co and worked in a laboratory adjacent to maltings near the town centre.

Although my memories of childhood summers are mainly of long, sunny days I also recall a few occasions when it actually rained and we couldn't all be out playing as a gang. Cooped indoors Malcolm and I would eventually, tire of playing with our train sets and other toys and of being housebound. Although Malcolm's mother was always patient with our complaints and generous with orange squash and biscuits, I am sure she in turn also tired of our constant moaning, 'We're bored. What can we do?'

'Put your coats and Wellingtons on and take Sherry out,' she would suggest. Sherry was their golden Labrador who would respond by enthusiastically wagging her tail. 'No, it's boring.' (Children haven't changed.)

One such day, we had parted company and I returned home for lunch. I had barely finished when Malcolm arrived at the door and excitedly told me 'Dad says we can go back to the laboratory with him this afternoon!'

It was the first of a number of such occasions. Mr Davies showed us how to use a binocular microscope. He taught us how to focus the instrument by setting the object lens very close to the slide table and then winding it out as to do it the other way would likely break the slide and possibly damage the microscope. He sent us out to collect water from rain puddles or the water butt which we then examined. We looked at hair, blood, the eye of a needle, a maggot (not quite sure where we got that from) and anything else small enough to be worthy of our investigation. We were even introduced to diatoms. It was really exciting and looking back on those days we were very fortunate. Not many parents would have trusted two small boys with such a valuable instrument.

We were given a note book which we carefully labelled 'Malcolm and Andrew's Lab-Book' wherein we were encouraged to make notes and drawings of things we observed. Using a monocular microscope, Mr Davies showed us how to make sketches by alternately blinking one eye while looking onto the microscope with one eye and at the notebook alongside with the other. It was a simple trick and one which many years later was to proved useful when studying plankton off the west coast of America—but more of that later.

I was a teenager when I learned what Malcolm's dad's job really was. He was a Botanist and Research Geneticist employed to develop strains of barley. The objective was to produce barley with a high resistance to mould giving a high grain yield for making malt.

Who thinks genetically modified crops are a new innovation?

## *My Brother Stephen*

I have already commented that there were many occasions on which I was held to account for Steve's misdeeds (of which more later), but there were occasions when he managed to get himself into Father's bad books entirely without my aid.

He became very friendly with an Irish boy who lived just down the road. Steve and Johnny Whelan were catalysts, each bringing out the mischief in the other. They both ran away on several occasions and I remember returning from Wolf Cubs one evening when there was a major search going on for the two boys, which involved most of the parents in the neighbourhood.

There had been an American rodeo visiting the town football ground for a one-night show. It was well after dark when the errant lads returned home. They had been to the show and my father was even more furious when they admitted they had gained admission by crawling through the hedge.

Life was most unfair, I thought. I had asked to go to the rodeo but was firmly told that it was Cub night and I could not just take a night off because there was somewhere more exciting to be. I felt really rather bitter when I got to the scout hut and there were but six or so of us. Everyone else was at the football ground.

Steve and I were taught to share things and even our carefully garnered rations of sweeties had to be offered around when there were visitors.

Steve devised a solution.

When the occasion arose, he would surreptitiously remove all but two or three sweets from the bag before proffering it. His generosity was invariably declined. 'Thank you, no. You only have one or two left. I couldn't possibly take one of your last ones.' Eventually, he was careless enough to let Dad see what was going on and that was the end of his ruse.

There was, though, one piece of mischief I admit to putting Steve up to. Two elderly spinster sisters, the Misses Lyons, lived not far from St John's Church in what had once been a tollhouse. It projected out onto the pavement slightly giving a view along the pavement in both directions from the hallway. One lady, Alice, was very quiet and seldom spoke to any of us boys but her sister, whom we thought spent most of her time sitting in the hallway watching the pavement, would tell us off for the most minor infringement. A crooked tie was irresistible and would always be grasped and pulled straight with an appropriate admonition.

Steve and I cruelly thought we should have some fun at Miss Lyons' expense. We obtained a length of cotton. I borrowed one of Mother's sewing needles and carefully threaded the cotton through the shoulder seam on Steve's coat. A short end was left hanging outside, the remainder carefully coiled and concealed inside the coat.

We thought that if we made a little noise as we walked up the pavement Miss Lyons would come out to see what mischief we might be engaged in. In her view, small children, most especially boys, were never *not* involved in some misdeed or another. We also felt certain, that once she saw it, the cotton end would be irresistible.

We were correct. 'What is this?' Miss Lyons asked imperiously as she plucked at the offending thread.

We struggled to keep straight faces as looking more and more dismayed, she continued to pull a seemingly un-ending length of cotton from the shoulder seam of Steve's coat. Undoubtedly she was beginning to wonder what she had done and at what stage the seam would totally unravel and the sleeve fall off. Eventually, we could contain our mirth no longer and had to run for it. We left Miss Lyons shaking her head, looking puzzled and holding three or four yards of cotton in her hand.

That was the first occasion when we tried that trick and it never failed. Looking back on it, the prank was probably a lesson in psychology as we could usually identify those people unable to resist such things and unable to keep their hands to themselves.

A few years later though, the quieter sister, Alice, had passed away and the surviving Miss Lyons had invited me to tea. While sitting with her, I came to realise that she was really a rather nice lady, a kindly soul but quite likely somewhat lonely. Mother first fostered this notion when she told me that after the death of her sister Alice, Miss Lyons was alone in the world with no other family. I don't remember why she had invited me to tea but I did enjoy the occasion, and even though it was something of a well-deserved lesson in humility for me, I actually became quite fond of her and we would often have a natter whenever I was passing the tollhouse.

Miss Lyons' perception of small boys and mischief was probably borne of long experience. After all, she had once been an infants' schoolteacher and Steve and I had done nothing to persuade her that she may have been mistaken.

## *Visiting family*

The annual summer visit to our grandparents at Royston in Yorkshire was decidedly not an occasion that Stephen and I wholeheartedly enjoyed.

There is no doubt that the small market town of Warminster was a very pleasant place in which to spend our childhood. Even though it was a garrison town with a large transient military population, there was seldom any trouble with soldiers. On the few occasions that I can remember stories of scuffles in town, local youths (who invariably came off worse!) had usually provoked it.

The surrounding countryside had lots of woodland to explore and the nearby estate of the Marquis of Bath had a very large lake in which we used to swim. During the summer holidays, groups of us would often disappear all day on our bikes. Parents never seemed worried. They knew the truth of safety in numbers—also that hunger or darkness would eventually bring us home.

On the duty visit to Royston, we missed all this; we missed our friends too, and the two hundred mile journey north seemed interminable. The further north we travelled, the more the houses in the towns seemed to crowd closer and closer together and become progressively more drab and soot-stained.

Of course, we looked forward to seeing Grandma and Granddad Parks but Royston was a small grubby colliery town. There was a permanent and pervasive odour of coal gas from nearby Monckton Colliery coking ovens and everything was grimed with smuts of black dust. To make matters even worse, some upright and God-fearing residents of Royston insisted that the swings and roundabout in the play area of the local park were chained and locked on Sunday. Heaven forbid that children should enjoy themselves at play on the Sabbath day!

Twice while on the annual visits to Royston, Dad took Mother off to attend a conference of Municipal Engineers, leaving us behind for nearly a week. Granddad Parks was still working as a winder and absent on shift work for much of the time so Grandma often took us out for picnics or on the bus to Roundhay Park in Leeds. Steve and I enjoyed these outings and riding on the trams in Leeds but I do remember once or twice when we misbehaved

Grandma had threatened, 'Your Granddad will fetch Toby to you when he gets home.' Toby, we knew, was the name of his razor strop hanging behind the kitchen door. 'Your father will remember what Toby feels like,' she continued. 'He and your uncle Fred had a taste from time to time.' That thought alone was sufficient to ensure that we ceased misbehaving forthwith.

On one occasion, the conference was in the Isle of Man and within a day or two of Mother and Dad leaving, we received a postcard from them. It was a picture of the ferry 'Manxman' in which they had made the crossing to Douglas. I remember being quite frightened at the thought of their journey and thinking that I should not like to be on anything with so much water beneath in case it sank. I could never have believed then, as a small boy, that I should spend much of my life travelling the oceans of the world!

How different, then, to other holidays in the summer when, as a small child, I had gone to stay with one of Mother's elder sisters, Aunt Doris, on the farm at Toller Porcorum in Dorset. Mother would drive me down in her green Austin Ruby. Steve sat on the passenger seat while I stood up with my head and shoulders out of the roof trying to catch my breath in the wind and waving at anyone we passed.

The farmhouse at Toller was attached to a mill that straddled a small stream from nearby water meadows. There was a sluice under the mill that my older cousin Jimmy would sometimes close, leaving fishing lines in the mill pool to hook trout. He also kept ferrets for catching rabbits, but my memory of eating rabbit is one accompanied by a warning not to eat any of the lead pellets from the shotgun cartridge.

On one occasion, Cousin Judith (from Cranbourne) was also staying and we were in trouble for our table manners when we had a competition spitting lead pellets at the roasting tin.

Judith and I had great fun in the river at the back of the mill when Aunt Doris' elder daughter Peggy, who was much older than Judith and me, fetched the tin bath from the farmhouse. It made a great boat, even though it was rather unstable and we spent as much time in the river as on it.

There were several horses on the farm. The daily trip with Peggy's brother Jimmy, when he drove a horse and cart down the track with the milk churns, was an eagerly awaited treat. There was a special platform at the roadside from which the milk was collected.

When they were harvesting, Jimmy often took me on his knee as he sat on the cast iron seat and drove the horse-drawn binder but what I most enjoyed was sitting way up on top of all the sheaves carried on the large four-wheeled cart as the harvest was brought down from the steep hillside fields for threshing. Uncle Jack always drove the big cart. It was painted blue and red with white lettering on tailboard, 'John Powell and Sons'.

There was a widow living in one of the farm cottages near the milking parlour. She had a daughter somewhat older than me. 'I reckon thick there Edie Crabbe do 'ave her eye on you fer when thee bist growed up,' Uncle Jack often teased me, eyes twinkling.

There was an Italian prisoner of war called Rudolph working on the farm. I remember he was always singing but I couldn't understand why he never ate his meals in the big farmhouse kitchen with everyone else. He was given the same food but it was always taken out to him where he sat at a scrubbed table set for him in the back scullery. Rudolph's English was limited but he had picked up a little and, not surprisingly, it was broad Dorset. After his meal, he would knock on the kitchen door before putting his head round and thanking Aunt Doris, 'Thank e missus. Thick were awright.'

Aunt Doris used to make all her own butter. She would sit for what seemed like hours with the glass churn between her knees, her pinafore stretched tightly supporting it, slowly turning the handle geared to the wooden paddles. I always wanted to take a turn but she would seldom allow me. 'Thee do churn un too quick 'n makes the butter white.' Apparently, the more slowly the cream was churned, the more yellow the butter.

Only the ground floor of the farmhouse had electricity but often a Tilley lamp was used. Upstairs it was candles or the paraffin lantern. To this day, the smell of burnt paraffin at an airport is powerfully evocative of time spent on the farm at Toller.

Another strong memory I have of Toller is an unpleasant one of being chased from the orchard at the side of the farmhouse by a flock of hissing geese, much to the amusement of Peggy who would eventually chase the gees off, often with a wooden butter pat!

## *The close of The Close*

During my final year at primary school, a new school was under construction on the other side of town. It was to be called The New Close and so, of course, the school I was attending became The Old Close. It closed at the time my year left to go on to secondary schools.

That last year, our eleven plus year, my contemporaries and I had been moved into a class taught by Mr Bott. He was, compared to Mr Brody the headmaster, a rather short man but what Mr Bott lacked in stature he made up for in other ways. He was a tough disciplinarian and I was sure that his short moustache used to actually bristle when we was beginning to lose patience with us. He pushed us hard, to the extent that in those last terms at the Old Close, we gained a good grounding in the decimal system, even to understanding the disadvantage and problems of recurring numbers. We still called the subject arithmetic not having ascended to the heights of learning mathematics, but it was more than that. We had been taught how to handle fractions, even to multiply and divide them. It was down to Mr Bott and much to his credit that our entire class passed the eleven plus examination and went on to attend either Frome Grammar School or Trowbridge High School. I was accepted into the former as the school of my parent's choice.

## *Other foundations*

During that final year at primary school when the foundations for secondary education were being well laid, Dad had acquired piece of land and foundations of an entirely different kind were underway. He had always said he wanted to design and build his own home.

The 'plot', about two thirds of an acre, was formerly the orchard of a large house on the outskirts of Warminster. The plans for the house had been drawn, by Father, and the site was being cleared in readiness for the builders. There was much to do as the orchard had been neglected and was very overgrown. Steve and I were youthfully enthusiastic in helping at the weekends and despite our young age, we were taught the rudiments of how to use a long-handled woodman's axe.

Dad had faced something of a dilemma when laying out the site as there was a fine mature walnut tree right where the front of the house was to be. In the end it came down to either build the house another sixty or so feet further back, or lose the tree. I remember that both Mother and Dad were very saddened the day the tree was felled. Steve and I, not fully appreciating the loss of such a fine hardwood were far more disappointed that we should no longer be able to climb it.

We followed the whole building process, albeit impatiently, watching the house slowly grow from muddy footings into a dwelling. The day eventually came when the house was 'topped out' and Steve and I were permitted to climb the scaffolding to the very top. It was with great excitement that we actually sat side by side on the chimney pots.

Now living in Warminster. I had started attending St John's Primary School

Walking home from school with my pal Bobby Still

Mother with Stephen and Doris Hedges' mean-spirited dog, c 1947

At the Old Close.

This was about the time of the 'higher and higher' competition

66 Boreham Road, the family home Father designed, under construction. It was built in the orchard of Prestbury House, seen in the background, a former prebendary home

## CHAPTER 3
# SECONDARY SCHOOL DAYS

*A small fish in a big pond*

The day I started attending Frome Grammar School was a day of mixed emotions and of twofold excitement. I wanted to go to the new school—but I couldn't wait to get home at the end of the day. It was also the day on which the family moved into the new house.

Those early days at Frome Grammar were bewildering. With around 450 pupils, it would not be considered a large school by modern standards but after the Old Close it seemed enormous. There was more staff than I could possibly have imagined and they all seemed, in their black gowns, to swoop around the school rather than walk. The rules about not walking on the grass quadrangles and other places that were out of bounds to 'first-formers' all took some assimilating. Unlike the girls, who were called by their Christian names, we boys were referred to solely by our surnames, which felt very unfriendly, and not at all what we had been used to.

It was made very clear to us that standard of appearance both within and out of school and the proper wearing of our uniforms was important.

'You are,' we were told, 'the school's ambassadors. Townspeople will judge the school by the behaviour and appearance of its pupils.'

Walking to or from school without wearing a cap, or beret in the case of the girls, automatically incurred a detention for anyone unfortunate enough to be spotted by a member of staff. What amazed me was the unerring accuracy with which, on little more that a brief glimpse, teachers could name a non-conforming pupil!

We were introduced to timetables for classes, timetables for homework, double maths, Latin lessons and rosters for sweeping the assembly hall of food debris after school lunches.

Of those first few terms at grammar school, I remember little except that I didn't care for it too much.

## *The trouble with golf*

Not long after moving into the new house, Mother's younger sister Aunt Joan came to visit, bringing with her our cousins Judith and Simon. When the adults went out that first evening, we had all been despatched to bed with admonitions about behaving ourselves. From our visits to the farm at Cranborne, the four of us had already acquired a reputation for getting into mischief. On one occasion when we had been playing hide and seek, Steve had hidden inside a solid mahogany and walnut wardrobe. So many years have passed, I'm not exactly sure who actually tipped it over—probably Judy, but it could have been me. Steve was left trapped inside until some time later when Aunt Joan succeeded in finding Uncle David and had the help she needed to lift it up again.

Judith, being the eldest, was usually the ringleader and left on our own in the new house, it wasn't too long before we were all in Mother and Dad's bedroom where there was much more room for some serious pillow fighting. I have no idea where the golf ball came from but we all ended up sat on their bed and were stripping the white plastic covering from its outside with a penknife. We were curious as to what was inside. Underneath the outer covering, the ball was a mass of what appeared to be rubber bands and we took turns pulling them off and twanging them at each other.

Eventually, Judy lost patience and with rubber bands strewn all over the bed, wanted to find out what else, if anything, was inside. She grabbed what was left of the golf ball from Simon and decided to stick it with the penknife we had used to remove the outer covering. As she did so, we were all taken by surprise when there was a squelching sound and a jet of what appeared to be brown paint squirted out under some pressure.

It was bad enough juggling the golf ball, trying to stop the paint splashing onto the Mother's new candlewick bedspread but I think it was Steve who first looked up and saw the state of the ceiling. None of us could believe that there could have been so much liquid inside something the size of the remains of that golf ball. There was splurge resembling a brown lightning strike zigzagging the pristine white ceiling for most of the length of the bedroom—and it was a big room!

Judy thought it was hugely funny and dissolved into gales of laughter. Steve and I did not. We both knew what the likely outcome would be for us, given the enormity of what had happened. Simon looked on in bewilderment, not knowing which camp to join.

As it was, Judy eventually owned up and shouldered the blame, confessing coyly from under lowered eyelashes, reasoning that my Father could hardly give her the threshing Steve and I would have received. We were all given a sound telling off, Judy and Simon from Aunt Joan who, I suspect, actually thought the whole episode rather amusing; Steve and I from Dad who went on muttering for weeks about 'Other people's ill disciplined kids.'

And he was not too pleased about having the re-decorate the bedroom ceiling either.

## *School and bullying*

Compared to the often extremely vindictive and vicious bullying reported in today's schools, what went on at Frome Grammar was quite innocuous. The worst we experienced was the dreaded first year initiation of being thrown into the holly bush at the entrance of the driveway to the Headmaster's house. The fear of the event was far, far worse than the reality.

There were occasional scraps but more often than not the jeering and excited shouts of 'Fight! Fight!' usually attracted a member of staff who broke it up before any physical confrontation really got started—much to everyone's disappointment.

In the year above us though, there was a small gang of boys who did cause trouble and were often in trouble themselves as a consequence. It wasn't that they would pick upon someone in the way of bullying today. It was more a question of getting their own way. They would always barge to the front of the bus queue or if a group of younger boys were kicking a tennis ball, they would likely commandeer it for their own game.

I fell foul of them once, after school. Bobby Still and I had managed to board the bus back to Warminster ahead of them and get a front seat on the bus. Our seat was on the left side and thereby gave us a view from the front window alongside and behind the driver's cab. We hadn't gone very far before the gang of second formers, from the seat behind and from the other front seat pushed and dragged Bobby off our seat. One then climbed over and was trying to shove me out also. When I realised that I should not be able to stop him, I decided not to go without resistance, without a scrap, so I stood, suddenly and very unexpectedly punched the other gang member sitting across the isle from me. The element of surprise left the others looking on in disbelief as he tried to stem the flow of blood from his nose. Bobby and I casually made our way back down the bus to another seat.

Unfortunately, the bus conductor had only seen my action and not what had brought it about. As he finished clipping and issuing tickets to recently boarded passengers, he came up to our new seat.

'Will your mother keep your tea aside for you?' he asked me.

'I suppose so,' I replied, wondering why on earth he was asking.

'That's good then,' he said, pressing the bell three times to signal the driver to stop. 'Get off,' he ordered, 'you can wait for the next bus. I won't have fighting on my bus.' There was a definite emphasis on the 'my'.

I was about half an hour later getting home than I would usually have been. I dared not tell my parents why I was late and made some excuse about missing the bus but it was worth it because the gang of second formers never bothered us again.

## Herbs o' the earth

Whenever I could during the school holidays, I went to stay with Mother's eldest sister Aunt Olive, staying at their flat over a butcher's shop near the town centre. Uncle Tom, a master butcher, was then manager of an abattoir on the outskirts of town. The area was called Skilling which always seemed to me an unfortunate name and evocative of what went on there. He often brought home meat and offal that are far less common in our present days of supermarket shopping. Tripe, chitterlings and sweetbreads—both throat and pancreas—were regularly on Aunt Olive's table and she often served cold pressed tongue accompanied by Gypsy sweetbreads. The latter was rather like the fat from cold sirloin of beef but was actually roasted cow's udder.

During one of these visits, I was introduced to jugged hare. I found it rather rich but quite enjoyed it—until I saw how long it was hung and how Aunt Olive made the gravy!

Uncle Tom was a keen gardener and had quite a sizeable vegetable garden alongside the slaughterhouse. He was always very boastful over the size and quality of what he had grown and whenever they visited Warminster would always want Father to show him around his garden. Uncle Tom's was always far more advanced.

'I was digging potatoes a week ago, Bill,' he would say, in broad Dorset, 'and you should see the size of my leeks. Herbs o' the earth!' Father would look on tolerantly and usually say nothing. He had heard about herbs of the earth many, many times before. Just occasionally, though, he had had enough of Tom's boasting and would retaliate.

'It's alright for you, Tom. No-one ever sees whether you are working in your office or spending your time in the garden.'

And on another occasion, 'Maybe, but you don't have eggs as fresh as ours.' When we moved to the new house and had space in the garden, Dad had resumed keeping a few hens again. Uncle Tom couldn't let it go, though.

'Told thee afore. You want to get rid o' they Rhode Island Reds. Get some decent layers like they gleenies Doris did keep at Toller.'

Uncle Tom always had to have the last word. Dad said his somewhat older brother-in-law was a 'Cantankerous old b . . .' He usually stopped short, leaving us to guess the last word, perhaps wondering if he was going to make some reference to parentage—but actually he and Dad got on quite well.

When I was staying in Bridport on one occasion, Uncle T was late coming back from work one evening and Aunt Olive, who was preparing a cooked meal, asked me to walk down the road and see if he was coming. It was summertime and the town was crowded with holiday makers. I had only gone about two hundred yards when I noticed that the people ahead of me on the pavement were pressing to the side to make way for someone. Some were even crossing to the other side of the street. It was uncle Tom, although I could barely recognise him at first. He was covered in congealed blood which was hanging from his clothing in slimy dollops. He was clearly totally unconcerned with the reaction of other people nor was he bothered about either his appearance or the awful odour. Not surprisingly, the latter preceded him by some distance.

'Better run on back and tell your Aunt Olive,' he said, as soon as he saw me. 'She won't want me in the house like this,' which, I thought, was something of an understatement.

I did as he bade, ran back and told Aunt Olive, 'Uncle Tom's coming up the street. He seems to be covered in blood.'

'He's fallen in the blood well again,' she replied wearily and prepared to meet him with a garden hose at the back of the butchers' shop.

Apparently, when leaving the abattoir, Uncle Tom had walked across the yard. Near the gate, at the end of a series of channels cut into the concrete was a well into which the blood from the slaughtered beasts gravitated. It was usually collected every couple of weeks by a tanker from a glue or fertiliser works. Uncle T had, evidently not for the first time, slipped on some offal and fallen headlong into the well. On this occasion, it was at its fullest but he just heaved himself out of the congealing mess and carried on, walking home oblivious of his appearance and the affect on others.

Much to Dad's irritation, and occasionally to Mother's catering embarrassment, Uncle Tom and Aunt Olive would sometimes arrive for a visit, entirely unexpectedly, just as Sunday lunch was being served. Their timing was impeccable.

On one occasion, during lunch which, of course, they were invited to share, Mother was telling them how some three weeks earlier one of the gamekeepers from Lord Bath's estate had given her a shoulder of venison.

'I hope you hung it first,' said Uncle T.

'Of course I did,' Mother replied, a true farmer's daughter, 'but when Bill saw the state of it, he refused to eat it. Said it was too gamey even to put in the bin. 'T wouldn't be fair on the dustmen.'

'Well what did you do with it?' asked Uncle T.

'I buried it in the garden. It seemed the least objectionable way to dispose of it,' Dad joined in and explained.

'Where's it to, exactly, then?' Uncle Tom wanted to know, pushing his chair back from the table, making to leave the dining room and starting to roll up his sleeves.

'It's staying where it is, Tom.' Very firmly.

There was no doubt in any of our minds that Uncle Tom would have dug it up again had Father told him. As it was, he went on eating his lunch muttering occasionally about 'Wasting good vittuls,' and 'Herbs o' the earth.'

## *School Reports and systems*

From the outset of my time at Frome Grammar School, my school reports were never to Father's satisfaction and during the school holidays whenever I asked to do or attend something, it was always met with some remark about 'I'd be more inclined to agree if you made more effort at school.'

Eventually, this would become so wearing that even Mother had had enough and would risk being accused of being soft. 'Can't you give it a rest, Bill? I think you've made the point.'

Many years later, my own daughters saw some of these reports; one in particular caused them considerable amusement. They noted that I had been just about bottom of the class for geography and they couldn't help relating it to my earning a living as a navigator and travelling the world's oceans. They thought this was really funny. Despite my poor class performance, though, I know that when I left school I knew far more of the world's geography, its seas and oceans, countries and capitals, than any of my grandchildren are being taught at school now!

Father was something of a disciplinarian and I can remember Aunt Olive and one of Mother's other elder sisters, Aunt Kay, agreeing with each other on more than one occasion. 'Bill's really hard on those boys,'—but it was never discussed within Dad's hearing!

Because Stephen was relatively close to me in age, Dad had systems for bed-times and pocket money. The bed time system kicked in at eight years old when I had to be in my bed with the light out at seven thirty. If I wished to read, which I usually did, I needed to go earlier. Thereafter, there was then an annual increment of fifteen minutes and by the age of fourteen, I was permitted to remain up until nine o' clock—which was far earlier than any of my contemporaries. Steve, at three years younger, was forty-five minutes earlier.

Similarly for pocket money where the system started from the age of ten with three (old) pennies per week for each year of age.

We knew the system. It brooked no argument and we accepted it.

## *Escaping to Bridport, with all mod cons*

The nagging over school reports was the primary reason I elected to go and stay in Bridport whenever I could during school holidays. Mother's was a large family and there were many cousins, some quite distant. Most of them were in some way or another involved in farming but I always stayed with Aunt Olive who undoubtedly spoiled me somewhat.

Her younger daughter Jenneth, four years or so older than I, was usually busy with various boyfriends and I saw little of her. However, she did give up one evening when she spent some time teaching me to dance the quickstep to the music of her wind-up gramophone.

On one occasion Steve was also staying and he played a trick on Jenny that I will never forget. The flat, although over a butchers' shop, was on two storeys with bedrooms on the upper floor. Unfortunately, the bathroom was on the floor below so it was usually expedient to use chamber pots in the bedrooms.

In Jenny's room the floor was covered with linoleum but there were two or three rag rugs around her bed. Steve thought it would be interesting to sneak into her room and place some folded newspaper in the bottom of the chamber pot. It had the desired effect.

The following morning at breakfast, Jenny, who fortunately had a sense of humour, was getting her leg pulled over using the pot during the night. 'Well, it kind of didn't sound right. I thought I was already over the carpet—so I moved over,' she told us, laughing.

## *Things that go bump in the night*

I recall another breakfast time when Uncle Tom came down and started talking of someone having died during the night. Auntie Olive quickly shushed him up saying something about frightening me. Later in the day, we learned that he had been correct and one of the distant family had passed away in the small hours. At the time, Aunt Olive refused to discuss the matter but Peter, Jenny's boyfriend, quietly confided that evening that he believed Mr Staples had made such a statement on several occasions over the years and had always been correct.

Many years later, probably when she considered I was old enough to be told, Aunt Olive explained that often when a family member or close friend had passed away during the night, Uncle Tom claimed that he always received a visit. Aunt said that she didn't have Uncle Tom's 'sense' but she always knew too.

'I have never experienced any visitations but your uncle always closes the bedroom door last thing,' she stated. 'Some mornings it's ajar. Uncanny but it only ever happens when Uncle Tom has had a visitor. He reckons that the person comes to pay his last respects as we always hear later that someone has passed away during the night.'

Everyone seemed totally unconcerned at the prospect of ghostly goings-on but I was glad that I had been spared the story when I was a small boy!

## Fresh fish for breakfast

Another of Mother's distant cousins owned a small fishing boat, which was moored in West Bay. Uncle Albion employed the Harbourmaster to operate his boat, *Redwing of Weymouth.*

Often on a summer visit, I would borrow Jenny's bicycle and ride the two miles or so down to West Bay for five in the morning and go out on the boat with harbourmaster Frank to empty and set the lobster pots. On our return, we would always spin for mackerel and usually caught several. Although I have never been particularly fond of fish with small bones, I must admit I was always ready to enjoy one of those freshly caught mackerel; a tasty grilled breakfast.

Uncle Albion had an elegant half-timbered house. It was surrounded by manicured lawns with those in the front of the house being tiered to accommodate a series of rockeries with no fewer than five fish ponds cascading from one to the other. He was a very keen gardener and had two large greenhouses of fruits. It was when visiting him that I first tasted nectarines which, at that time, most people had never even heard of.

'Uncle Albion has had two silver weddings you know,' Aunt Olive told me once when we were visiting, adding how unusual this was.

Of course, I didn't 'know' and misunderstood. I replied that I thought such was illegal. She had to explain, 'No he isn't a bigamist, you dope! Aunt Phyllis is his second wife. His first wife died.'

Aunt Phyllis was much amused by this when she was told.

Irrespective of the weather, I never cycled down to West Bay without taking an old raincoat Uncle Tom lent me. The slightest onshore breeze was always welcome. It made the journey back up to Bridport much easier. I used to put on the coat on, and riding no-handed, hold it spread wide with both arms and sail between West Bay and Bridport. It was, after all, slightly uphill all the way.

## CHAPTER 4
# OUR DEN AND OUR TOOLS

*Not in My Garage*

In recounting some of the previous events, I have intimated that Father was strict. He was, and no more so than in how we used his tools and workbench. With the knowledge I acquired later that he was actually a time-served joiner, and with the understanding that any craftsman will take pride in the care of the tools, Dad's refusal to give us free access is not surprising.

Under the window at the far end of the garage, near his joiner's bench, Dad kept a large black tool chest. It was fitted inside with two sliding tills with wells underneath for larger tools. All the compartments were lined with green baize and the lids on the tills and the inside of the chest lid all highly varnished. The entire chest was sturdily constructed and all corners were jointed with stopped dovetails. Uncle Horace, when he told me about Dad having served an apprenticeship and how his mate had been killed falling down the pit shaft, explained that Dad had crafted the toolbox toward the end of his apprenticeship. It was, said Horace, customary to do this as a demonstration of proficiency and of having acquired the necessary skills.

The box was always kept locked.

Nevertheless, from the time either Steve or I were big enough to hold a handsaw or grasp a hammer, Dad had started to show us how to use woodworking tools. As we became more proficient we were permitted access to the tool chest—but only on an *ad hoc* basis.

Whenever we asked to use tools, the request was always met with, 'What are you going to do?' and 'are you sure there are no old nails or screws in the wood?' The retribution that would have followed had we run a smoothing plane over a nail head, or struck one with a saw, doesn't bear thinking of!

Then the time came when Dad thought it would be far better if we had a few tools of our own and, apart from the usual gifts for birthdays and Christmases, we would each also be given one or another kind of tool. Some of them I still have, which does prove his rather cynical outlook that anyone will often take less care of something belonging to another than they will of their own possessions. My own collection of tools was started with a Spear and Jackson handsaw given on my eleventh birthday.

In due course, this gave rise to another problem in that whenever Dad came to work at his bench he often had to clear away our tools, bits of wood and off-cuts. He solved the problem by building us a six foot by ten foot shed in a corner of the garden behind his garage, at which location it was easy to provide power for lighting. The shed, our 'den', was wood-framed, covered with flat asbestos sheeting and had windows over a built-in bench in the far end and along one side. Steve and I actually helped in the construction.

Naturally, we kept it locked. Just like Dad's toolbox. Naturally, too, Steve and I were the only key-holders; we trusted no-one with *our* much-prized tools.

## *Pythagoras and his hippopotamus*

My father was always keen to foster Stephen's and my interest in anything that related to mathematics, physics or the natural world.

Post war, there was a great deal of construction taking place in Warminster and even before I started at grammar school, I often used to go out with Father when he was attending the various building sites. Sometimes, he worked with one of his assistants, who were in training, in 'setting out' some of the roads and building plots. I loved nothing more than to assist in this and felt very important when I was asked to set up his engineers' dumpy level, which I had been painstakingly taught how to do. I often wrote down the readings for them but if Dad was working alone, it was much better because then I got the really important task of actually holding the staff.

Measuring distance was usually done with a special chain, each link of which was twelve inches long. I learned how they set out ninety degree angles using a triangle of chain with sides of 3-4-5 units and something they called Pythagoras's hippopotamus.

Later, when I started to learn trigonometry I found out that Pythagoras never did have a hippo but I could relate what I was being taught to the practical application I had seen used when surveying.

Dad was always keen to demonstrate the practical uses of his favourite subject, mathematics. When Steve and I assisted with the construction of our shed, we were tasked with making a calculation of the diagonal and setting it out so that Father could ensure the shed was a perfect rectangle, with ninety degree corners. I had already learned how to make rudimentary calculations using a slide rule.

I suppose, looking back to my last year at the Old Close primary school our teacher Mr Bott, too, was keen on mathematics. I recall him referring to a cat he had named Ptolemy-Apollonius.

## *In a Spin*

As well as being a den, the shed was also used for storing our cycles, which were often being dismantled for one or another reason. We were also frequently undertaking some project or another; collecting five gallon oil drums to build a raft, collecting much-prized pram wheels for a go-kart, whittling an ash stave to make a long bow, or some other undertaking.

On one occasion we had been replacing a wheel in a bicycle and the machine was inverted, standing on the handlebars and saddle. I don't recall how it came about but we ended up peddling the bike furiously and then holding a large pram wheel set on a short axle against the rapidly spinning cycle wheel.

We found that when the pram wheel had been set to spin even more quickly—it was smaller than the cycle wheel—it seemed to develop a mind of its own and it became quite difficult to move around with it. This was very curious and after Steve and I had tried the 'experiment' several times with the same result, we decided to ask Dad what was going on.

Later, while we were at the table, I tried to explain what we had found. He smiled knowingly.

'Do you still have that old swivel chair from my drawing office that I gave you for the shed?' he asked in response to my question. Steve replied that we had.

'Well try sitting in the chair while you're holding the spinning pram wheel. Lift your feet from the ground and see what happens when you try to move the wheel. You may be very surprised,' Dad stated. 'Tell me what you find—and try it with the wheel spinning the other way as well and see if there is any difference,' he suggested.

This was really intriguing and we could barely wait to get back out to the shed.

We did as Dad had suggested and found that when holding the spinning wheel with the axle horizontal, the wheel resisted any attempt to tilt it but to our amazement, the chair stated to rotate! Acting on his suggestion about trying with the wheel rotation direction reversed, we then found that the chair moved the opposite way.

We reported our findings. 'You have just found out about a thing called gyroscopic inertia,' Dad told us. He started to explain more as well but we were far too excited over what we had found to pay much attention.

The event was, however, typical of Father's approach to teaching us some rudimentary physics and encouraging us to be inquisitive of such things. As it was, we had tremendous fun repeating the experiment and amazing our friends on many subsequent occasions.

Several years later, when studying at college and learning how a gyrocompass worked, I remembered Father teaching us about gyroscopic inertia and progression, giving cause to realize how fortunate we had been.

## *From gyroscopes to hydrostatics*

Stephen and I were often asked while at the tea table what we had been doing at school during the day. One time, I told Dad that we had been discussing the aqueducts in the Limpley Stoke Valley, near Bath.

'Mr Gregg said the Romans were not as clever at engineering as people think,' I told him, believing that I was about to impart something really knowledgeable.

'And why did he say that?' Dad asked.

'Mr Gregg said that they didn't need to have built aqueducts,' I replied importantly.

'How should they have got the water from one side of the valley to the other, then?'

'Well, he said they could have piped the water down into the valley and up the other side. It would have reached the same level on both sides,' I said, confident in the infallibility of our teachers.

'That's quite correct,' said Dad, 'but the Romans knew better than that. I am sure they were very well aware indeed that they could never have constructed a culvert that would have withstood the pressure of the water when at the bottom of the valley.'

He went on to explain just how great that pressure would have been one hundred or so feet down on the valley floor.

To my surprise, the conversation concluded with the closest comment to a criticism of one of our teachers that I ever recall my father making.

'Mr Gregg would probably be better sticking to teaching languages. He is evidently far more knowledgeable about their language than he is of Roman engineering practices.'

Another lesson in physics. Dad knew that Mr Gregg was our Latin master.

## *The big bang*

Although slightly out of chronological order (this event happened after Steve had also started at Frome Grammar

School), I should not close this chapter, which started with a description of our 'den', without recounting one of Steve's misadventures.

He very nearly succeeded in demolishing our shed.

He seriously frightened Mother.

And I, typically, was blamed for it.

Studying chemistry and physics was, I suspect, rather more exciting when I was at school than it is now with the ever more stringent health and safety requirements.

We all knew how to make gunpowder and had enjoyed the experiments making hydrogen, both chemically and by electrolysis, and then igniting it. We knew about the properties of oxygen and we learned how to make hydrogen sulphide for stink bombs—although I didn't understand just how dangerous the gas is until many years later when learning about tankers carrying 'sour crude'.

Then we carried out an experiment with coal gas to show how, when the mixture of gas and air reaches a critical point, it becomes explosive.

The chemistry master had an old Golden Syrup tin with a small hole pierced in its base and in the top. The tin was inverted over an unlit Bunsen burner and filled with gas. Then the lid was pressed on, the tin stood on a Bunsen tripod, and the gas coming from the top hole ignited. The class was then instructed to stand back. We were all jostling for the best position, craning over each other's shoulders trying to get the best view as we waited impatiently. The pale blue flame of burning gas at the top of the tin was barely discernable. It seemed to take far longer than it probably did before a small explosion blew the lid off the tin and it struck the ceiling of the laboratory.

This was fantastic! A simple bomb! I could barely wait until we were on the bus on the way home from school. I wanted to share this with Steve.

Annexed to the side of Mother's kitchen, there was a room which in modern terms would be called a utility room. We referred to it as the 'gas house' for it contained a gas copper for laundry and a gas cooker which Mother used in the summer when the Yorkseal (similar to an Aga) was unlit.

At the first opportunity, Steve and I repeated the experiment, filling a small tin using the gas ignition-wand on the cooker, and taking our gas-filled tin out to the shed where it was ignited.

Steve was well impressed—but I never thought for one moment that he would later repeat the experiment to show a pal of his. The trouble was, he used one of the five-gallon oil drums which we had been collecting to build a raft.

It was a school holiday and I was out on my bike in the woods with some pals. Apparently, brother Stephen and his friend Simon Fitzsimmons waited until Mother was out of the way and upstairs in the house. Then, having first pierced the drum top and bottom by hammering a large nail through, took it into the gas house and held the cooker ignition wand at one of the holes until, as Steve later told me, 'We couldn't stand the smell of gas any longer.' Then they carried the drum to the shed, stood it on a couple of pieces of wood, and lit the gas emitting from the top hole.

Steve elaborated 'We watched for a long time but couldn't see the flame and thought it had probably gone out.' Fortunately for them, they decided not to take any chance by trying to re-ignite it and decided to abandon the experiment. They closed the shed door and both boys went off to play elsewhere.

Some time later, in Mother's words, 'There was a hell of a bang!' Not knowing what on earth it may be but realising it was outside the house, she rushed out and around to the back to find that there was broken glass over much of the lawn and some of the shed roof was missing. After a quick search confirmed that none of us had been present, Mother, very agitated, returned into the house and telephoned Father who left his office and returned home immediately.

The fact that he had no shed key and had to force the lock served only to add to Father's ire. He gained access only to find the twisted remains of the oil drum.

By the time I arrived home, totally unaware or the incident, Steve and his pal had been home some for time and had already been questioned but their reprimand was insignificant by comparison to that which I received. I was in very serious trouble for 'Having no more damned sense than to tell Stephen how to do such a fool thing.'

That was when I started learning how to re-glaze windows.

## CHAPTER 5
# THEN WE WERE THREE

### *A family announcement*

As I was starting my third year at Frome Grammar School, Mother was admitted into hospital in Bath. My brother and I didn't understand what was going on but Aunt Kay came to stay and looked after us all during Mother's absence.

Each weekend, Stephen and I accompanied Father on a visit to the hospital. We were assured that Mother was making good progress. Meanwhile, Aunt Kay fed us well and Dad instigated an even stricter regime of table manners, also adding clearing the table, washing and wiping up to our list of pocket-money chores. 'It is the least you can do when someone has taken the trouble to prepare a good meal for you.' Steve privately pointed out, though, that the washing-up rule seldom seemed to apply to adults.

In the past, Stephen and I had often been admonished over the way we handled cutlery. Our parents were particularly strict about not pointing our knife and fork up in the air. 'The only time your cutlery need not point downward at your plate is when your fork or spoon is travelling to or from your mouth,' and 'keep your elbows in while you are eating,' was another common instruction. (Years later, when frequently travelling by air and trying to consume food in what seemed to be a two-dimensional space, I had very good cause to be grateful for this latter training!)

Now, we were also encouraged always to express our thanks after enjoying a meal and seldom left the table without a grateful 'Thank you Auntie. That was very nice.' This expression later became something of a family ritual and whoever had cooked the meal, the thank-you was invariably to 'Auntie'.

Not long before Christmas 1954, Father told us the reason for Mother's long absence in Forbes Frazer Nursing Home and in the following February she returned home bringing us a baby brother.

Steve and I, meanwhile, having by then acquired some basic knowledge about these worldly matters, viewed our parents in a rather different light.

William seemed to pass the infant baby stage quickly and before long Steve and I became resident baby-sitters and often took our baby brother out in his large and luxuriously-sprung Silver Cross perambulator.

Dad would sometimes come out with us but never pushed the pram. He had only ever pushed the pram out alone once. In those days, Steve and I were aware our parents were considered as rather senior to be adding to their family—indeed, we certainly thought they were past such things! On the one occasion that Dad took the pram out unaccompanied, he walked right through the town and reached home before he discovered that Steve had fixed an 'L' plate on the front. To say he was displeased hugely understates the situation.

I thought we were facing a severe threshing (Steve was seldom punished alone; I always had some culpability) but

Mother and Aunt Kay's intervention saved us. 'Come on Bill, where's your sense of humour?' they chided.

I think what really made him back off was them reminding him of the amusement he had gained at Mother's expense on an occasion that she had been proudly pushing William through the town.

Aunt Kay had been accompanying her when a lady stopped them to admire the new baby. Father, in his position as the town surveyor, was quite well known and the lady evidently also knew Mother. She, however, had no idea who the lady was. According to Aunt Kay, Mother tried to resolve the situation but instead of asking 'Do you know my husband?' actually said 'Do you know who his father is?'

When told, Dad had thought the incident extremely funny and the story was, to Mother's embarrassment, told many times.

Several years later, when Steve was leaving home, Mother was clearing up some of his things and came across a diary. When she realised it was written during the year that William was born, after her long spell in the nursing home, the temptation to look at the entry on his birth date was irresistible. Steve had been ten years old at the time and in his penultimate term at The New Close primary school.

"Got ten out of ten for arithmetic today. Sir was very pleased. Had a baby brother."

I suppose we all have different priorities.

## *School holidays*

I never tired of being in Bridport and whenever I could, I continued to spend my holidays there.

Although I always stayed with Aunt Olive, I spent much of the time at Manor Farm in Eype. The farm (and two others) was the property of Mother's cousin Aunt May and her husband Uncle Reg. Aunt May's elderly mother lived with them too. Great Aunt Annie was a spirited lady who, as a consequence of her deafness, always shouted. She had a zest for life and loved nothing more than a good card game or attending race meetings. She had several times owned and invested in race horses.

I was told that, not too long before I knew her, Great Aunt Annie had felled a runaway bull with a pitchfork. I could well imagine it.

One of the farm employees was a little bow-legged man called Archie. He was the same age as my mother and had been employed at Manor Farm since he was a small boy. Mother had told me that she and her younger sister Joan, when they were children, knowing that Archie was a bit 'slow', used to egg him on to try and jump the pond. He never succeeded, she said, but was always game to try and never seemed to mind the inevitable wetting when falling short on his jump.

'Archie's a bit simple. He's actually certified,' Uncle Reg told me one time, 'but he's not as daft as people think.' Apparently, if he thought no-one would notice, Archie would often leave the farm early and if caught, would explain "Tis me shave night.' Archie's shave nights were well known and regarded with tolerant amusement by the other farm staff.

On the occasion of the trouble with the bull, Archie was leading it using a halter, disregarding instructions always to use a pole attached to the ring in the beast's nose. Evidently, something spooked it and the bull got away from him then chased Archie across the front of the farmhouse. Archie dived for shelter into a wooden henhouse nearby. Aunt

Annie, who had seen what had happened through the kitchen window, ran from the back of the house with a pitchfork in time to see the bull demolishing the henhouse trying to reach Archie. It would, I was told, have succeed had not the redoubtable Annie brought it down with her pitchfork.

I recall a time when I was working with Uncle Reg with some penned sheep. He would point at an animal and I would grab it and drag it into a separate pen. Archie was watching with amusement over the top of one of the hurdles. Of course, I realised we were segregating young rams from the ewes but thought it would be interesting to hear what Archie had to say.

'Why are we picking out some sheep and not others?' I asked him.

'Aar, well, we can't tell that to no little boys like you Andrews,' he responded. Reg thought this really funny. I must have been nearly a foot taller than Archie—and Archie never did get my name right. It was always plural.

## *The Shorthorn Show*

The Easter holiday in Bridport was always a good time to visit. Uncle Reg had a prize herd of shorthorn cattle, which was something of a hobby for him. Not many farmers raised the breed but every Easter there was a dedicated show and sale in Yeovil and farmers travelled some distance to attend.

Preparation of the few cattle selected as worthy to be taken to the show was painstaking. For a week or so preceding the show, they were kept in a byre and I helped as they were washed and groomed like horses. Their horns and hoofs also received attention and were filed and rubbed down with fine glass-paper before conditioning using olive oil.

On one occasion, two or three days before the show, we were drenching them for worms or some other parasite. The heifers' heads were locked into the restraining devices over the manger and Uncle Reg, standing alongside, would grab the beast with a finger and thumb of one hand in its nostrils and with the other hand, grasp its bottom lip. There was then something of a struggle while he pulled its head upwards by the nostrils and its mouth open by the lower lip. This was the opportunity for me, standing on the other side, to thrust a squash bottle containing dissolved green powder way down its throat. With eyes rolling and head held firmly upward the animal had no choice but to swallow a pint or so of the noxious solution.

Eventually, I wanted to change places and have a go at holding the heifers myself. I succeeded, but in the struggle the animal stepped on my toes—more than once. This amused Archie who had turned up to watch a 'townie' at work. Archie did a lot of watching.

Uncle Reg gave me the nod. 'Grab him,' he said. I didn't realise quickly enough what he meant so he stepped out and man handled Archie in the same way as he had the heifers. With no reluctance whatsoever, Archie tipped his head back and opened his mouth.

'Go on. Give him a dose!' urged Uncle Reg. I hesitated, unbelieving, as Archie tried to nod in acquiescence. He had no qualms at all in gulping down the dregs which had been left in the bottle as I poured them into his mouth. On his release, as he went off, I swear Archie was smacking his lips. I could hardly believe what we had done,

'Won't it make him ill?' I asked.

'Not at all,' said Reg, 'Archie doesn't know that I know, but he often helps himself to a dose. Thinks it's good for his stomach, too.'

Apart from helping to prepare the animals, there was another thing I particularly liked about the Yeovil Shorthorn Sale and Show. It was quite lucrative. I took turns with John, the cowman, in leading the heifers around the show and auction rings. I was very proud, smartly dressed in a white dairy coat—and extremely grateful for Uncle Reg's generosity after each occasion!

## *Other Bridport attractions*

Although I spent most of my time on the farm when I was in Bridport, sometimes there were other attractions.

Another of Mother's numerous cousins, Aunt Freda, who lived in a large bungalow on the seafront at West Bay, sometimes had a niece to stay. Suzanne was of a similar age to me and we always enjoyed each other's company.

Sometimes we would walk over the cliffs to Eype's Mouth; other times we would go swimming or play tennis on the court at the rear of the bungalow, and if we called in for a hot drink after swimming in the sea, we were always made welcome by Aunt Freda. She owned a restaurant on the seafront and the crab teas or home baked scones were something of a speciality.

Suzanne's father was the manager of Lloyds Bank at Ashburton in Devon and in the most incredible of coincidences, very many years later I learned that her Godfather was one of the senior staff at Lloyds Bank in Frome and that Suzanne was also a close friend of a classmate at Frome Grammar School.

Aunt Freda's husband, another Uncle Reg, was the Lloyds Agent (marine insurance, not banking) in West Bay and he was always joking and pulling my leg about something. On the last visit I made before I left home to go to sea, he was very interested to hear about the career I had chosen but his humour still prevailed.

'Do you get sea-sick, lad?' he asked.

'I don't know,' I replied. 'I haven't been to sea yet, but I hope not.'

'Well if you do, you should eat bread and jam,' he advised.

'Is that a cure for sea-sickness?' I had already heard of various remedies.

'Not at all. It won't cure it—but it'll taste just the same when you bring it up,' he promised.

## *Not in my kitchen*

Brother Steve had passed his eleven-plus and had joined me at Frome Grammar School and, during his first year, as his big brother, I was required to 'keep and eye on him' and ensure that he came to no harm.

I have earlier made reference to the standards of uniform and dress we were required maintain for school and clean shoes was one of them.

'Molly, don't fuss with the boys. They are quite old enough to clean their own shoes,' Father had insisted. We were, but of course seldom did so the night before with the consequence that in the morning, we had to adjourn outside as Mother would not permit such activity in the kitchen while she was preparing our breakfast.

One particularly frosty morning, having stood outside, breath condensing in the cold air, with alternately one foot then the other on the dustbin while buffing his shoes, Steve returned to the kitchen shivering. As he was rubbing his arms trying to generate some warmth, Mother looked up from frying our eggs and asked, 'Is it cold outside then, Stephen?'

'Cold?' Steve replied through chattering teeth, 'It's cold enough to freeze the brass balls off a pawnbroker's shop!'

'I will *not* have language like that in this house!' Mother replied, emphatically.

'What language, Mum?' Steve said, all innocence, 'I don't know what you thought I said but I wasn't swearing.'

Mother thought about this for a moment before blushing and turning back to her frying pan. Dad, meanwhile, had a small fit of choking to disguise his laughter.

A year or two later, there was another incident as a consequence of the rule of only cleaning shoes outside.

Steve was up in his bedroom having an illicit cigarette and when he had finished, he flipped the butt out of the side window.

Shortly afterwards, when he came down to the kitchen, he was more than surprised to find Dad was waiting and accused him of smoking. 'And there is no use in denying it. The end landed on my head—and it was still smouldering.'

There was punishment, but for once I had no involvement whatsoever. I had been outside waiting for Dad to finish with the shoe brushes when it happened.

## *Fire training*

We didn't exactly have drills in the manner that I later became used to on board ship, but undoubtedly influenced by his fire service work during the war, Dad was always fire conscious. He wanted us to understand what the risks were and what actions we should take.

We were instructed that if, at night, we thought something was burning we should shout and yell but never open any closed doors. Steve and I were told how we could escape from a bedroom window by hanging by our finger tips from the sill at which point our feet would be only a few feet off the ground. Being boys, of course, we had to try this and Dad obligingly positioned himself outside where he easily held our feet before inviting us to let go, making sure we came to no harm. What an adventure, pretending to escape from a burning house!

There is no doubt, too, that all this made Mother fire-conscious as well—but it didn't stop her setting fire to the kitchen one morning.

Aunt Margaret, yet another of Mother's ubiquitous cousins and who lived nearby, was with Mother when it happened. It was she who recounted the story.

Mother had a Ronson cigarette lighter and she had just refuelled it before she and Aunt Margaret lit cigarettes. The lighter was returned to a patent-leather handbag standing on one of the worktops and it is probable that it was saturated with excess lighter fuel that had, un-noticed, continued to burn.

With no warning, the handbag erupted into flames and before either could react, some adjacent newspapers and the fitted cupboards above the worktop were on fire too.

Apparently, Mother grabbed a sweeping brush and dragged the burning handbag and adjacent newspapers from the worktop to the middle of the floor. Aunt Margaret, meanwhile, swiftly filled a bowl of water in the sink and threw the contents at the worktop, refilled the bowl and threw water at the burning mess of paper and handbag on the floor. The situation finally was brought under control when Mother smothered what remained on the floor with a heavy rug from the adjacent hallway.

Father was telephoned.

Not surprisingly, he returned home in very short order and both Mother and Aunt Margaret, whom Mother had persuaded to stay for moral support, were concerned that he would most likely loose his temper when he saw the damage.

As it was he looked at all the damage, then concluded 'It's all this damn smoking,' and, taking his own cigarettes from his pocket proffered them.

'Have a cigarette, Margaret.'

When Steve and I returned from school, Dad told us what had happened, saying that it was entirely due to Mother and Aunt Margaret's quick action that disaster was averted and the house hadn't burned down. He then took us to the bedroom above the kitchen. There were lessons to learn on just how quickly fire can spread.

William, at this time, was a toddler and unable to reach the bedroom door handles. To overcome his lack of height, he would fetch the stool from the bathroom to stand on.

The stool was still in the doorway where William had left it that morning. Close to the floor, the white paint on its legs was brown and blistered. It had indeed, been a very close call.

## *Household chores*

The hallway and dining room were fitted with oak parquet floor tiles and it was one of Steve's and my Saturday tasks to wax and polish them. Although there was an electric floor polisher, we thought it was much more fun to tie felt and dusters on our feet and would happily chase each other skating around the dining table or between hall and dining room. Dad didn't really approve—but it got the job done.

The kitchen floor was covered with thermo-plastic tiles, in those days, a very new innovation. Unfortunately, they were prone to show dirt and while we could all wipe our shoes, Linda the cocker spaniel, had still to grasp the concept and was the biggest offender for bringing in mud.

Eventually Mother became tired of getting to her knees and scrubbing the floor each morning. When she complained about it to Dad, he thought the solution was simple.

'I can't think why you don't polish it. It will be much easier to just wipe it clean.'

The floor was painstakingly waxed and polished. Several times.

Once again, the story was related by Aunt Margaret. She had been present when Linda came scampering into the kitchen. Having bounded over the threshold, cleared the mat and landed on the gleaming floor, her brakes failed. Aunt Margaret said she had never realised a dog could actually have a look of astonishment. Linda was unable to stop before, after several pirouettes, she fetched up against the door to the hall.

The next person to come through the door was Father, returning for his morning coffee.

'He didn't pirouette,' said Aunt Margaret, 'but he came damned close to turning a perfect back-flip. I had never thought of Bill as a gymnast'

The mat from inside the door disappeared. We never saw it again.

## *Other canine capers*

Having mentioned Linda, our blue roan cocker spaniel, I am reminded of two other incidents in which she featured.

When brother William was an infant, he would often be left sleeping in his pram on the back lawn. Linda would then usually be found lying underneath, her front paws outstretched and her head laid along them. Dad had a notion that the dog was actually guarding the pram. Protecting William.

He decided to put his theory to the test. Knowing that the dog was likely to recognise his footfalls, he disguised his gait by wearing Wellington boots. An old raincoat used for gardening and a flat cap which he never wore, completed the disguise. He was correct and as he shuffled up the garden path towards the pram, Linda bounded out and was certainly going for him. When Dad called out to her, she recognised the voice and stopped dead, but she was very wary and continued growling until he approached close enough to be identified with certainty and welcomed with a wagging tail.

As part of the dog's health programme, after a routine visit, the local veterinary surgeon recommended that she be given a daily Doc Martin's yeast tablet. Steve thought she would probably simply eat the tablet but was told he didn't know what he was talking about.

All attempts to hide it in her food failed and the tablet would be nosed to one side and left in her dish, in solitary splendour, after all other food had been consumed.

Dad then elected to show us how to make a dog take a tablet forcibly. Linda was unceremoniously grabbed, her mouth opened, and the tablet thrust deep into her throat.

She suffered the indignity gracefully and stood placidly unresponsive while Dad continued to rub her throat for some seconds.

'That'll have done the trick,' he assured us, releasing the dog. She moved away a few paces before turning to look disdainfully at Dad, and then spat the offending tablet across the kitchen floor. Steve retrieved it.

'Lyn, Lyn,' he called, and held out his hand with the tablet in the middle of his palm. She walked over to him, licked the tablet off his palm, swallowed it and walked off again, unconcerned and happily wagging her tail.

Much as he may have wanted to, Steve had more sense than to make any remark about having predicted that this was what Linda would do, but Mother was brave enough to say 'You were right Stephen.'

Dad, with a face like thunder, was muttering something about 'What do you expect, the dog *is* female.'

Despite his statement having a seeming gender contradiction, I suspect that in these circumstances, even Dad was not sufficiently courageous to have used the correct term for a canine female. Such a remark may very well have been misconstrued.

## CHAPTER 6
# MEANWHILE, AT SCHOOL

*Upper school and music*

Those first three years at Frome Grammar passed quickly and before I realised it, I had reached the dizzy heights of becoming a Fourth Former. Things had settled down—although I still was not achieving the standards that Father required.

One thing had changed. In the fourth year I took the opportunity to cease learning Latin. Whew! I thought I had learned nothing whatsoever of the language and that it had been a total waste of time. Many years later though, when I started to study Spanish, I was quite surprised to find how much Latin I actually remembered—and how similar the verbs, even the irregular ones, were to those in Spanish.

Another thing that had changed; I quit learning the piano. I had started with lessons when we lived in East End Avenue and I was seven. By the time I reached the second year at Frome, I was having so many rows with Father over practising that for the sake of domestic harmony, I ceased. I had found it difficult enough to spend time on homework each night without having to fit in an hour of piano practise as well.

All Dad's family were accomplished musicians, Dad especially so, and music was an important part of their family life, as it later became for mine. I remember looking at Dad's book of Mazas Etudes for violin. They were exercises and I noted how his tutor had marked off the dates of his competence on very difficult fourth-position pieces. Dad had been only ten years old and at that age he routinely practised for two hours daily. Clearly, I was never going to achieve his level of accomplishment.

So I quit, despite his admonitions of 'You'll come to regret it, lad. Mark my words.' Of course, my father, as parents so often are, was eventually proved to be correct. I do regret not having persevered as I had really wished to progress to playing the church organ.

Four years later, I took up playing the clarinet and the grounding in musical theory I had received when learning piano was a definite advantage. As it turned out, it was probably as well because I could not have continued with the piano once I went to sea, and I certainly had great enjoyment on board ship with the clarinet—but I'll come to that later.

Frome Grammar School had a strong tradition of music and was always a very active participant in the annual Bath Festival with an orchestra and choirs and when in the senior school, I also enjoyed singing at Wells Cathedral on occasions with one of the school choirs.

## *Prize and Prejudice*

Despite all Father's admonitions, I was still failing to bring home end-of-term reports of the standard that he required and when the time came for the annual speech day and prize-giving he always declined to attend on the basis 'Why would I wish to come and see other pupils receiving prizes? It would be different if you had some achievement to recognise,' or words to that effect.

While I was in the third year, a squadron of the Air Training Corps was formed and, with an interest in aircraft arising from making models, eagerly, I joined up. Because it was a school squadron there was a strong academic focus, unlike the squadron that met in Frome town where the set-up was more that of a youth club with greater emphasis on social activities, table tennis and the like. One period in the school's weekly timetable was allocated to club activities, which in our case was used for instruction in navigation, principles of flight or some other aeronautical subject.

At least once each term we went on a 'flying day', usually to RAF Colerne, near Bath. It was on such days that the academic level of our school squadron paid off. Because the cadets had all studied towards proficiency to some extent, we were often afforded the opportunity to fly in twin-seated training aircraft instead of being merely one of seven passengers in an Avro Anson. Usually, the pilot would ask 'Aerobatics? Or do you want to fly it yourself?' I opted for aerobatics once and enjoyed the experience but on subsequent occasions always took the opportunity to try flying the aircraft myself. It was far more exciting! It probably depended on the pilot's nerve, but often control was handed over while the aircraft was still in the climb, very soon after take-off, instructions being given via the intercom as to maintaining rate of climb and establishing direction.

Sometimes, the pilot would ask 'Where do you live?' and, as it was only about twenty miles away, we would fly to Warminster and back. Mother and Dad were always on the lookout for me on these Saturday afternoons when we circled the aircraft above our house.

All this was really good fun and it was interesting but when a number of us had to sit an unexpected mock examination for proficiency in air navigation, engineering and armaments, I was totally unprepared and, somewhat dismally, failed.

Because we were a school squadron, cadets' progress was duly recorded in a small, separate report enclosed with the normal end-of-term school report. That term our commanding officer, Flight Lieutenant Greg had written 'I hope Parks will not let the squadron down by being the first cadet to fail the Proficiency Exam.' I thought the remark was partially a consequence of personal prejudice. Father had earlier had a very serious altercation with Greg over an injury Steve had suffered at his hand. The report was also misleading by inferring that all who had taken the examination had been successful. In reality the squadron had been so recently established that no cadets had even taken the exam at the time my report was written.

When Father read it, however, he was predictably angry. 'You can't even apply yourself seriously to your hobbies.' he exploded. 'You'll never make anything of yourself.' Et cetera, et cetera. I knew this set the tone for the remainder of the school vacation. I couldn't wait to go to Bridport.

All these years later, I am still unsure whether it was Dad's castigation or whether, with such interesting subjects, I should have spent significant time on revision anyway, but I passed with a marking of 92%. I had answered one question incorrectly but my mark was exceeded by one other cadet in our squadron.

In the same term, there was an art and essay competition in senior school which had to be themed on the New Testament of the Bible. I decided to enter and chose as my essay topic that of occasions in which the word 'shepherd' was used, the inferences and implications. For the art part, as I enjoyed calligraphy, I prepared an illuminated scroll of the Twenty Third Psalm. Somewhat to my surprise, I won.

At Speech Day that year, the guest of honour handing out prizes for achievement was the RAF Group Captain controlling Transport Command. He presented me with a book for the art and essay competition. He also presented Certificates of Proficiency to cadets who had sat the examination and in his address, the Group Captain commended our squadron for its academic achievements. We had achieved the two highest marks in the country for the Proficiency Examination with Brian Pike, one of my classmates, being marked with an unbeatable 100%. Brian was told he would receive a special reward for his outstanding achievement.

Although my parents had known that Speech Day was imminent, at the time I hadn't bothered to tell them about the proficiency award, or the book prize.

During the summer vacation, Transport Command arranged a tour and flew Brian to the Far East and back. He stopped over at Cyprus, Aden, Gan Island, Colombo and Singapore. It must have been a fantastic trip—and I was as envious as hell!

The Air Training Corps report at the end of that term was a very different one from the previous term. Mother was pleased for me, and referring to my successes in the proficiency exam and to the art and essay competition, made some comment like 'Hasn't he done well, Bill?!'

'Yes—but it's not much damned use to him for earning a living.'

So I thought longingly about Bridport again, wondering about a career and what life held for me. Just a few weeks later, it was while listening to Brian recounting his adventures, of his travelling half way around the world, that a small seed had begun to germinate.

## *Hand and tooth*

The incident between Father and Mr Greg alluded to above was a result of minor misbehaviour by Steve during a Latin lesson.

His class had been set some task and Greg, as he often did, stood at the back of the classroom. It was one of his favourite positions and if he thought someone was misbehaving, he would throw a board rubber the length of the room so that it bounced off the blackboard. It was never intended to strike anyone, nor did it, but it was very effective in getting attention and maintaining order.

On the occasion in question, the board rubber had already been thrown when Mr Greg, feeling the need to further instil some control, invoked another of his disciplinary repertoire and started to walk forward. He did this sometimes and as he passed, the offending pupil, who dared not look round, would receive a glancing swipe across the top of his head with the flat of Mr Greg's hand. It was never a serious blow, and clearly was not intended to be, usually doing little more than disturb the errant scholar's coiffure.

Steve, who had thought he may well be the target on this occasion, had crouched forward towards his desk, ducking, his shoulders shrugged. For some reason, just as the blow was being delivered, Steve unwittingly raised his head slightly. This resulted in quite a hard clout to the back of his head at which Steve's head snapped forward and he walloped his chin on the desk top. Unfortunately, at the moment of impact he had his tongue between his teeth and bit it quite severely. The event was a really an extremely unfortunate accident and Steve fled from the classroom, spitting blood as he went.

This occurred during the first of the three afternoon lessons. At the end of my first lesson I had called by the boys' toilets where I found my brother. He was in an awful mess, standing in the wash area, leaning over a washbasin dribbling blood into it. There was blood all over his shirtfront and part of his blazer and Steve was unable to speak coherently.

I removed one of the roller towels from its wooden mounting, held it to his lower face and bundled Steve round to the sick bay, calling for help as we went.

The French Master, Mr Moran, was our designated first-aider. He did little but fuss and said I should take Steve home, immediately. We were fortunate in that there was a bus due at the front of the school within a few minutes and after asking that someone telephone our father at his office to request he meet us, armed with great wads of cotton wool, Steve and I anxiously embarked on the thirty minute journey back to Warminster.

Dad, very evidently worried, was waiting for us. He took one look at Steve and immediately drove us to the accident unit at Warminster Hospital, while commending me for my part in getting Steve home. The staff there had a similar reaction. After a swift examination, fearing that he may lose a large piece of his tongue, an ambulance was summoned and Steve was taken at high speed to hospital in Bath, some twenty miles away.

Although the situation had been critical, the outcome was eventually favourable and Steve returned home after a couple of days.

Furious, though, is barely adequate to describe Father's reaction. He was not angry at the physical punishment and the fact that Steve had been struck. Dad never had any problem with corporal punishment and he realised that what had happened was never intended as blow to the head (which he would not have found acceptable) but was very unfortunate accident. What really aroused his ire was that when Steve left the classroom spitting blood, there had been no follow-up whatsoever on the injury and it was I who found him some time later. Father thought this was irresponsible in the extreme.

We were never apprised of the details—nor should we have been—but I was aware that Dad had a 'heavy' meeting with our headmaster, Mr Fairs, and I believe that there was a letter of apology from the Latin master.

## *Summary justice*

The seven-mile journey to school each morning was by coach and from home to the coach pick-up point was about three quarters of a mile. Steve and I were usually in good time (timeliness something Dad was a stickler for!) and often, being in no hurry, we would amble along the main road pavement towards town.

On our way, we passed a terrace of three-story houses that fronted right onto the pavement. One of them was occupied by Miss Marsh who frequently sat at her window observing passers-by, many of whom she knew by name.

One winter morning, Steve and I were dawdling and idly kicking a large piece of ice along the pavement. There had been a heavy snowfall a few days earlier and the road had been cleared by a snowplough and then salted. A thaw set in but had been followed by heavy frost which caused the slush debris at the roadside to congeal into large chunks of ice. It was one of these that we had liberated and were amusing ourselves with, alternately kicking it and sliding it along the frozen pavement.

As we passed the front of the house in question, Miss Marsh bustled from her front door and started to admonish us.

'You boys should have more respect for your shoes. Your parents pay good money and all you do is to scuff them,' and more in the same vein, wagging her finger emphatically. Then she had to pause for a few moments as she could not make herself heard above the engine noise from a heavy lorry coming along the road, probably carrying stone from one of the nearby Mendip quarries.

Before she could speak again, a shattering crash was clearly audible above the roar of the truck engine and the glass from a large sash window imploded into Miss Marsh's front room. Evidently, the lorry had clipped one of the ice chips at the roadside and the pinch of its tyre against the road had caused the ice to squirt out, rather as a plumb stone squeezed between thumb and forefinger. The window had been in the direct line of fire.

For a few seconds we all stood in speechless surprise, viewing the wrecked windowpane, then Miss Marsh recovered and looked at us accusingly.

'It's all your fault,' she said. 'If I hadn't had to come and speak to you, this would never have happened.'

Her statement seemed somewhat devoid of logic but privately, I thought it was fortunate that she *had* been outside because she could not then claim that we had actually kicked the ice through her window. I felt sorry for her but surely, common sense would prevail.

Steve and I decided that perhaps, after all, possibly, maybe, we didn't have quite as much time to catch bus as we had thought and a hasty departure was needed. As we ran off, between breaths, I called an explanation over my shoulder. Steve said he thought it was unfair, she would probably tell Dad.

By the time we returned home from school that night, Mother and Dad knew all about the incident. Common sense had *not* prevailed and we had been blamed but, for once, our version of events was believed. It wasn't the first time Dad had had dealings with Miss Marsh. She always had something about which to register a complaint—street lighting, refuse collection and such—but complaining about Steve and me was a first.

'It's unfortunate her window is broken but it is summary justice for her interfering,' Dad muttered quietly to Mother, somewhat unsympathetically.

We did, though, receive a fairly severe telling-off for scuffing our shoes.

## *Lightning does strike twice*

Before the end of that school year, there was an accident which affected the entire school.

The school was raising money to construct an outdoor swimming pool and one of the events planned for a special day to be held at the end of the summer term was a display of gymnastics. In late June, there was a week when the weather was particularly hot and oppressive and gym equipment had been carried out onto the sports field for the team to practice as it was too hot in the gymnasium.

The boys in my form had just changed for an afternoon cross country run when the weather broke and there was a thunderstorm of a magnitude that I later came to associate with those when the Southwest Monsoon broke in Bengal.

The rain was sudden and torrential. Our PE master directed us to carry the equipment back into the gymnasium with the utmost haste, before the rain could soak in and damage the leather covering on the vaulting horses. We were split into two groups and as my group was making its way onto the field and passing the back of the domestic science rooms, the end of the building was struck by lightning and some brickwork was dislodged from the gable.

The flash and bang were instantaneous and the noise was deafening. Debris fell into the playground. Our nervous laughter and banter was a poor disguise the terror we all undoubtedly felt. It was alarming but we were urged on to collect the equipment and only moments later there was a second lightning strike, this time to the French windows of the adjacent French room.

We collected a vaulting horse and spring board and as we were scurrying back to the gym with them, the second group passed us on their was back to the field to collect mats and other equipment.

The horse and spring board had been restored to the gym and we were on our way back out again when the third lightning strike crashed to earth in the field not far ahead of us into the middle of the other team. This was too much, too close, and we turned and ran back to the safety of the school building

We lost a classmate that afternoon, Colin Owen. Several staff from the classrooms on the north side of the school who had seen what happened through the French windows, had rushed out onto the field uncaring for their own safety, and there were attempts to resuscitate Colin. I later learned that it was token attempt and recognised as probably futile. Amazingly, Colin had appeared unharmed, but the soles of his gym shoes had been completely burnt off.

The mood of the entire school for the remainder of the term was very sombre indeed.

During my years at sea, I experienced several lightning strikes and one of the most noticeable after-effects is the smell. The ionised air has a strong odour similar to that of bleach. On each of those later occasions, it was the smell of chlorine that I found very evocative, reminding me of the tragic time a classmate had been killed by lightning.

## *Euphonium player wanted*

In a lighter vein.

It might be supposed from my description of home events that my father had no sense of humour. He was certainly a tough disciplinarian, a martinet even, but he also had a good sense of humour and was more than capable of the occasional prank himself.

One Saturday morning, Aunt Margaret was in the kitchen with Mother. I walked in on them when they were almost convulsed in laughter. Naturally, I wanted to share the joke but at first, Mother was reluctant to do so. 'Go on Molly. Andrew would appreciate knowing what Bill has done,' Aunt Margaret urged. Between them, they went on to explain that Dad had played something of a prank on Uncle George, Aunt Margaret's husband.

Uncle G was a rather short, rotund jovial man—almost as wide as he was tall. Surprisingly, for his stature, he was a very competent golfer and the South African international Bobby Locke, was a personal friend and Godfather to his son Chester. (He who wrecked all the garage doors with Steve and another friend.) Uncle George and Aunt Margaret lived nearby in a large property called Donum House and I think Bobby Locke sometimes referred to Uncle George as The Sultan of Donum.

Occasionally, Uncle George and he would play a round of golf for charity at the local West Wilts Club. Uncle G's glove factory (later becoming Dents of Westbury) patented and made the first golf gloves, initially under the Bobby Locke label, later, Henry Cotton. However, I digress.

Warminster Town Band had had to disband through lack of support and all the instruments and equipment the band had owned were handed in to the council offices. There was also some printed stationery that for some reason ended up in Dad's drawing office.

Within a day or two of all this being handed in, Uncle George, who knew nothing of the erstwhile Town Band, received a letter advising that they were in urgent need of a euphonium player. The writer had heard of Mr Jefferies' 'great prowess as a wind instrumentalist' and implored him in other gushing terms of similar double meaning to join the Town Band.

Apparently, Uncle G really thought the letter to be genuine and had taken it to the Yew Tree when he met with Father and other cronies the night before. Dad later told me that he had great difficulty keeping a straight face, especially when the assembled group, with some jocularity, kept making reference to the 'wind instrumentalist'.

What particularly amused them all was that, apart from having no musical ability whatsoever, Uncle George was profoundly deaf and could hear nothing without his hearing aid. Indeed, he had developed advantageous use of his disability to a fine art. It never failed to surprise me how the battery would often fail just when Aunt Margaret was giving him some instruction.

'George. Will you just . . . .'

'It's no good, Doe. The battery's down. I can't hear you,' he would interrupt, with unerring accuracy of the best moment to do so.

I was then just fourteen—and all the while, that little wanderlust seed was continuing to germinate. The notion of some sort of a career that involved travel was slowly taking root.

'The Sultan of Donum'

George Jefferies, with my father.

Written on the back of the photograph by golfer Bobby Locke:

His Serene Highness the Sultan of Donum snapped in the paddock prior to the Hunt Cup—his ADC in the rear.

## CHAPTER 7
# DECISION TIME

*Preparing for the dreaded GCE examinations*

During the Fourth Year, those of us that had not already made up our minds (most of us), were being encouraged to give serious thought to what we wished to make of our lives and what careers we should train for or embark upon.

Apart from our futures, there were implications for the school staff as well, as they faced the complex task of designing timetables to offer the appropriate course subjects in a multitude of permutations. Whatever the combination of subjects required, the core ones would in all cases be English grammar, mathematics and a science subject.

At the beginning of that school year, I had no firm employment ideas and, like many of my classmates, started attending the career advisory sessions, which were being co-ordinated by school staff.

I did have a notion, triggered by Brian Pike's good fortune, that I should like to see something of the world (wouldn't any teenage boy?) but beyond that, had no idea how this could be tied into any future employment—nor, frankly, did any of our careers advisory teachers. They, I suspect, regarded it is little more than romantic nonsense.

## *You want to do what?!*

The eventual outcome really only started to develop when Mother had some friends visiting to play solo one evening and I picked up on an overheard remark.

'Gordon came home on leave yesterday,' her friend Joyce was telling mother. I had met her girls who were closer Steve's age and I had heard that she had a much older son from an earlier marriage.

'Is Gordon in the Royal Navy then?' I asked, interest aroused.

'No dear, he's in the Merchant Navy. Just came off the *Queen Elizabeth* in Southampton.'

'What's the Merchant Navy?' I asked. As Warminster was not too distant from Southampton, I knew of the famous Cunard liners, The Queens, but had never given any thought as to how and by whom they were operated. Joyce explained briefly before continuing 'Why don't you talk to Gordon while he's home?' she suggested, taking a sip of her gin and tonic. 'Would you like me to arrange for you to meet him? He's ever so interesting.'

This seemed like a good idea and I thanked her.

Later, I asked Dad about the Merchant Navy but he evidently knew little and seemed very cagey, reluctant even, to discuss it. Then I told him about my conversation with Mother's friend and that Joyce had offered to arrange for me to meet Gordon as I quite thought I might like to go away to sea.

'You want to do what?!' he exploded. Dad had already met Gordon and the meeting had clearly prejudiced his notions about Merchant Seamen. 'You want to go and work with a bunch of poofters!' The question was rhetorical. He was never one to mince his words, especially in those days before political correctness. 'A bunch of queer bloody stewards. On the *Queens*. Right bloody ship for them,' he continued. The reason for Dad's reluctance to discuss the Merchant Navy was now apparent. There was no point in pursuing the matter and I let it drop. He thought all ships were manned entirely by homosexual stewards.

A few days later, however, in a calmer moment Dad had evidently been giving the matter some thought. His sense of reason had prevailed and it was he who raised the subject with me. 'Andrew. Were you serious when you asked about the Merchant Navy the other day?' he asked.

Dad had now acknowledged that the entire British merchant fleet could not possibly comprise solely of stewards and catering staff with, to his notions, perverse standards of sexual behaviour. There were, he recognised, navigating and engineering officers on all ships and the position of a ship's master was certainly one of responsibility and prestige. That of becoming a chief engineer was also an admirable achievement. They must have been specially trained.

I confirmed that I really was interested, adding that I found the practical application of mathematics in what we had learned of air navigation to be interesting and the idea of navigating the world's oceans was fascinating. Trigonometry, triangles of velocities, parallelograms of forces. This was certainly grist to Father's mill!

'Let's thee and me see what us can find out,' he concluded, surprisingly enthusiastically. Always a Yorkshire accent, but occasional lapses into the un-grammatical idiom generally only ever occurred when Dad was emotional.

I think in the end, it was he who talked to Gordon. I certainly didn't.

## *The Southampton Shipping Office*

Always methodical, my father set about discovering as much as he could about the Merchant Navy. I think he started out with visits to the local library and he soon found out about the Mercantile Marine Office, the Shipping Federation, and their rôle in manning merchant vessels. He certainly made numerous telephone calls and it wasn't too long before we made a trip to Southampton when he took me with him on an appointment to meet an august gentleman called The Shipping Master.

From this Dad learned about some of the British shipping companies who offered indentured apprenticeships, training midshipmen to become navigating officers. He found out that it was these officers who could continue training and on becoming a Master Mariner, may eventually progress to become a Captain, the ship's Master.

Marine engineers he was told, did not train as sea-going apprentices. They were recruited directly from heavy industry, usually from shipbuilding, often from railway workshops. They entered directly as junior officers and many of them in those days had 'signed on' solely as a means of avoiding National Service with one of the armed forces. Five years in the Merchant Navy was an alternative to conscription.

We also gleaned that there were basically four categories of ocean-going merchant vessel: passenger liners, cargo liners, tramps and tankers. Liners, we were told, only meant that the vessel sailed on a fixed route and schedule, unlike a tramp which sailed anywhere there was a cargo to be carried and at any time.

Dad wrote many letters, painstakingly by hand, and it was not long before he had amassed quite a file of information from which he made a basic analysis. Viz.

Tankers had a poor reputation for safety with an unfortunate tendency to catch fire and blow up. They spent little time in port and often at remote, smelly and inaccessible terminals.

(Fortunately, now, we know much more about static electricity, explosive limits and spontaneous combustion and tanker safety is as high as that of any vessel.)

Passenger liners, too, spent little time in port and their routes were rather limited. (The days of cruise ships had yet to arrive.)

Tramps were often considered to be rather inferior vessels which could be away for extended periods, sometimes years at a time, with the crew captive until the vessel should return to a home port.

Cargo liners, well they may not have the glamour of the passenger liners, although they frequently carried up to twelve passengers which was the maximum permitted without carrying a ship's doctor, but their areas of service were less restricted. The routes were more diverse and thereby, potentially more interesting. They also tended to spend much longer in port.

Cargo liners, then, seemed favourite.

## *But what about farming?*

In this narrative so far, I have frequently recounted events involving my father and this is likely because we were quite often at odds. Tacitly, Mother usually supported Dad's discipline, but privately, later, she would often be sympathetic. 'Dad may be hard, but it's for you own good you know, dear,' and often continued 'You know he thinks the world of you boys.' The inference was plain but the word *love* was not one that was ever used.

Nevertheless, when I first expressed an interest in seafaring, Mother, proud of her farming heritage did say to me one time, 'Are you sure about going away to sea, Andrew?' and then went on to remind me of a proposition Uncle Reg had made after I had spent so much time working with him at Manor Farm.

'Uncle Reg has offered to put you through agricultural college so you can go and work for him if you want to. You could work up to becoming one his farm mangers, you know.' I did know, and I also knew that what mother had left unsaid was the inference that as he and Aunt May had no family, I may ultimately have been very well set up indeed. I also knew that for someone else to finance sending me through college would have been hard for Dad to take. He was a proud man.

Looking back, my life could have been very different. I always thoroughly enjoyed school holidays spent with Uncle Reg on the farm. I was fond of Uncle Reg and genuinely enjoyed his company. This being so, my working hard was a natural consequence from his approbation. Nevertheless, I was aware that some of the other labour viewed my presence with suspicion and I thought that were I to take up farming as a career move I should never be able to hold my head up as the Boss's relative without striving to be the hardest working person on the farm. It would become an invidious situation.

Anyway, by that time I had already been bitten by the wanderlust bug—and Master Mariner did sound rather a grand aspiration.

## *Thos. and Jno.*

Eventually, all Dad's research into the shipping companies who operated apprenticeship schemes was narrowed to one strong contender, Thomas and Jonathon Brocklebank of Liverpool.

The Brocklebank Line was reputedly the oldest shipping company in Britain and had been started by one Samuel Brocklebank. Although a Master Mariner, he had been a shipbuilder in Massachusetts when the Boston Tea Party took place and subsequent colonial events firmed his resolve that it was time to move back home to England. On his return, he ceased shipbuilding and started acquiring a large fleet of sailing vessels.

Eventually the company was handed over to his sons Thomas and Jonathon and later still, was amalgamated with Cunard Line who purchased a significant shareholding.

At the time of Father's research, about twenty eight Brocklebank vessels were operating a cargo liner service from UK and the near Continent to India and the East Coast of the United States.

After considerable discussion as Dad tried to make very sure that going to sea was something I really wanted, application was made to Brocklebank Line for an indentured apprenticeship.

I was only fourteen years of age when they asked me to attend for an interview in Liverpool.

## *The family responded*

Up until now, it would probably be generally correct to say that all the family were either engineers of some sort or from the farming community. When it became known, my desire to go to sea caused something of a ripple. No-one had ever heard of such a thing.

Soon after the invitation to attend Liverpool, Uncle Tom and Aunt Olive turned up on one of their un-announced Sunday visits. True to form, their timing coincided with that at which Mother was starting to cook the vegetables for lunch.

The rhetorical question of 'Are you *sure* you have enough, Molly?' went unanswered as Steve and I were told to lay extra places at table.

I suppose it was inevitable that after Uncle T's routine account of how much bigger his vegetables were than those Dad had grown, followed by his customary 'erbs o' the earth homily, the conversation at table turned to my forthcoming interview in Liverpool.

'Do you know Liverpool, Bill?' Dad was asked, and before he could respond, 'Bin there a couple a times. Reckon we should go up together an' I could show 'e the way.'

Thus did Uncle Tom inveigle himself into the expedition.

I think I minded less than Dad, although I had been looking forward to a couple of days when just he and I would make the trip to Liverpool. I had been recalling the last occasion we spent some time together. It had been shortly after passing the eleven-plus examination and I had been interviewed and accepted for Frome Grammar School. As a reward, Dad took me to London for a week of sight-seeing. I thoroughly enjoyed it and to this day have special memories of visiting the Kensington Science Museum. It was full of exhibits to interest a small boy and I recall the fascination of seeing Focault's pendulum, marking the hours of the day, swinging in relationship to space as the earth slowly turned. I also experienced my first flight. It was from Heathrow and we were airborne for thirty minutes, flying low over central London in a DeHavilland Dragon bi-plane.

## *Liverpool Bound*

The time for our trip to Liverpool soon arrived and Dad, Uncle T and I set off in Dad's Ford Prefect. There had been much discussion and planning of the route and of course, Uncle T knew the best way to go. I was given a set of maps and, sitting in the rear, designated the 'official navigator'.

'You want to be a navigator. May as well start,' Dad had suggested but I suspected in truth was he was providing me something with which to amuse myself on the journey.

Dad was driving and it very soon became apparent to me that he was not following the route Tom had decreed. When I started to say something, a knowing wink reflected from the driver's mirror silenced me. Uncle T was unaware—he was good naturedly telling me about an event a few years earlier when he had been the butt of a New Year prank carried out by Father and Uncle David. This was good stuff; I was hearing more of Father's sense of humour.

They and wives had, apparently, all been to a New Year's Eve Ball at the Bull Hotel in Bridport. It had been, said Dad, joining in, a somewhat 'liquid' occasion and Uncle T had over-imbibed. The following morning, suffering somewhat, Tom had been complaining that he thought he had lost some money. The truth was that he had spent it but was unable to remember doing so.

Uncle David, well known for his very acute sense of humour, immediately spotted an opportunity for some fun at Tom's expense.

'Can't you remember when we left the Bull this morning?' he asked Tom, knowing full well that he couldn't. 'Don't you remember knocking that young constable's helmet off when we left the pub yard?'

'No,' replied Tom, 'Did *I* do that?'

'Well you did—and you probably haven't heard the last of it.'

'What do you mean? Surely he would have taken it as a bit if New Year fun?'

'He *did*,' said Uncle David '—until you tried to bribe him not to take it any further by giving him a fiver for the Police Benevolent Fund.'

By this time, Uncle Tom was beginning to get rather worried. Father got in on the act.

'If I were you, Tom, I shouldn't wait. I should get up round to the police station and see the Chief Inspector,' Dad suggested.

'What for?' asked a very contrite, puzzled Uncle T.

'Explain. Tell him it was just high spirits. New Year and all that. I reckon your best bet is to get in first and make an apology. He'll probably understand.' And more along the same lines, backed up by Uncle David.

Between them, they could be very convincing.

Later that day, Uncle Tom went to see the Chief Inspector and proffered a profuse apology.

Some time after the event, he learned that it had all been a put-up job made possible by Dad knowing the Chief Inspector personally. Before Uncle T went to the Police Station, Father had telephoned, explained what was going on and the Chief Inspector had played his part to perfection.

'Your Uncle Tom received a severe telling off for something he had never even done,' concluded Dad.

Uncle Tom, I recall, then retaliated, getting his own back, taking mischievous delight in reminding Father of a time when he was the butt of a joke. He recounted the occasion when I put water in the petrol tank of his Dad's car—and he took great pleasure in pointing out that their mother-in-law had been on board at the time.

With these and other family stories being told, re-told and undoubtedly embellished, the long journey to Liverpool passed quite quickly.

We were approaching the outskirts of the city and they had changed drivers. Uncle Tom was behind the wheel. Then we were in the Mersey Tunnel in dense traffic, and Uncle Tom, quite a big man, suddenly started bouncing and wriggling in his seat, rocking the little car and narrowly missing oncoming traffic.

'What the hell are you doing, Tom?' demanded Dad, obviously concerned for our safety.

'Bloody cigarette!' he replied.

That was another story later told around the family; how Tom dropped a lit cigarette between his thighs while driving through the Mersey Tunnel and had to wriggle his backside and sit on it to extinguish it. Burned a hole in the seat of his trousers. It was another tale that improved with the telling. The more often the tale was recounted, the bigger the hole in Tom's trousers became and the closer we were to having a crash in the Mersey Tunnel and log-jamming the Liverpool rush hour traffic.

'They damned near had to get the breakdown truck into the tunnel!'

## *The Cunard Building*

After some difficulty, despite Uncle T's professed knowledge of the city, (or perhaps, because of it) we eventually located the Shaftsbury Hotel where Father had booked accommodation for two nights. That evening we went to see a film *Brothers-in-Law* which Dad thought rather appropriate, having in mind his relationship to Uncle Tom.

Brocklebank's office occupied one floor in the Cunard Building near Liverpool's Pierhead. In good time the following morning, Dad and I attended for my interview. Initially we met a senior clerk, Mr Danny Roberts, who had responsibility for all the apprentices and after a short session during which Brocklebank's and the apprenticeship scheme were outlined, I left Dad in his company and was taken to what I believe was a boardroom.

It was a massively impressive room, panelled in dark mahogany and with numerous glass-cased models of ships around the perimeter. Many of the models were of vessels in full sail, others were only half of a ship but had been mounted on a mirror to give the illusion of being complete. Glowering down from the walls above were several large, gloomy oil portraits of bearded gentlemen in frockcoats. The patina on the surface of a huge mahogany table standing in the centre of the room was probably indicative of its antiquity. It was surrounded by heavy leather chairs upholstered in hide, pinned with domed brass nails.

It was awesome.

My interview was carried out by Captain Charles Cadwallader, the Marine Superintendent, who was an imposing white haired gentleman dressed in a morning suit, set off with a very colourfully flamboyant bowtie. After half an hour or so during which I was quizzed about my school studies, Dad was ushered into the room to join us and was seated beside me, facing Captain Cadwallader across the table. Although I don't remember much of the initial interview, I do recall what happened soon afterwards.

'Well, young man,' said Captain Cadwallader, 'You seem to be interested in physics. Can you tell me ways in which you might magnetise a piece of steel or soft iron?'

I thought I was on fairly safe ground here and quickly responded 'Yes sir. One way would be to stroke it with another magnetic,' and went on to define what the polarity of the new magnet would be.

'Not quite correct,' he replied. 'You would need two magnets and using opposite poles on each, commence stroking from the centre to the ends.'

'Yes sir, but...' and tailed off on receiving a surreptitious kick on the ankle from Father.

Later, Dad, who knew all about residual magnetism and hysteresis, admonished me, 'You were both correct—as you well know—but it is not a good idea to contradict someone when you are a candidate for interview!'

A few days after our return home a letter arrived offering me an apprenticeship. It was, however, conditional upon achieving acceptable grades in at least five subjects in the General Certificate of Education examinations. They had to include maths, English and at least one science subject, preferably physics.

I had not then reached my fifteenth birthday but I suspect that Father's relief was probably on a par with my excitement at the first positive steps toward selecting my career.

Charting a career might be a rather apposite way of putting it.

## CHAPTER 8
# FINAL SCHOOLDAYS

*Air Training Corps*

I had been promoted to Corporal in the Air Training Corps and during the Easter holiday in 1957, was the senior cadet in charge of a group from our squadron that went for a week's camp at RAF Halton.

As on previous such occasions, I enjoyed myself immensely. We met up with a bunch of cadets from the Wirral with whom we had struck up a friendship the previous year when on camp at RAF Hawarden, near Chester. While on these ATC camps we were always required to enroll on a short programme of related study. On previous occasions I had attended courses on Airmanship and Engineering and as a flying day was guaranteed anyway, I allowed myself to be cajoled into joining the others of our little group on a PT Course. Definitely not my scene as I have never been particularly keen on sport!

Nevertheless, I enjoyed it—even the obligatory cross country run we undertook before breakfast each morning, followed by a wheelbarrow race across a football pitch. The race didn't finish on reaching the far side of the pitch as we then changed places before racing back to the starting side again. The race always gave rise to great hilarity as the arms of the 'wheelbarrow' always gave out before the finish, resulting in the cadet being pushed chin-first through the mud. A quick shower and we were more than ready to attend the cookhouse for breakfast!

One of the objectives of the PT course was to introduce cadets to as many different sporting activities as possible, often ones which would not be undertaken at school. I recall that we tried our hands at judo and at fencing and we received some boxing coaching from an RAF instructor called Jimmy MacTaggart. When he achieved Olympic Gold for boxing not long afterwards I was proud to say that I had received some instruction from him. The instructors also showed us some elementary un-armed combat. This was really good stuff for teenage boys—but it was clearly not sufficiently advanced to be dangerous.

## *Last term at school*

Apart from the foregoing, the two or so terms of final preparation leading up to the General Certificate Examination passed quite rapidly and were mainly uneventful. The end of the Summer Term arrived all too quickly and for many of us the trepidation we felt at facing a programme of such important examinations was only slightly offset by the fact that on days when we had no examination, attendance at school was not mandatory.

Eventually, the GCE examinations had been completed and we anxiously awaited the results. It was mid July and the majority of my year were preparing to leave school. Those planning to remain and enter the sixth form—subject to a good outcome in the GCE examinations—were reviewing their A-Level options. Their studies would continue for another two years when success in passing two or perhaps three A-level examinations would gain entry to Oxford or Cambridge University. In those days, there was not the proliferation of universities available to today's students nor, indeed, such a diverse choice of degree courses.

Frome Grammar School was proud of its VIth form with the availability of all the true academic subjects. There was a steady stream of pupils entering well established universities and when staff recognised any with even higher quality, they were entered for Oxford—and were accepted!

It was quite usual for school-leavers to perpetrate some final act of mischief or a prank and my year was no exception. I am not certain, all these years later, who actually came up with the idea but it was I who, shortly before the final assembly, being assisted over the fence enclosing the outdoor swimming pool, actually carried out the deed. Our idea originated from an experiment in chemistry earlier that term which involved using potassium permanganate. We had been shown how just a few crystals could be dissolved in bucket of water, turning it pale red.

During the weeks leading up to the end of term, four or five of us boys visited the local chemist's shops each purchasing a small quantity at a time. On the final morning of the term, several ounces of permanganate of potash were dissolved in half a dozen or so bottles of water. When I emptied the mixture into the swimming pool, the convection currents set up in the water by the summer sun shining on its surface mixed the solution and the entire pool slowly swirled into pale pink.

Task accomplished, we attended the final assembly, aware that for most of us it was a momentous time as we would no longer be schoolchildren but would soon be commencing our careers.

After the final assembly, reciting the General Confession and singing 'Jerusalem' one last time, we all parted company with promises to 'keep in touch' and several of us had autograph books into which classmates—and some of the staff—wrote ditties and good wishes.

## *Many years later . . .*

As to the 'prank', those of us involved thought we had been very daring. We believed we had gotten away with it and that the staff were entirely unaware. How wrong we were!

Almost thirty years later, with our own daughters in secondary schools, Ruth and I had several times met up with our former English teacher and one time Form Mistress, Miss Reed. She lived nearby in Cinderford and we enjoyed pub lunches at various hostelries in the Forest Of Dean. Joan Reed was only a little older than our headmaster's daughter and a close friend of the family. More than once, Mr and Mrs Fairs also joined us. I would never, ever, have believed when I was at school that in the future we could have enjoyed such a relaxed occasion in their company! Gilbert Fairs (Joe, to all the pupils) had also been a lay preacher and was held in very high esteem by both staff and pupils and, indeed, by all the parents.

While writing this, I also recall Miss Reed's advice before the GCE English Grammar examination. In the first part of the paper, an essay was compulsory but in the second part it was an option with sentence analysis being the alternative. Miss Reed suggested that, with a little work on the subject, it would be far easier to achieve a high mark in the latter as sentence analysis, unlike an essay, is entirely objective—either right or wrong. At these later meetings, I also dared to pull her leg for the book choice she made for our English Literature GCE. The Jane Austen book, Northanger Abbey, would never be particularly inspiring to 15-year old boys!

The first time we all met for lunch, just as we were leaving the restaurant, Mr Fairs looked at me and said, eyes twinkling with humour, evidently anticipating my surprise,

'By the way, if you think, young Parks, that I don't know who put the potassium permanganate in the swimming pool nearly thirty years ago you would be very much mistaken.'

His comment had come entirely out of the blue and although I was amused that he prefixed my name with the adjective 'young', the remark was so unexpected that I was left speechless.

I was thinking that he had just uttered what must be the most perfect of last-words on a subject when Mr Fairs smiled, before going even one better and continuing, 'You boys had the school talking for some time but it did no harm. I don't suppose you were aware that permanganate is sometimes used as a mild disinfectant and you did a very good job of killing off a developing problem.' He paused before concluding, 'The pool was beginning to grow algae.'

Mr Fairs was correct. At the time we hadn't known its disinfectant properties, but by the time of this last-word comment, I was familiar with its use in mild solution to wash fruit and vegetables. In my early days at sea we always carried potassium permanganate in the ship's dispensary and its use when washing produce was a common precaution against cholera.

Sadly, not many months later but after several pleasant luncheon meetings, we attended Hereford Cathedral. Gilbert Fairs' memorial service was a very moving and well-attended occasion. Esteem and respect had not diminished with Joe's retirement.

## CHAPTER 9
# HONEST TOIL

*Summer Holiday Job*

School days now behind me, I was waking to the reality that I could no longer spend a summer vacation in Bridport, subsisting on what little pocket money I had saved, supplemented by generous top-ups from Auntie Olive (who always spoiled me) and earnings on the farm from Uncle Reg. Father made it very clear that having left school, I was expected to be more financially self-dependent and pocket money was no longer an option.

Until such time as the GCE results were published and my apprenticeship with Thos and Jno Brocklebank commenced, a holiday job was a necessity. Fortunately, Malcolm's Dad, Mr Davies, came to the rescue and employed both of us to assist with the harvest of the experimental barleys.

Arthur Guinness and Company annually leased a plot of land from one of the arable farmers in Southern Wiltshire. Each year, for rotational purposes, the lease was in a different location and this year it was part of a large field on the downs between Warminster and Shaftesbury and some distance, several miles in fact, from any proper road.

The day started at seven when Mr Davies and Malcolm arrived with the Land Rover and collected me from home.

On our way through the town another member of Mr Davies' staff, Horace Jones, was picked up before making our way out to the trial ground.

It was quite painstaking work. Horace drove the combine harvester, which had been constructed with a six-foot wide cutter specially for Guinness barley trials, while Tom Davies rode on the back. At the end of each pass and as a trial bed was harvested, Mr Davies would first label, then dump a sack of barley.

Malcolm's and my task was to follow behind with tractor and trailer collecting the bags, identifying the particular strain of barley from the plan of trials before weighing and recording the yield.

Any teenage boy would enjoy the sense of power emanating from driving a tractor and Malcolm and I were no exceptions. We took turns to drive and never took the shortest route.

We were however, in serious trouble on one particular occasion.

I should explain that for some years after the War, and still at that time, tractors often used a paraffin-like fuel called tractor vaporising oil. It was relatively inexpensive but it had a disadvantage. As the octane rating of TVO was very low, it would not vaporise until the engine was hot. To overcome this the tractors had a second, smaller, fuel tank containing petrol which was used when starting from cold

One afternoon our tractor came to a stuttering halt. The engine stopped and was silent apart from the occasional spitting of hot oil. We had run out of fuel. When Mr Davies jumped off the combine to come and investigate, he found we had exhausted not the TVO but had run out of petrol. A burst of Welsh expletives followed, concluding, 'That's it! That's enough! You bloody boyos can stop the damned joy riding!'

Mr Davies was irate because apart from the higher cost of petrol, the field was so far off the beaten track that all the fuel had to be manhandled and brought to site in the Land Rover.

That morning, we had started the engine on petrol as usual but in our exuberance and enjoyment of driving the tractor, had completely forgotten to switch to TVO once the machine was hot. The oversight only became apparent when the petrol ran out but the subsequent tongue-lashing we received served well to ensure we didn't forget a second time!

## *GCE Results*

The harvest was finished, summer was drawing to a close and I had managed to save a little of the money earned. Examination results were imminent.

Then the day came and the results so eagerly awaited, arrived on the doormat.

I could scarcely believe what I was reading. Although I had worked harder during my last term at Frome than in any of the previous years, the unthinkable had happened. I had satisfactory passes in all the other subjects but I had failed to achieve the grade that Brocklebanks required in that subject most important to a navigator, mathematics.

From previous experience of such shortcomings, I fully expected to be on the receiving end of a tirade of castigation and recriminations from Father. To my amazement, I received very little—which was almost as bad. I felt guilty. I had let him down very badly after all the efforts he had made on my behalf. The multitude of letters and telephone calls, finding out about sea-going apprenticeships; the visit to the Shipping Office in Southampton and then the trip to Liverpool for interview. I suspect he sensed how I felt and thought it punishment enough. He had also been surprised at the examination result, having seen my prior study and revision efforts.

Dad prided himself on 'good Yorkshire common sense'. His approach to what I thought a disaster was pragmatic and after a comment with, surprisingly, a mixed metaphor about spilt milk and salt in a wound, concluding with what a fool I was, he started planning.

'What's needed now is damage limitation.' It was the first time I had heard the expression. He continued, 'We need to draw up an action plan.' Action plan, that was another first, too. He then sat with me at the kitchen table and started to write a list. Failure was not a part of it.

The first task was to contact Mr Fairs and seek his help to arrange a re-take in the December examinations. It was exceptional as the school normally never entered candidates for the intermediate sitting but Dad was evidently persuasive and Mr Fairs agreed to make the necessary arrangement. Dad had drawn the plans and written the specification for the construction of the new swimming pool gratis—the one I had coloured. I think, to use the modern expression, he may have called in a favour.

As I would not actually be returning to school, a programme of home study and revision of the syllabus was next on the list. This was accomplished with assistance from my former maths teacher and a study timetable was drawn up which I would follow under Father's scrutiny and guidance.

That accomplished, he contacted Brocklebanks, optimistic that by showing them positive steps were already in hand to rectify the situation, they would hold the position open for me. Evidently, it actually suited Brocklebanks rather well as they would not have been able to offer me a berth until early in 1958 but I was not told that at the time. I suppose Dad thought it better to keep the pressure on. So, subject to eventual success in achieving a higher grade in the next GCE maths examination, Mr Roberts, the superintendent in charge of apprentices agreed to keep the opportunity open. Now, I think another favour may have been called in.

I only found out several years later, long after I had completed my apprenticeship, that when we had been in Liverpool for my interview, Dad had established a special relationship with Mr Roberts. Danny Roberts (as, later, all us apprentices referred to him) had a son slightly older than I who was keen to become a civil engineer. Dad had been able to help him with some career advice in return for which, Mr Roberts reported on my progress. It explained how Dad came to know so much about my correspondence course work. It had puzzled me at the time and when I once asked, 'How did you know I was late sending in the assignment on meteorology?' Dad simply tapped the side of his nose and winked but he refused to be drawn any further.

The final task on the list Dad compiled that fateful day was that of finding a job and since, all being well, it would be only temporary employment what that job may be was relatively unimportant. I just had to acquire some self-sufficiency.

In those years, not too long after the war, Warminster was undergoing considerable development and several estates of council houses were under construction. Much of this development was being carried out by one local contractor. In due course, I was given employment on one of those estates as a Chippie's Mate.

Mother, I recall, was not too sure about this and remonstrated.

'Bill, what will people think? The Surveyor's son working with a carpenter—and on a building site too!' I overheard. Clearly, she had other worries as well and continued 'And what about all the foul language he'll hear?'

Father would have none of it.

'I very much doubt that Andrew'll hear anything he hasn't already heard—and what about when he goes away to sea? I'm sure he'll hear it all then, and plenty of it, I wouldn't wonder!'

I noticed the positive *when* he goes away, rather than *if* he goes away.

'It'll do him no harm to get his hands dirty and he'll likely learn some skills which will stand him in good stead in the future,' he continued. 'You are from farming folk, Molly. You should know as well as anyone, there's no shame in honest toil and it will do him good to realise it.'

That was the end of it. I went to work on a building site but the truth of Dad's statement about honest toil has stayed with me throughout my life.

## *On 'The Buildings'*

By the time schools were re-opening for the beginning of the new academic year, I had already started working for Thomas Holdoway and Son. The carpenter to whom I was assigned, David, had not long completed his National Service in the Army. At first, he was somewhat suspicious, thinking I was a dodger and planning to enter the Merchant Navy only as an alternative to National Service with one of the Armed Forces. He soon realised that is was not the case, that it was a career move. Conscription had ceased a couple of years earlier.

We soon became firm friends and I enjoyed working with David. He taught me several of his skills, not least of which was to swing a hammer vertically upwards in front of my face when nailing plaster board to a ceiling—although I did rather more than 'bruise' the plasterboard a few times before I finally got the hang of it! David was left-handed which was a distinct advantage when we were 'bumping'—nailing down—floorboards and other similar tasks. We never got in each other's way.

When I first started on site, some of the other workers, including the foreman, were very suspicious and thought that I would go running to tell my father of all the things I saw, especially mistakes. I never did. Although Dad was always interested to hear what I had been doing he never asked me anything that could have even remotely involved me in tale telling.

Several times, David came to my aid when I was being slagged off and being referred to as 'The effing surveyor's son,' or given the cold shoulder by other workers during our tea break. I took little notice of them anyway as tea breaks didn't last that long.

I was no telltale he would affirm and eventually when they came to believe it, there was quite a lot of leg-pulling and practical joking. More than once, as we came to leave, I found the haversack containing my thermos flask and sandwiches had been nailed to the floor. Another time, when we were working inside, it was cold and David used some small off-cuts of floorboard to light a fire in the hearth. We were soon coughing and spluttering and rushing to open windows to clear the smoke. 'Chimney must be blocked,' said David. Later, we spotted the tile over the chimney pot but never found out who put it there. David had his suspicions that it was the foreman, Bill Hicks.

At tea break, one time, I recall some of the brickies had been complaining about the foreman. 'Reckon his parent got it wrong,' David replied. 'Don't think he had two. Should have called him Boll 'Icks—and dropped the aitch off his family name.'

Spelling wasn't David's strong point and it was a moment or two before anyone realised what he meant but the laughter was heartfelt.

David Seviour had a very good reputation. He was a firm believer in the adage that a job worth doing is worth doing well; he had little patience with skivers and was one of the few carpenters, I learned, that could oversee the full construction of a roof including, in those days, fabricating all the trusses. Hipped, gabled or mansard, David was recognised as the man with both the skill and knowledge and was respected for it.

When we were working inside houses on so called 'second fixings', there was concern that the floors should be kept as free from the site mud as possible. David came up with a simple solution and made stilts for us both so that we could keep our footwear clean.

'Always know where you two are skiving,' one of the plumbers let slip one morning at tea break. David raised his eyebrows questioningly. 'Stilts. Outside. Propped on the wall. Gives you away every time.' We had never thought about it but we had wondered how the foreman always seemed to know exactly where to find us. Thereafter, the stilts were always laid on the floor of the hall with just the muddy tips protruding through the door. We saw rather less of Mr Hicks.

Meanwhile, I was spending several evenings each week at my maths and if I struggled with any of the algebra, Dad was always more than willing to help me. His approach was that solving algebraic problems should be done as though telling a story of logic.

'First write down all the things you know about the problem. Then write down all the things that are readily deduced, their relationships. Define what you are planning to prove and you are more than halfway there,' he told me. 'And if it helps the logic by including phrases explaining the steps, then do so.'

Practicing what he said, Dad's proofs would contain phrases between the lines of algebra such as 'but because . . . or . . ., it follows that . . .,' and something else would be logically deduced. His method made much more sense to me. He was painstaking in his explanations and would often reason through something several times, but once I said I had grasped what I had been shown, the paper would be torn up and I was on my own.

Christmas was rapidly approaching and with it, the time to re-sit the examination. Soon, both were behind me. We had enjoyed spending time in Bridport over the Christmas which saddened me a little as I realised I was potentially on the threshold of leaving home and I recalled all the happy holidays I had enjoyed there. Now, once again, I was waiting for examination results.

Soon, the result arrived and this time it was cause for celebration. Brocklebanks were contacted and things started to roll, gathering momentum as the New Year receded.

I received an extensive list of all the uniform and other kit I should require. Bearing a special chart from the Company's uniform suppliers in Liverpool, I was taken to a local tailor to be measured for my double-breasted black doeskin naval uniform, which I had now learned, was called a 'reefer'. The information was sent off and in due course my sea kit arrived. There was a lot of it.

I had received my reefer uniform, a battle dress, two uniform hats and three or four white covers, white buckskin and white canvas shoes, black shoes, denim work clothes and I had never seen so many shirts! Six with starched white fronts and even more detachable collars—some of them wing collars,—six shirts with short sleeves for wear in the tropics with an equal number of white shorts. I also had two sets of midshipman's epaulettes and two long white uniforms, number tens, for formal tropical wear. It cost Dad a small fortune!

There were trips to Southampton and to Bristol for pre-sea medical and a special sight test, which involved the use of an oil lantern and a rotating slide of pinholes in red, green and white glass. It was a stringent test simulating the appearance of distant navigation lights and made more difficult with the lantern being shone at a mirror to increase the apparent distance.

I was photographed for my seaman's Discharge Book and a full set of finger and thumbprints were taken for my seaman's identity card.

Finally, Dad took me to one of the local solicitors (one of his Masonic pals) where signatures were formally witnessed and the red seal fixed on my Apprentices Indentures. This impressive linen document obligated me to obey all lawful commands of any Master on whose ship I may be serving and he in turn would ensure I received sustenance, linen and a very meagre payment. My indentures also stipulated: *Nor will the Apprentice visit any alehouses or taverns unless upon the Master's business.* That puzzled me until Dad's friend explained that historically, contracts to carry cargoes had often been agreed between Masters and shippers in just such establishments.

Later, I saw documents of apprentices only a few years older than I whose indentures also included a clause *nor houses of ill repute* among the other restrictions that could only be waived *when upon the Master's business*. How, I wondered, would Mr Knight have explained that one!

The Indentures were sent back to Liverpool. I was ready. My kit was packed and we had been down to Bridport when Aunt Olive catered a farewell dinner for me. Dad made a little speech wishing me safety and success on the high sea. I responded and thanked him for all that he had done for me in helping me to achieve the ambition. It was all rather emotional. I was only sixteen and about to leave home and would soon be on my way to India. Journey to the so-called far-flung corners of the earth as the family perceived it.

My days working with Holdoway were drawing to a close just as the Munich air disaster occurred when many of the Manchester United football team perished.

I was waiting now only for Brocklebanks to advise where and when I would join my first ship.

Mother was a little upset.

I was a little apprehensive.

Father was a little relieved. Relieved, I think, that after all the worries of my poor school reports, I was about to embark on what he thought was a worthwhile career.

Apprehensive I may have been—but I was also more than a little excited.

JUST A SIMPLE SEAMAN

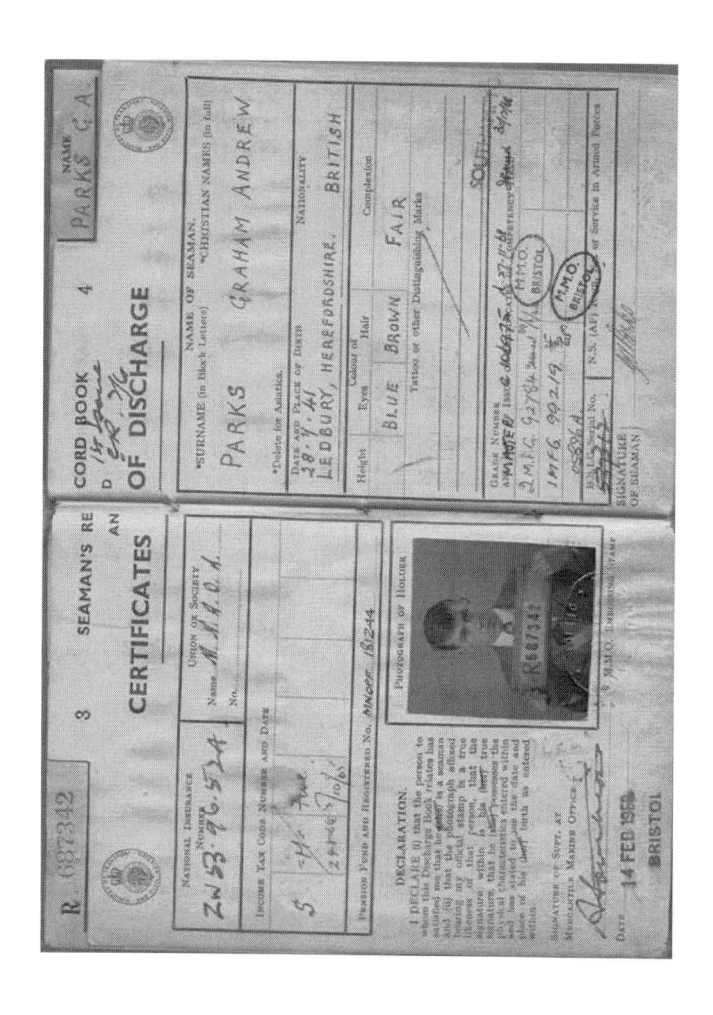

# Andrew Parks

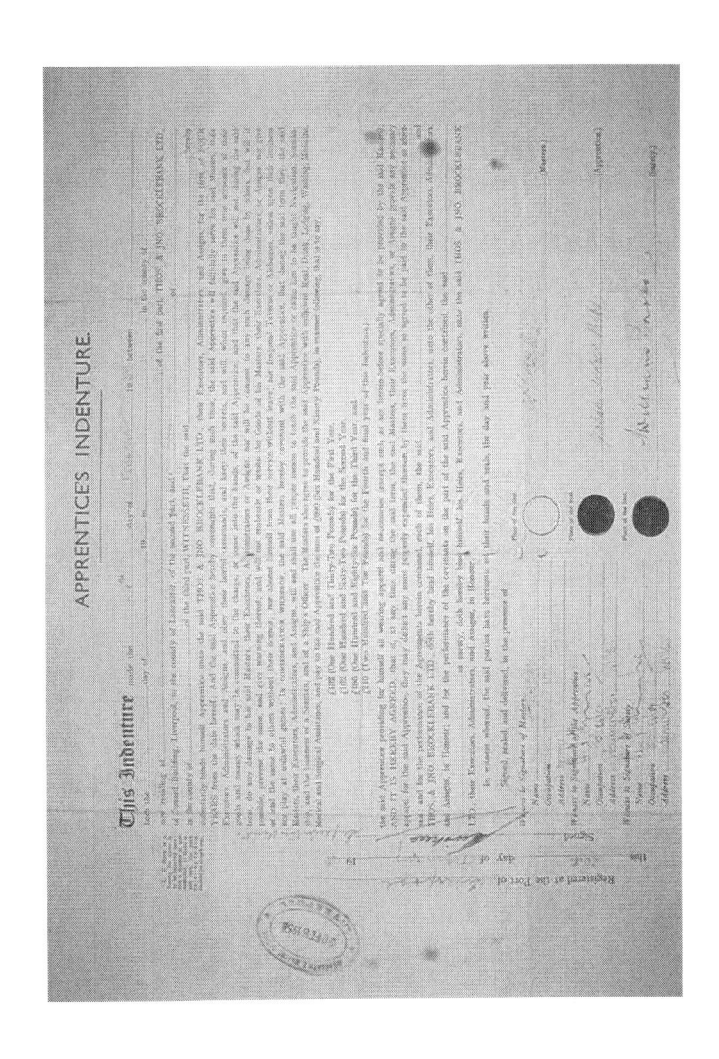

## CHAPTER 10
# FIRST SHIP, FIRST DAYS

## *Joining Day*

I suppose it is because the *ss Manipur* was my first ship that it carries many vivid memories. All the experiences were so new. Also, of course, as one gets older it is often difficult to recall what happened last week but memories of events years in the past remain as clear as ever!

Mum and Dad had driven me up to London where I was to join *Manipur* in the Royal Docks. They had, I was aware, both been struggling to maintain a brave face on the journey up from Wiltshire. After all, at the tender age of only sixteen, their eldest son, their firstborn was leaving home—and not just to attend college or live somewhere nearby.

Much of the journey was in silence, each of us, probably, having our own thoughts of my future but at one stage Mother had broached the subject of going ashore in foreign ports. We knew that after leaving the near Continent, the ship's first real foreign port of call outbound to India would be Algiers I had already had my leg pulled about getting lost in the Kasbah. Mum was trying to caution me against the dangers of loose women and was clearly embarrassed, not quite knowing how best to express her concerns. Father, typically down-to-earth and forthright, came to her rescue.

'I think Andrew knows what you are trying to say, Molly.' Then turning his head slightly towards me as he drove, 'Keep your nose clean. Right? Enough said.' That was very clearly the end of *that* conversation and it was also obvious that Dad, too, had been embarrassed by the topic.

When we arrived at the Royal Albert Dock, the dock police scrutinised my letter of appointment before, seemingly reluctantly, granting permission to enter. We drove along between the dock warehouses looking for a glimpse of the *ss Manipur*. There seemed such a bustle of activity and eventually Dad spotted her curved stern between to two warehouses where he also found a spot to park that seemed safe from all the traffic. A crane was unloading chests from one of the holds and there was a wonderful aroma of tea leaves.

Climbing the ship's gangway, I felt very apprehensive and was self-conscious in the unfamiliar uniform—despite Mother's assurances about how smart it looked.

As we stepped onto the ship's deck, we were met by a seaman wearing a white topped sailor's hat with the designation Quartermaster woven into the hatband. We identified ourselves.

'You'll be needing to see the Chief Officer,' he said with a vague wave of his arm. 'Bridge deck, amidships accommodation, aft, port,' Port and starboard were no mystery to me but these directions to the chief officer's cabin seemed a contradiction. Amidships *and* aft?

Eventually, after some wandering around accommodation panelled in teak and smelling of wax polish, we happened on an open door leading into a cluttered office. It had a small, highly polished brass plate above the lintel. 'Chief Officer.'

I knocked, timidly, half expecting to be told I had no business being on board.

'Enter!' Very peremptorily.

Fumbling my peaked cap behind my back, I peered round the inner door of the office while Mother and Dad remained in the alleyway outside.

'Parks,' I said, and after a long pause during which I was scrutinised, 'Apprentice,' breaking the silence, but not realising that being in uniform this was a statement of the obvious.

The Chief Officer was in shirt sleeves with his tie partly undone and his reefer jacket was thrown carelessly across a built-in settee. He removed his slippered feet from the corner of a coffee table and discarded a magazine he had been browsing.

A tanned hand was outstretched.

'Davis, *Mr* Davis.'

'How do you do sir.'

'Welcome aboard lad.'

Mr Davis then explained how to find the accommodation I was to share with another apprentice, a Rhodesian. He was not on board at the time, I was told, as the *ss Manipur* had docked on her return from the Far East only two days earlier. Apprentice Verran had been given the weekend off and shore leave to visit an aunt in Portsmouth. (Later, I learned the 'Aunt' was nineteen, a shapely five foot six with blue eyes and blond hair.)

The directions to find the apprentices' quarters caused me more confusion in these unfamiliar surroundings. It must have been evident from my expression as the Chief Officer, who until then had spoken in carefully modulated BBC English, suddenly bellowed 'Boy!'

In the ensuing silence I began to wonder what I had done—or omitted to do—and was starting to feel decidedly uncomfortable when an Indian, wearing the black trousers and the white jacket of a steward, and of seemingly very advanced but indeterminate years, insinuated himself into the cabin.

'Burra Sahib?' obsequiously.

'Show Chota Sahib to cabin.' (I soon learned that all apprentices were 'small sirs'.)

'Sir,' I asked before following the 'Boy', 'Will it be alright for my Mother and Father to come to my cabin?'

'Where are they?'

'Outside Sir.'

'Bring them in.'

In the short time it took to usher them through the office, the Chief Officer had donned his jacket and tightened his tie and while introductions were exchanged, I couldn't help but notice that he was still wearing his slippers and the discarded magazine was a copy of 'Playboy'.

After bidding them welcome, small talk was exchanged. Mr Davis, evidently aware of my parents concerns, was oozing charm (which I later found was always the case when any member of the opposite sex was present) and was trying to reassure them that I would be entirely safe and would be under his watchful eye. Dad was speaking as usual with just a trace of his Yorkshire upbringing and Mother using what my brother and I often unkindly referred to as her best telephone voice. Clearly, the vast amount of gold braid on the Chief Officer's cuffs was creating an impression and he had a way of standing with hands in his pockets, thumbs hooked outside, which tended to give prominence to the three gold bands.

The 'Boy', who had meanwhile discreetly retired to the office, was summoned back and given instructions in Hindi.

'The Boy will escort you to the apprentices' quarters and bring you afternoon tea,' the Chief Officer translated.

We followed and were eventually shown into a cabin fitted for double occupancy. The steward then left us while he went off to another part of the ship to return shortly with a tray bearing the afternoon tea.

It was something of a disappointment.

The teapot, which was of brown earthenware, had a piece missing from the spout making it reluctant to deposit its contents anywhere but the saucer. That is was obviously freshly brewed and very hot was a saving grace. The biscuits were vintage but certainly not a good year, and the hot-buttered toast had a most peculiar taste. 'It's garlic,' Mother said. I later found out this was due to someone having stowed garlic next to the butter in the ship's dairy.

However, this was rather an emotional time for the three of us and such matters were trivial. I think we were struggling to make small talk, all of us dreading the moment of farewells. I recall Dad was urging me to ensure that I wrote home regularly. 'For your mother's sake—she will worry about you,' he explained. He always attached great importance to corresponding and ever since I could remember, had exchanged a weekly letter with his father, usually sitting quietly on a Sunday evening to write, relating the events of his week.

A knock at the cabin door interrupted us.

'You'll no mind iffen I come in for a wee while? The Chief Officer told me you'd boarded'

Thus the ship's carpenter, William Carroll, introduced himself, making us feel at ease.

He was a wizened Scot with a wry sense of humour and in no time he and Dad were conversing as though they had known each other for years.

We all talked for what seemed to be quite a long time, but probably wasn't. Chippie meanwhile demolished the remains of the tea, attacking the biscuits and toast with gusto, before taking his leave of us and assuring Mother that I should come to no harm and would be under his guidance for the voyage to come.

'I'll keep a wee eye on him,' he promised.

'Anyway,' he quipped, looking at me round the door as he was closing it with what can only be described as a twinkle in his eyes, 'The mair I see youse, the mair I like ma wee Doug."

Chippie was right. I came to no harm under his kindly guidance during the long months that followed. He kept his promise to Mother and kept an eye on me. I spent a great deal of time working with this hardy Scot who had served his own apprenticeship many years earlier in the tough world of Govan and the Clyde shipyards. I had heard how rough an area it was. It seemed totally alien to Wullie Carroll's humorous and gentle nature.

I hadn't been on board long before I learned that his only living relative was a much loved niece. He certainly had no-one called Doug but that dug was the Scottish pronunciation for the canine species.

But I digress.

Some three or so days after I had joined, with Chippie Wullie's help, I was just beginning understand some of the new terminology and was able to find my way unaided around the vessel when the other apprentice returned.

'I don't give a monkey's fist if you are always called by your second name. I shall use your first—or call you Parks'

I had just introduced myself, rather self-consciously, and had told Ian Verran my full name, adding that I was always called by my second Christian name.

'Yes,' he continued, 'I shall call you Graham.'

His emphasis on the pronoun 'I' was unmistakable and made me wonder if this was arrogance or the result of the command training which had been promised during my interview with the Marine Superintendent at the company's head office in Liverpool nearly two years earlier.

With his deep suntan and two inch height advantage, this self-assured Rhodesian seemed friendly. Anyway, I thought, I had survived the leg pulling and ribbing meted out when I had started work on the building site well enough, why would I worry about what I was called? Nevertheless I asked,

'What's the objection to my second name then?'

He seemed to study me for a moment or two, perhaps contemplating whether his answer might shock me, before replying, 'The Fourth Officer last trip was called Andrew. I don't want to drag his parents into it but I doubt that they were married,' he paused, perhaps wondering if I understood what he was implying before continuing, 'I'd rather have nothing to remind me of him.'

## *Settling in*

My new home was reminiscent of many older British Railways carriages of the day. Dark mahogany with heavy brass fittings, once-white ceiling (deckhead, as I now had to call it) and yellowing cream paint on all the bulkheads. As when near a steam locomotive, there was a pervasive odour of steam and oil.

The fabric upholstery on the day bed was as old as the ship. It had had a slightly musty odour and if treated violently, would retaliate with clouds of dust, redolent of spices, which had accumulated during years spent in distant ports. Even the light fittings and power outlets had a second-hand appearance; the plastic, once white, had become dull brown and acquired the texture of an old biscuit.

Although I was rather disappointed with the accommodation, which bore little resemblance to the glossy photographs in the company's recruiting literature, it was far better than that on many ships—or so Verran knowledgeably assured me. We were fortunate, he pointed out, that the accommodation was in effect a self-contained flat and located in solitary splendour, away from everyone, at the after end of the boat deck. It had two double cabins with a bathroom and a dayroom in between and the facility was, overall, superior to that allocated to many junior officers on the ship.

In the central alleyway between the two cabins, a small bell was screwed on the bulkhead. Not, as I first supposed, like a door bell ashore, but used as a peremptory summons to the Chief Officer's office.

The bell itself and the surrounding area of bulkhead bore witness to past frustrations and was scarred where objects had been thrown at it. In the following months I developed a strong empathy with the generations of previous apprentices at the whim of that accursed bell during the fourteen or so years of the ship's life.

Verran was frequently missing one shoe—which later often manifested its presence on the deck under the bell by tripping him. Eventually, the ship's electrician established a fixed price of two ginger ales for repairing the bell before the Chief Officer found out and suspended all shore leave.

When I had joined, although absent at the time, it was clear that Verran was using the lower bunk. On his return, he was anxious that I continue to use the upper. I later came to realise that he was not motivated entirely by unselfishness.

It is far from easy to make up an upper bunk when standing precariously on the lower bunk board with the ship rolling, which it seemed to do much of the time when not in port. The procedure for knotting the corners of the bottom sheet beneath the mattress to keep it free of wrinkles and securely tucked in, became a test of both tenacity and balance.

There was, I learned, a special way of folding the upper sheet and counterpane together to form an envelope where only the foot was tucked under the mattress, and which, when properly executed, was both practical and neat.

'The Mate,' Verran declared on more than one occasion, 'Is a bugger for Sunday morning inspections and insists on the bunks being made as sea-beds,' and invariably continued, 'Worse than bloody hospital corners!'

Evidently, the 'Aunt' referred to earlier was a nurse.

There seemed so very much to learn in addition to all the normal daily tasks at that time—running errands for senior officers, cleaning accommodation, making our bunks, checking stores on board, tallying cargo and a miscellany of other new activities. I was also having problems understanding two of the other officers and they were rapidly becoming impatient with me. 'Are you bloody deaf, Parks?' I always understood that without difficulty.

The Second Officer (always muttering to himself something about optional discharges, and over stowing) was a very broad Scot from a small village near Inverness, Drumnadrochet or something like that, and the Third Officer spoke with a very thick Scouse accent.

With officers from all parts of the United Kingdom, becoming familiar with all the different dialects was a steep learning curve. It was something I had never thought of before, but I, too, had an accent. West Country accents were something of a rarity in a Liverpool based company.

I recall one time in the mess being asked where I came from.

'Warminster,' I replied.

'Where in the pig is that?' from the Third Officer.

'It's a small market town mid way between Bath and Salisbury.

'Baath. Baath—you mean Bath.'

'Well, I suppose the people who live there know how to pronounce it and I'm just copying them,' I responded, only to receive a kick on the ankle from Ian. 'Don't push your luck,' he hissed.

On another occasion, also in the mess, the word shirt had come into the conversation.

'Why do you pronounce the word and sound the 'r'?' Mr Roberts asked in his broad Scouse.

'The word's sheht,' he stated. I can't accurately write his pronunciation phonetically, with a virtually non existent 'r' but anyone familiar with the Liverpool accent will know how it sounded.

'Actually, Mr Roberts, I prefer to sound the 'r' because without it the word is something I'd prefer not to be wearing.' There was a moment or two of silence while he worked out what I meant.

'Don't be bloody impudent, Parks! You smart arse!' he exploded while some of the other Junior Officers at the table lifted their napkins to hide their sniggers.

Meanwhile, I had received from the Chief Officer what my cabin mate disparagingly referred to as 'The Mate's pep talk.' I had been threatened with the most dire consequences if I neglected my correspondence course, 'Like that bugger Verran.'

The Chief Officer had a favourite adjective for describing people, especially apprentices. We were often challenged, 'Where do you buggers think you are then?' all in very well-spoken English. Then, 'Daddy's yacht? Eh? Eh?' This was usually accompanied with a pointed finger, jabbing in time to the Eh, Eh.

He was convinced that the younger generation had it too soft. (Nothing changes there!) It had been much harder in his youth. I remember him illustrating his point by declaring to Verran one time, 'In my day, lad, the Senior Apprentice had to sit and warm the Mate's lavatory seat for him each morning.'

I was therefore trying to find odd moments to commence my book learning and to complete a correspondence course assignment—despite a definite attitude of disparagement from my colleague. However, I feared the Mate's threats far more than Verran's chiding and was determined that the Mate should not be afforded the opportunity to refer to me as he did my colleague, 'An academic eunoch.' Ian, though, was totally unconcerned at such an insulting remark and cared little for the Chief Officer or his opinion of him—or, it seemed, anyone else's for that matter.

On a ship where all the ratings were Indian, it was part of the officers' macho image (at least, in the eyes of some) to be able to eat the hottest, spiciest curries that either the ratings' Bandari (cook) or the officers' Chef could prepare. I was trying hard to conform and find a liking for the lunchtime curry, always an option on the menu in the officers' mess. Much of the Indian cuisine I came to thoroughly enjoy but I couldn't then (nor ever did) find any eating pleasure in some of the more brutal dishes which were specially prepared only for our mess. The crew wouldn't touch them.

I also lacked the courage to tell Verran that on the many occasions we passed the crew galley, the smell he enthused over was, to my unworldly nostrils, far more suggestive of stale vomit.

Nevertheless I persevered, following his advice on curries and sauces but which, to his evident amusement, sometimes totally anaesthetised all my taste buds and left my lips numb for some time. It was my Scottish mentor, Chippie, who eventually realised that Ian was mischievously advising I try all the hottest curries, misleading me and telling me they were mild. It was Chippie who explained that by any standards Vindaloo is likely to be a fierce one—all the while re-assuring me that he still preferred his wee dog to my own company.

## *Captain on board*

At the end of that first week in London, the *ss Manipu*r completed discharging her cargo of tea ('optional Manchester, optional Liverpool, optional Dundee' according to the Second Officer, Mr Milne) and I became excited at the prospect of the ship actually moving, albeit only into the nearby Victoria Dock to Brocklebanks' general cargo loading berth.

During the afternoon, we had been sent to the monkey island, the deck immediately above the wheelhouse, to rig two red lights on one of the signal halyards in preparation for moving later in the evening.

I had been puzzled when Ian explained that the signal meant 'not under command' for I knew the captain to be on board.

My Scottish friend again eventually clarified that which appeared to be an anomaly explaining that 'not under command' only indicated the vessel could not manoeuvre properly under her own power, in our case because one of the rotors from the steam turbine engines was ashore for balancing. It had nothing at all to do with the ship's commander as a person.

My reluctance to ask my cabin mate arose from an incident a day or so earlier when I had seen a figure slouching around the fore-end of the boat deck. Unlike other officers on the ship, this person wore no uniform but was very casually attired in an ancient trilby hat, a tweed sports coat and a pair of baggy flannels which, through want of pressing (and possibly dry-cleaning) had acquired shaped knees which bore some resemblance to that of the crust on a pork pie.

'Father,' Verran had pointed out, knowledgeably.

'Why do we have a priest on board? Is he going to India as a Missionary?' I naively queried.

'Idiot!' was the scornful response.

'That's the Captain. His Nibs. Himself. The Gaffer. God. The Old Man. Captain Walter Cowling.'

SS Manipur, my first ship

## CHAPTER 11
# ON THE MOVE AT LAST

### *Shifting the Ship*

The discharge of the inward cargo had been completed during the afternoon and the dockers were making their way down the gangway, incessantly hurling good natured abuse at each other and anything in their way. I stood near the ship's side watching the crane drivers climbing down the ladders from their working eyries. I had daily observed an end-of-shift ritual when all the shoreside crane jibs were turned parallel to the quay and left pointing like accusing fingers as the last of the sun's rays disappeared, casting a roseate hue behind the sheds at the far end of the dock.

Once more, *Manipur* was quiet but this time her derricks had been swung inboard. I recall the noise of the electric winches as they cooled slowly, the contracting metal protesting sometimes with small cracking and creaking noises, recovering from the constant thump of the brakes punching at their insides all shift.

But, despite the relative quiet, other less familiar noises were becoming evident as a veritable army of Indians moved around the decks tidying the ship and preparing her for loading. There was even a sailor moving along the edges of the cargo decks spraying disinfectant in all the scuppers from the rose of a gardener's watering can.

'Dockers,' said Verran, deprecatingly, 'Would piss in their mates' hats if they left them around!' Always straight to the point.

'Of course,' he continued, 'It would be better if we were putting to sea then we could run a fire pump and wash-down properly, but if we did it now there'd be hell to pay with those damned barges still alongside.'

The barges were soon to be moved and their places taken by four steam tugs.

'Pilot's on board. Better get to stations,' Verran advised not long afterwards. He instructed me to attend the poop but warned me to stay clear of the towing and mooring wires. 'And stay out from under the Mr Milne's feet. The Second Officer doesn't like first-trippers!'

With some apprehension, I made my way aft to the poop where strange orders in English were issuing distortedly from a tannoy, before being readily translated into fluent Hindi and bellowed at a group of scurrying Lascars by the Second Officer.

'Stay in the centre of the docking bridge lad, by the tannoy. Relay my messages to the bridge and for Heaven's sake stay out from under my feet.' Verran had been right about that.

I remember, too, the Second continuing in his broad Scots and making a remark about first trip apprentices being less use than a one-legged man in an arse kicking contest. The colourful metaphor certainly conjured up an image and I remember chuckling at the thought of it, but he had already turned his back to resume shouting at the crew.

'Singled-up aft. Tug fast port quarter . . . . well dammit laddie, don't just stand there. Tell them on the bridge!'

Thus was I introduced to the bewildering intricacies of un-mooring aft.

The order 'let go aft' crackled from the tannoy, was duly translated to Hindi and relayed to the crew and, as the ropes became slack and were cast off from the quay with what I now realised were just mindless profanities, customary on the London dockside, the tug slowly took the strain. To my surprise the ship had begun to move. No vibration or any other indication but she was clearly no longer a captive of the land.

The Second had shouted something which sounded like: all gone angler.

I hadn't a clue what he meant, or if it was even English and was just bending to press the Tannoy transmit button to relay the message phonetically when I was thrust to one side and the Second impatiently advised the bridge 'All gone and clear!'

Slowly, the tugs pulled *Manipur* out into the middle of the dock and I was becoming aware of just how cold it could be over water in mid February. Things were quiet for a while and the Second Officer used the opportunity to lecture me on the dangers of ropes parting, 'Not breaking, Parks. Only fools ashore say ropes break. They're not brittle.' He followed this with gruesome tales of unwary seamen sustaining terrible injuries, losing limbs or even being severed in two when mooring ropes under tension parted and snapped back on board like a giant rubber band.

The Second had been in fine form.

'And another thing, Parks, when I tell you anything, an order that is, repeat it back to me so I ken you have nae got it wrong,' he admonished.

During the next half hour or so as the ship was inched across and along the dock, with his breath coming out as vapour, Mr Milne explained that a ship is a peculiar construction where you can walk on the ceiling and climb through the floors. The floors he explained, were the heavy vertical plates like ribs in the ship's bottom, and the ceiling, wooden sheathing at the bottom of the ship's holds. I was totally bewildered.

Having shared this wisdom, he proceeded to delve into one of the capacious pockets of his duffle coat and produced a packet of sandwiches. I was asked to hold his flashlight and looked on curiously as, in the beam of the torch, the Second Officer carefully peeled back a corner of the top piece of bread on each of the sandwiches and peered at the contents.

'Another thing, Parks. Take my advice. Never eat your sandwiches in the dark and always look under the lid of any pie with a crust.' I must have looked puzzled. 'That way you'll eat fewer cockroaches.'

There was so much to learn. Life seemed to be filled with 'And another thing, Parks.'

## *At sea—at last!*

'No, bloody no!. You can't possibly wear a steaming revvy like that. Looks like a sodding dinner plate. Take the damned grommet out!'

Verran was lecturing me about my uniform hat, affirming that you could always tell a first-tripper by his bonnet.

He succeeded in convincing me that there would be no repercussions from the Mate at any endeavours to make my hat look more lived in. Out came the thin steel grommet and the chin strap was lifted over the top of the hat to pull the sides down in the hope that while unworn, the hat would acquire what I was knowingly told was a 'shag'.

All this had taken place in the afternoon before our scheduled undocking from the Royal Docks in London.

Now, we were well on our way down the River Thames and I would shortly be experiencing my first spell at watchkeeping—the eight-to-twelve. During dinner that evening I had been told that it was very cold up on ther bridge and that I should go on watch well prepared and protected.

## *Watchkeeping*

Fifteen minutes before eight, the Indian lookout, the purri-wallah, appeared at out cabin door.

'Quarter bell, Saab' he muttered from somewhere inside a set of voluminous oilskins. A few minutes later and well wrapped in heavy clothing, I was groping my way in the darkness up the ladders to the bridge.

Two hours later, I seemed to have been on the bridgewing for half a lifetime. Could it really only be ten o'clock! I was cold, wet through, thoroughly miserable, totally bewildered by the array of lights from shore and passing ships, wondering how the Indian lookout could tell one from another, and was beginning to think the whole idea of coming away to sea had been a disastrous mistake. My self pity was aggravated by thought of home where there would undoubtedly be a log fire burning in the living room and where I could at least have a smoke and make myself a warm drink.

The Third Mate (Officer) loomed in the darkness.

'Right lad. It's four bells. Go and have your smoke-ho and be back here in fifteen minutes sharp.'

'Ay ay, sir.' The world was a better place already as I replied in true nautical fashion.

Back in our accommodation, I was obliged to remain in the day room as Verran was already asleep in the cabin and destined for the middle watch, the twelve-to-four. He had threatened me most vociferously with a multitude of consequences, all of which would be painful and some biologically impossible, if I dared to awaken him before the appointed time!

Trembling with the cold, I struggled to light a cigarette but only after discarding my first two attempts, when the Woodbines became soggy with the water running off the sleeves of my oilskin, did it dawn on me that success would only be realised when I removed the dripping garment.

After rather less than fifteen minutes of introspection I was back at my post on the port bridgewing, nearly blind in the extreme darkness after my smoke-ho in our accommodation.

Some five minutes or so after my return, the Third Mate walked unerringly through the wheelhouse door and round the large brass engine room telegraph which was still barely discernable to my eyes.

'Where in the hell do you think you've been, Parks? I told you to return after fifteen minutes.'

'B-but I was only fifteen minutes, sir. I have been back for at least five,' I stammered, somewhat taken aback.

'Well you'd better learn damn fast Parks. You only leave the bridge when I say so and you always report on your return.' So saying, the Third turned on his heel and quickly returned to the warmth and dryness of the wheelhouse. Alright for some, I reflected, as I heard sounds of laughter from within. 'Got a first-tripper out there' I overheard the Third telling the pilot. 'Doesn't know his arse from a hole in the ground.'

The thought that he had been the same only a little over four years ago was scant consolation and did little to dispel a rapidly forming dislike of the Third Mate.

My reverie of wondering how he had fared on his first trip was interrupted by the Third reappearing, this time wrapping a towel round his neck while struggling into an oilskin. He paced up and down for a while, obviously in very poor humour, muttering to himself something mainly unintelligible apart from the odd words I caught about 'Time the old bugger went to his bed.'

The Captain had put in an appearance in the wheelhouse which later turned out to my advantage. The Third had been ignominiously booted out to the bridgewing, he shortly confided, going on to explain that the Old Man would not permit his officers to remain in the wheelhouse in his presence. We were now in the same boat literally and figuratively—and the Third Officer unbent sufficiently to start explaining how the various ships' lights identified the direction in which they were heading.

The next hour passed with surprising rapidity and the lights were beginning to make some sense, although a lecture on 'boxing' a compass in quarter points was to remain as mystifying as a tic-tac man's code for quite some time.

I also learned an interesting quirk of human nature. The Third Mate had very strong objections to being called 'Third'. 'My name is Roberts. As a junior member of the ship's company, you, Parks, should address me as Mister Roberts.' But, in his very early twenties and with a recently acquired certificate of competency qualifying him as Second Mate, Mister Roberts never showed any disapproval at being addressed as 'Sir' and almost visibly preened when called such!

My first experience at watchkeeping was over! Verran was on the bridge and in a mood as black as the night. It was still raining but we had moved further away from the shore lights and the night had become darker than I had ever imagined possible. My lookout duties having been handed over, I had returned to our cabin and was now snug in my bunk after a warm drink and a hotter shower. Drowsy. Perhaps it wasn't such a bad world after all, and with these almost unformed thoughts I drifted of into a self-satisfied sleep.

Suddenly, the cabin door was thrown open with a crash against the headboard of my bunk. The cabin was bathed in light. For a moment I had no idea where I was or what was happening then realised my cabin mate, clearly not practising what he had been preaching only hours earlier about one's sleep being sacred at sea, was struggling to remove his sea boots, light a cigarette, slip off his oilskin coat, towel his hair dry and open a drawer all at the same time as cursing most fluently.

'What time is it?' I asked, when I perceived that Verran was sufficiently in control of himself and the situation to formulate a comprehensible reply.

'Two bells. Have you seen my spare bloody sea boot socks?' By this time he had achieved a measure of success and with a cigarette, which should by all normal standards of physics and combustion have been entirely extinguished, smoking damply in one corner of his mouth, Verran up-ended his sea boots and to my amazement, proceeded to pour water from them onto the already well-stained carpet.

'They're on the clothes line in the bathroom,' I replied.

Shortly, he returned bearing one slightly and one very off-white heavy sock, clearly odd socks. I recall that my observation he had another pair like them on the line was ignored as Verran stumbled around the cabin trying to don his boots again. Without another word, he soon disappeared back to resume his duties on the bridge and I once again surrendered myself to the arms of Morpheus while reflecting on Verran's lack of common sense or 'nous' which he was always saying I was devoid of.

As long as he continued to stuff his waterproof trousers into his boots, the latter would necessarily act as a repository for all the rainwater draining downward from his sou'wester, coat and trousers.

## *The Noble Art of Skiving*

The first time he disturbed me this way, it was the source of some private amusement but as the same procedure was repeated twice more, once each hour, on the hour, it had lost all aspects of humour. I was more than just a little peeved at Verran's lack of consideration and when he finally came off watch at four o'clock, I was wide awake and remonstrated with him.

'Is this what they taught you at that damned pre-sea school? If you want to be a walking, talking rain gauge, that's alright by me—but you might show me the same consideration you insisted on when *you* were trying to get some sleep!' I was under a full head of the steam of righteous indignation.

'Anyway, why don't you keep your trousers outside your boots? Even a half-wit can see your boots will fill if you tuck them in!'

I waited for a similar outburst in retaliation. Verran merely looked at me quizzically for a few moments and with more than a hint of suppressed amusement.

'Okay, smartarse,' he eventually replied, 'How many smoke ho's did you get on your watch?'

'Naturally you wouldn't know—I didn't wake you.' I was still annoyed but was becoming curious as to what this had to do with his boots filling up with water.

'Well, anyway, one. From four bells for fifteen minutes' I conceded.

'Well. There you are then.'

I still failed to see the relevance. Verran raised one eyebrow, questioningly.

'You really can't see it, can you?' and as I shook my head, 'Well, you daft bugger, I had three!'

Thus did my colleague introduce me to what he considered to be the skilful art of 'skiving'. He was an inveterate work-dodger and some of his schemes were complex in the extreme. On later occasions when I expressed the opinion that the 'skive' involved more effort that it saved and questioned why he bothered, his reply would leave me wondering.

'Yes, but that's not the point. See. It's a matter of principle.'

## Changes in the mess

The next morning I had been called at seven o'clock and arose reluctantly in sufficient time to make my way to the officers' mess—dining room—for breakfast at half past—seven bells. I remember my eyes were still gritty with lack of sleep, and I was thinking the night had been far too short.

Although I had been told things changed at sea, I was more than a little surprised just how much. I arrived at the mess to find all the officers smartly dressed in their 'blue' uniforms, their reefers. The tables were gleaming with white linen tablecloths and napkins and all the silverware and cutlery had been carefully polished. The stewards, too, were immaculate in starched white jackets and black trousers. This standard was to prove the norm when the ship was at sea and officers were not involved in loading operations or the like. The less formal 'duty mess' was then largely unused. For the first time since I joined the Captain was present in the mess, also resplendent in full 'blues'.

Blue, with reference to uniforms, always seems to be somewhat of a misnomer as the standard British Merchant Navy uniform, like the Royal Navy, is black.

I was interested to find that many of the officers carried their own personal silver napkin rings. For those of us not so equipped, our place at table was designated by a napkin ring having a rank engraved on it, in my case, 'Apprentice 4', with the company's flag before and after.

The breakfast bill of fare typed on a stiff white menu card, also bearing the blue and white Brocklebank house flag, offered a wide variety of appetising choices and I noticed that several of those present made a very resolute effort to work systematically through the entire menu. 'Gannet', Verran later told me was the name given anyone at sea having a healthy appetite, referring to the sea bird which feeds so greedily it is frequently unable to fly until it has lightened itself by digesting some of its repast.

I, too, ate heartily in the time available, before making my way to the bridge well fortified for the forenoon watch, the eight-to-twelve again.

## *Starting to learn my trade*

The outward pilot had been taken off by boat as we passed Dungeness Point while Verran was on watch during the small hours and our course around the south coast of

England, on passage to Avonmouth, now left us exposed to the heavy swell and strong winds buffeting the English Channel after travelling unhindered across the vastness of the Atlantic Ocean.

From the navigating bridge, which was near the mid-length of the ship, the bow seemed to be rising and falling a considerable distance as the ship's buoyancy responded to the relentless succession of swells. I found the pitching movement rather unbalancing, the more so when very occasionally this see-saw motion became synchronous with the swell frequency and with but minimal help from the passing swells, the amplitude of the ship's movement progressively increased until with a bone shaking crash, the bow plunged right through a swell, throwing spray high into the air. It would be snatched by the wind and carried swiftly along the ship to hiss across the wheelhouse windows and the accommodation front. I soon learned to duck when this happened, the alternative being a face-full of salt spray so cold it stung, feeling rather as a nettle might.

To me, the weather seemed very bad and I was reminded of the phrase seen in some schoolboy's adventure book of 'man against the elements', but despite the sea's apparent severity, the sky was a clear, washed-out blue and the sun was shining weakly. Visibility was excellent with the horizon a well defined and sharp contrast between ocean and sky. The whitecaps with which the wind had crowned the waves, also stood out vividly against the blue-green hue of the sea. Altogether a most exhilarating sight, I thought, fascinated—while also being thankful that so far I felt no adverse affects from the unaccustomed motion.

For the next two hours, apart from reporting the occasional other craft I sighted to the Third, I was totally absorbed in thought. It was the first time I had been away from home, apart from holiday periods with farming relatives in Dorset and one-week visits to Royal Air Force stations with the school squadron of the Air Training Corps. Certainly the first time I had even come close to being out of England!

I was enthralled with new sights and experiences but my thoughts would keep returning to family and old school friends now behind me. By the time I saw any of them again, I should likely have travelled half way round the world and seen such far-away places as were currently beyond my boyish imagining. How very fortunate I was, I mused. Truth be told, I was a tad homesick, although I would never have admitted it.

My contemplations were interrupted by Mr. Roberts.

'Parks!' His first call barely penetrated my reverie. Again,

'Parks! Dammit, wake up!' He had my attention now.

'Yes Mr. Roberts?'

'It's nearly four bells. Come into the chartroom and make some coffee for me please, then you can go below for fifteen minutes for your own smoke-ho.'

In the chartroom were an electric kettle and the requisites for the watchkeeping officers to make sundry hot drinks. All were stowed in a corner on the top of a locker specially fitted for the purpose. It had a secondary top of plywood fitted about two inches above its upper surface and into which were cut holes of varying sizes, precisely accommodating all the drink-making accoutrements and holding them secure against the ship's movement. It was evident that someone was not too good at aiming the tin of condensed milk and there were glutinous runs of it down the sides of the locker. The paint on the bulkhead in the vicinity bore blistered testimony to occasions when a boiling kettle had been forgotten.

In addition to observing this disaster area where the drinks were concocted, I also seized the opportunity while waiting for the kettle to come to the boil and the Third remained in the wheelhouse, of sneaking a swift glance at the chart—all I dared lest I was caught, for I felt sure that I should be told to confine my interest to those things which concerned me.

The coffee duly made, I was handing it to Mr. Roberts, when, to my surprise, he stated that on my return from smoke-ho he would show me the vessel's location on the chart.

So much for my fears of being caught peeking!

I had returned after my smoke ho.

'Right then, Parks. Let's see if you know *anything*.' Back in the wheelhouse, Mr. Roberts obviously intended, despite his emphasis on the first syllable of 'anything', to put me to some sort of test. He was pointing out to starboard, 'See that headland over there? There, on the starboard beam.'

I peered at the promontory he was indicating and could just discern a red and white lighthouse on its tip.

'See the lighthouse?' he asked.

'Mm, I *think* so.'

'Right. Then go and look at the chart and see if you can identify it.'

My perusal of the chart suggested the lighthouse in question could well be Portland and the headland, Portland Bill—not that I could identify it with any certainty, but there was a heavily pencilled line on the chart, drawn below in a west-south-westerly direction and it seemed likely that this represented the ship's track. From the right hand margin, a series of small encircled stars followed this line. Each star comprised of three intersecting lines, like a rather angular spider. There was a time written near each, clearly indicating the ship's past location, and the most recent, '1000hrs', was a little to the south-east of Portland.

'I think it may be Portland Bill' I tentatively told the Third Officer and continued to explain my reasons. I was a little disappointed that Mr. Roberts seemed not in the least surprised, merely confirmed my deduction.

The remainder of the watch was spent showing me how to use the azimuth mirror, an instrument placed over the top of the compass which, when sighted through, indicated the angle between an object, in this case Portland lighthouse, and the magnetic meridian. This angle was then transferred to the chart, after being corrected for the magnetic errors of variation and deviation. Mr. Roberts explained that two or more such lines were needed to establish the vessel's position which would be at or near their point of intersection. The 'angular spiders' I had noticed previously.

My own first attempts at coastal navigation produced far larger triangles of error as I was told the inaccuracies were termed when the lines did not intersect at a point, 'Or, more often, a 'cocked hat',' explained the Third, before exclaiming after one of my efforts produced a particularly large triangle, 'Hell, Parks, Nelson and half his scurvy crew could get lost in that one! The chart's barely bloody big enough!' He was very disparaging of my navigational efforts but later owned to more than a little surprise that I actually knew what variation and deviation were. My studies with the Air Training Corps had not been irrelevant.

Despite his chiding, I enjoyed the remainder of the morning watch which passed very rapidly. I suspected the Third was gaining his first experience as teacher, rather than pupil, and was finding his new role, with its implicitly elevated status, privately gratifying.

And I was beginning to think my initial dislike of the Third had been ill judged.

All too soon it was eight bells—I was trying to think in a truly nautical fashion—twelve o'clock, and Verran had appeared on the bridgewing still sleepily rubbing his eyes and evidently trying to collect his wits.

'Right then, Parksy, let's have a proper hand-over. Not like this morning's cock-up. Where are we? What's the course and what traffic have you?' he demanded testily.

The traffic was the easy part and I pointed out the craft in our vicinity while the Third looked on in evident amusement.

'Go on then. Don't stand there. You should know where we are by now. Show him the chart while I take some bearings for the noon fix,' the Third instructed.

Verran studied the chart, took up a pair of dividers and with much esoteric bravado and a flourish, set the points a predetermined amount using the scale at the right hand margin of the chart, and swiftly stepped the instrument along the ship's pencilled course-line.

'Should be around the Lizard and approaching Longships by the time you come on tonight,' he declared knowledgeably, 'Aye, okay. Off you go then—check with Mr. Roberts first. See you at lunch.' So saying he glanced at the chronometers before rushing into the wheelhouse and striking eight bells as four couplets on the small brass ship's bell suspended above the wheel.

An hour later, thirteen hundred hours. Lunchtime—and I was ravenous, probably the result of all the invigorating fresh air I had enjoyed during the forenoon watch. I waited in our cabin for Verran to join me, thankful that unlike the Third it was not necessary for me to go to the bridge and take over while my opposite number went for his meal.

## *The Guilt Trip*

Earlier in the morning, at four bells when I was having my smoke ho, I was on my way along the boat deck headed towards our accommodation and had been accosted by Chippie.

'Hi-de-hi, Parksy.' It was unnecessary to turn to recognise the soft Scottish accent as he caught up with me.

'Where away, the noo?' he queried.

'I'm gonna give my cabin mate a taste of his own bloody medicine. It's my smoke-ho' I replied, as he fell in step alongside.

'So what's young Verran been up to this time?'

I explained all that had happened during the middle watch when Verran had consistently woken me each hour. Wullie chuckled as I repeated the bit about being a walking talking rain-gauge.

'So what do you plan then?'

'I'm going to our cabin and make as much noise as I can' I averred.

'And I suppose you think that will make him more considerate in future—or will it just make you feel a wee bitty better?'

'I don't know whether it will or not, but he deserves to be woken.' I ignored his latter question.

'Ah! So, it's revenge you're after. Dinna be so bluidy daft. There are far better ways tae handle Verran,' Chippie admonished.

'If you wake him—just to make yourself feel better—he will only do the same tae youse tonight. Think on it.'

We had reached the end of the boat deck and the entrance to our accommodation.

'Come and take your smoke ho and have a coffee with me. Leave Verran in peace.'

'That's all very well' I remonstrated, 'But when I complained to him, he just laughed at me.'

'Ah, so now we have it. It's the dignity that's affronted!' over his shoulder as Chippie clattered down the ladder to the after deck.

'Come on. There's mair ways o' killing a moggy than choking it on cream.'

I followed him into his mess, waiting in aggrieved silence while he deftly mixed two mugs of instant coffee, drawing the water from a gasping steam boiler affixed to the bulkhead.

'What you'll be havin' tae do,' as he briskly stirred in condensed milk, 'Is t'make Verran feel guilty, and the only way you have any chance is to make very certain you dinnae disturb him.'

'But he won't even realise it' I protested.

'He will if you make him feel uncomfortable aboot it.' Chippie was adamant.

'But how?' I wondered.

'Well, just ask him in front of everyone when you're in the mess if he slept well and tell him you hope you didnae disturb him and that you did your best to make no noise so you didnae go to your mess for smoke-ho. After all, 'tis quite true.'

'Do you really think it'll work?' I was not entirely convinced.

'It's worth trying, surely—hey, come on, you'll be late back on watch if you dinna shift your arse!'

I had thought about what Chippie said during the final two hours of my morning watch and his advice was still in my mind when the lunch gong was sounded.

The readiness of a meal was always announced, usually spot on time, by a steward walking swiftly through the accommodation striking a gong.

The gong's echoes had scarcely died away before Verran and I were seated in the mess in hungry anticipation of our lunch.

We had, I suspected, each made our selection of initial course by the same criterion—simply reading down the menu until reaching the first dish that took our fancy—and were eagerly awaiting the steward's return with the foods of our choice.

There was a murmur of polite conversation and Mr Milne, who had been relieved for his meal and who was seated at the head of our table, asked me how I had enjoyed my first watchkeeping experience. I had started to reply when the Junior Radio Officer, doubtless with the vast experience of having already completed one voyage, interrupted with a gratuitous comment. 'Watchkeeping. Mindless bloody boredom if you ask me.'

'But we *weren't* asking you,' the Second Officer replied very curtly, which presaged a rather strained lull in conversation.

Thinking of Chippie's ruse to shame Verran, I had deemed the time opportune to put his recommendation to the test.

'I trust you slept well?' I asked my cabin mate, around the arm of the steward who had returned and was now serving us.

Verran appeared more interested in his soup than in making any reply to my question, which was in any case rhetorical.

'Parks, I hear that you spent your smoke-ho with Chippie,' stated Mr Milne. 'Tis good tae hear that you are aware already that one's sleep on board is regarded as sacred.'

My Scottish mentor had, I realised, effectively primed the Second Officer, but Ian, I recall, kept his eyes firmly on his meal and was actually looking more than a little embarrassed. A faint flush was creeping under his tan. Chippie's psychological revenge appeared to having an affect after all, I thought.

Verran evidently preferred to change the subject.

'I should think that judging by your appetite the weather hasn't affected you Parksy!' Verran suggested, 'Not that it's that bad anyway,' he continued.

Mr Milne was having none of this conversational swerve and concluded, 'It's good that Chippie always welcomes you lads in his mess. You can learn a lot from him.'

Darned right, I thought!

The point had been well made with the Second's assistance and my sleep wasn't disturbed again.

Verran's estimate of our whereabouts by the time I was on watch again that evening had been slightly in error and we hadn't reached Longships. There were two reasons, I remember being told; the wind and swell had prevented *Manipur* from making the speed expected and the ship had been intentionally slowed down.

Because it was dark, I was not permitted in the chartroom as I had been in the forenoon watch but was again relegated to the bridgewing and told to keep a sharp lookout. I found the Third to be far less formal than he had been when we had a pilot on board and he spent much of the watch outside with me explaining more about ships and their lights. When I was told that we had reduced speed, I was curious and asked why. I had definitely revised my opinion of the man.

'Tides.' explained Mr Roberts. and since my expression must have conveyed my total lack of understanding, 'We cannot lock into Avonmouth until shortly before high water.'

'But I thought locks avoided the problems with tide.' I was still puzzled.

'I thought you said you knew Weston-Super-Mare?' His retort seemed irrelevant.

'Well think about it. The Bristol Channel has the second highest rise and fall of tide in the world. Avonmouth's like Weston. When the tide's out there *is* no water. It's nearly fifty foot rise and fall on a spring tide and we're on spring tides now,' he asserted patiently.

'Get there too soon,' he concluded, 'And there's no bloody pani-water—outside the lock gates! Only mud.' He paused for a moment to let this register.

'And before you say anything. I know damned well it's not Spring yet. Spring tides as opposed to neap tides. Neither has anything all to do with the seasons, only the moon's phases.' He chuckled, continuing 'And if you don't get some spring in your step and make some soddin' coffee for us you'll be here 'til Autumn!'

## CHAPTER 12
# OUTWARD BOUND

*Getting ready for Deep Sea*

Because *Manipur* had loaded a small amount of cargo in London, although she was not fully discharged, she was considered to have commenced the outward-bound voyage; soon to be designated deep sea, as opposed to coastal. We continued on to discharge cargo in Avonmouth and then back through the English Channel and up the North Sea to Middlesbrough where the discharge of cargo was finally completed.

In Middlesbrough, the vessel was briefly dry-docked. It was an interesting experience and I was surprised to find out the ship had quite a large area of entirely flat bottom, more or less in the shape of a leaf.

Interesting the dry-docking may have been—but it was also a somewhat miserable time. The ship was 'dead', that is to say with only shore power for lighting, no steam for the heating systems, no water for washing or showering, the toilets were all out of use and there was only somewhat limited catering—certainly not of the standard enjoyed when the vessel was at sea. It was the end of February, or maybe early March, and there had been quite a heavy snowfall. The ship was extremely cold and everyone had to trek ashore for toilet and bathing facilities which was a nuisance to say the least.

To make matters worse, the Chief Officer invariably declined any request by Verran for evening shore leave with a flat refusal. The Chief Officer didn't have to give a reason to mere apprentices but I think it may have had something to do with an unfortunate incident with a large snowball.

My cabin mate had rolled a snowball the length of the boat deck, outside our accommodation, and had stood poised with it at the top of the outside stairs down to the next deck. Verran was waiting, he later admitted, for me to start coming up the companionway from the promenade deck. Unfortunately, when he launched the snowball, which was about three feet in diameter, he had not looked properly. It was not I who was about to start up the stairs but Mr Davis. I suppose the only saving grace was that as the ball rolled down the stairs it burst—disintegrated—all over the Chief Officer. Had he been part way up, and the snowball remained in one piece it could have knocked him down and caused a serious injury. The prank had really not been thought through very well. That the Chief Officer was not best pleased is something of an understatement and just might have had something to do with refusing our shore leave for some time afterwards. Several times, Ian just went ashore anyway, waiting until the Chief Officer was comfortably settled for the evening with an after-dinner gin and tonic watching television in the officers' lounge. Should anyone ask, I was primed to say that he was only ashore in the shower block.

From Middlesbrough, the ship went across to continue loading in Rotterdam and then to Antwerp where we did manage a trip ashore. Now, I don't really remember much about it except that we saw a fountain where a the statue of small boy urinating formed the centre piece. I couldn't believe such a thing could exist in full public view! I could not imagine it ever being accepted in the park in Warminster. We also visited a bar where there was an incredible fairground organ complete with all the small figures playing the instruments.

Our final loading port was a return visit to London where, apart from loading general cargo, we lifted a steam locomotive onto one side of the foredeck and some London buses onto the other. The loading of the locomotive, which was a large one, was very interesting. The ship's 200 ton heavy-lift derrick was used and the operation took most of the day as it was accomplished only very, very slowly.

On our arrival in London, two more apprentices joined, John Churchill and Norman Segar. Churchill, from Fareham in Hampshire, was the senior among us, having a year or so more sea time than Verran, and was making what would probably his last voyage before being promoted to Fourth Officer. Segar, from Merseyside, was just commencing his second voyage.

From then on I was to spend less time working under Chippie Wullie's direct control but nevertheless, for the entire voyage, he was always there to give help and guidance whenever I needed it—which, I suspect, was rather more often than I remember!

As 'chota sarbs' (small sirs) it was inappropriate for us to be under the control of the Serang (Indian bosun) and should not be taking orders from him. So, as we were now a gang of four, the Chief Officer made us fully responsible for everything connected with number six cargo hold. We were a miniature crew, with John Churchill, who by then had gained the seamanship knowledge, acting as our bosun.

After this, the lascars did nothing whatsoever relating to number six hold. If a derrick needed topping or a winch wire changing in the middle of the night when the ship was working cargo, we were turned-to to take care of it. If a stevedore evacuated his bowels in one of the bilges, that, too, had to be taken care of. Later in the voyage, it was Verran I think, who having cleared up such a mess, retaliated and left some smeared under the edge of the hatch coaming just where the stevedores would grasp hold as they came up from the cargo hatch. Ian said it really did make him feel better!

The apprentices' hold, number six, had a special locker in the after end of the 'tween deck where we loaded hundreds of cases of different kinds of gin, whisky and other booze. It all had to be tallied and we apprentices were tasked with this and of ensuring that none was stolen. While this 'special' cargo was being loaded, we worked in pairs and I was teamed up with John Churchill. The first afternoon we went down into the hold before the shift of stevedores arrived, in good time to unlock and open the heavy steel sliding doors in readiness for this valuable cargo.

'Why are they all carrying tin mugs?' I asked John as the stevedores were clambering down the ladder. 'You'll soon see,' he promised and it soon became evident that John was an old hand at loading special cargo. He sought out the charge hand and appealed to him, 'Play fair, will you, mate? You know that if any of the cases are broached my mate and I will be in trouble.'

'Okay mate,' with a knowing wink. I was just beginning to get used to the idea of everyone calling each other 'mate'. It wasn't Wiltshire idiom.

None of the cases of whisky was opened and no bottles were stolen—but by the end of the shift the stevedores were having a sing-song and were barely capable of making it up the ladder to the after deck unaided. I think it was twice that they accidentally-on-purpose managed to drop one of the wooden cases containing twelve bottle of Scotch onto the steel deck in such a way that it landed on its corner. The box was then lifted as one after the other the stevedores held their tin mugs under the corner to collect some of the leaking contents. They clearly had this off to a fine art and were confident all the broken glass was contained in the wooden box—and by the end of the shift, they couldn't have cared anyway. John then endorsed the manifest, noting that two cases had fallen from the cargo net as it was being landed in the 'tween deck. 'Extent of damage to contents not ascertained,' although personally, I thought it unlikely there were any intact bottles remaining.

Later, I asked him about what had happened.

'Did you notice they were all carrying their dockers' hooks in their belts?' he responded. I acknowledged that I had. Indeed, they had been using them some of the time to handle the wooden cases.

'Well when you've been threatened that you'll get a hook in your face if you don't look the other way, and you know it is a serious threat, it's prudent to negotiate a compromise,' John explained.

I thought about this. The wooden handled steel hooks for handling sacks and other cargo, would have been the envy of a Caribbean pirate.

'As it is, they've had their drink. We've got no cargo that's actually been broached. Nothing *actually* stolen. Just some accidental damage where spillage was contained. Sometimes, Parksy, discretion really *is* the better part of valour,' he advised.

By the time we sailed from London, the poop deck was packed full of items that our crew had bought at local second-hand sales to take back to India and sell. I have never seen so many Singer sewing machines, old pianos and bicycles. It was almost impossible to move from one side of the deck to the other!

## *Other cultures*

Unbelievably by today's standards of minimum manning on ships, the *ss Manipur* carried a complement of ninety nine. I recall the exact number because while on watch with him one time, Mr Roberts had explained that it was the maximum number of persons a cargo ship could have on board without the need to carry a doctor. About thirty were officers and petty officers (the latter being the Carpenter and Quartermasters) who were British. The remainder were all Indian and mostly from Bengal. Twenty-seven were deck ratings, the rest were engine room and catering ratings.

The deck crew were under the control of the Serang. The Bo'sun. The next senior rating was the Cassab, historically the Lamptrimmer but by then with oil lamps no longer in use (although the ship still carried them), a storekeeper. The Serang had three assistants, the Tindals, one for each watch.

I very soon realised that among the Indian crew there were Muslims, Hindus and one or two Christians, the latter being from Southern India, not Bengal.

Muslims were in the majority and it was Chippie who first told me a little about Islam. He firmly believed that it was important to respect others' cultures and beliefs and strongly advised me always to treat the Serang and Cassab in particular, with respect and dignity. (I could have heard my father saying something very similar!)

'That way, ye'll earn respect yourself,' he stated. 'Respect is two-way traffic.'

The discussion had come about when I noticed that the Serang's beard was red and wondered why, since his hair was black. Wullie, was always patient with my questions.

'Red beard, lal dari in Hindi, is a wee mark to show Serang is a Hajji.' He went on to tell me that it meant he had made the pilgrimage to Mecca which every Muslim must do at least once in his lifetime, and how important is was to them. One of the 'Five Pillars of Islam'.

'When ye hae the chance,' he suggested, 'You should make the effort tae read the Q'ran. It'll stand ye in good stead when ye're a full grown officer and dealing wi' the crew.' Later in the voyage I did so and found it very interesting. I was quite surprised how many stories I recognised from the Old Testament, although some of the names were different.

Very many years later, I was presented with a copy of the Q'ran. It is a beautifully printed book with green leather covers tooled in gold leaf. It is printed in both Arabic and English, on opposing pages. The book was given me by a good friend who was a Muslim and who explained that they were encouraged to 'spread the word of Allah' in this way.

Returning to write of Chippie's advice on showing respect, I also recall an incident that occurred much later in the voyage, in Calcutta I think. I was in the forepeak store with Cassab where we were checking the quantities of paints. The Junior Fourth Engineer, whom I already considered to be one of the most ignorant people on board, came by for something and just proceeded to help himself from Cassab's store.

'Saab, my store. Don't please take. Please tell what you want. I give you,' with typical politeness from this elderly seaman, also a Hajji and who was much venerated by all crew members, not just the Muslims.

'Cassab, you can kiss my f***ing arse!'

I couldn't believe what I had just heard and feel sure I probably just stood with my mouth open in amazement.

Cassab looked at the engineer for only a moment or two with an expression of total disdain, as though the Fourth might have been something unpleasant on his shoe. His very politely worded response was, to my surprise, in well phrased and unbroken English. Almost 'Oxford' English.

'Saab, why should I bend to kiss what I can stand and kick?'

It was a perfect put-down and left the Fourth speechless in embarrassed anger.

Later, when I told Wullie about the incident, he roared with laughter, mainly at such an appropriate and witty reply but partly at the audacity. It would have been perceived as an enormous breach of discipline for one of the Indian crew, however senior, to address an officer in such a manner. But then, Chippie had little time for many of the engineers most of whom had served their time in a shipyard, as had he. The Junior Fourth in particular, was 'Nae mair nor a semi-literate bluidy jumped up pig-iron polisher. A rivet tosser.' At least, that was how Wullie colourfully described him.

But always thereafter, whenever we were alone and Cassab spoke with me, it was never in pidgin English but always very articulate and un-accented 'Oxford' English. It was as though we shared a small secret.

## *Suez Canal*

As scheduled, we had called at Algiers and I recall that we four apprentices actually managed to get an afternoon off and spent it relaxing on a nearby beach. The ship was only in Algiers for a couple of days and I was quite excited that my first *real* foreign port should have been in North Africa. The near Continent didn't seem to count, but Africa, wow!

From there we sailed on through the Mediterranean passing quite close to Malta and eventually anchored off Port Said. The others had been regaling me with stories about the port (which everyone pronounced as the 'said' in the past tense of the verb to say), and about the Suez Canal transit.

In due course, we weighed anchor and proceeded into the port, passing the remains of the statue of the canal's builder, Ferdinand De Lesseps, on the western breakwater. It had been destroyed by the Egyptians in protest during the Suez Canal Crisis only a couple of years earlier. *Manipur* was then manoeuvred and secured at buoys in Port Said Harbour.

As had been predicted, we were met by a flotilla of small craft, all sounding their horns, shouting in both Arabic and pidgin English and clamouring to be allowed on board. Brocklebanks' Agents were the first up the gangway, bringing with them a local guard appointed to prevent others boarding until the ship had been cleared by Port Health and our yellow flag, the international signal requesting free pratique, had been struck. The ship was no longer in quarantine and the local 'businessmen' swarmed on board.

'You want haircut mister?'

'You got rope sell? I make you best deal. Pay in dollars mister'

'I sell you picture your ship? In frame? Good price mister. You pay me in whisky,' and so the clamour went on.

A number of vendors set up their wares—from papyrus to postcards, clay pots to camel saddles—all laid out on pieces of threadbare carpet spread on the boat deck. The gilly-gilly man started performing card tricks and producing fluffy chicks and yards of silks from under his fez. He used one of the chicks and three small metal tumblers in a version of Find the Lady. 'You lose you give me one beer. Yes?' It was chaotic—and I savoured every minute of the experience! I bought a small souvenir camel of hand-stitched white leather which later stood on Mother's dressing table for as long as I can remember.

We had been warned, though, not to leave anything unlocked.

Soon, we apprentices were sent to drive the winches on the after deck and assist the canal boatmen to load their boats. All vessels compulsorily ship two rowing boats and crew during the transit as if fog set in, and it often does as the desert cools in the small hours of the morning, ships had to stop and moor using bollards set all along the canal banks. Modern radar makes stopping un-necessary, but the boats and men still have to be carried and paid for. Just in case. All part of the Suez Canal rip-off.

Then we had to go to the fore deck and assist the canal electricians load the canal searchlight. The searchlight had a special prism to split the beam into two, one to illuminate each bank. Throughout the night while it was in use, one of the canal electricians would have to be in permanent attendance as light was provided by carbon-arc and the carbon rods had to be continually adjusted as they burned down to maintain the correct gap for the arc. I recall that like many of the cinema projectors then in use, which were also lit by carbon-arc, there was a large permanent magnet immediately behind the reflector, which stabilised the flame. Nowadays, carbon-arc lamps have been replaced by lamps having a large bulb—but ships still have to pay for and carry an electrician, even when it is a daytime transit and the searchlight will not even be switched on! More of the Suez Canal rip-off.

Later, Wullie told me that when Egypt had nationalised the Canal causing an international furore just a couple of years earlier, the staff became employees not of the Suez Canal Authority, but of the Egyptian Government. They were, he said, classed 'working on government service' and their navy blue work shirts had the acronym W O G S marked across the back—but his eyes *were* twinkling as he recounted the story.

My first Canal transit took place in daylight and in the afternoon we had to anchor for a while in the Bitter Lakes while the northbound convoy went past us. The Canal was not wide enough for ships to pass each other. We apprentices took the opportunity to go for a swim, jumping from the bulwarks to do so.

A little further down the Canal, I was fascinated to see the 'walking' excavators Ian had been telling me about. They were two massive draglines whose jibs could span the canal as they swung their buckets to the far bank before dragging them across the bottom, dredging. The machines were so big that they each sat on a huge turntable and when they had to move two enormous legs, like the thighs on some prehistoric monster, swung down, one each side to lift and shuffle the machine forward.

That evening as we cleared the canal at Port Suez the former Canal Authority building and a nearby Mosque were pointed out to me. As we entered the Suez Bay I listened to the Muezzin in the distance calling from a minaret, his high-pitched, nasal chanting fading behind us as he summoned the faithful to their evening prayer and we sailed on into the Gulf of Suez.

I marvelled at the way the setting sun had thrown the mountains on both the Egyptian and Sinai sides of the Gulf into stark relief, the deep, deep shadows of the valleys cleaving the steep hillsides, contrasting starkly with last rays of the sun reflecting back from the ridges and craggy peaks. It was a truly splendid sight and fitting ending to an incredible day.

Nevertheless, much as I enjoyed the experience, during that first Suez Canal transit I gained an impression that has remained virtually unchanged throughout all the transits I have made since. The whole thing was, as I have already commented, something of a rip-off.

It's a little out of sequence from my first voyage but it is appropriate to recount here another incident that occurred while making passage through Suez.

Several voyages later, I was still an apprentice and on the *ss Mahout* as I recall. We had a most amusing and entertaining canal transit. It all came about because the captain was a member of the Magic Circle. Most of the captains were very aloof, seldom, if ever, spoke directly to an apprentice, and they generally seemed to lack any sense of humour—it might have appeared too human. The voyage in question was an exception.

It started when the gilly-gilly man was performing some of his tricks. The Old Man came down to where all the visitors had assembled and very casually showed the Egyptian magician a simple trick. The challenge was taken up and the gilly-gilly man responded with another, and so it went on for two or three exchanges while we all looked on in amusement. I don't recall exactly what it was the Old Man did in the end but the slight of hand and the trick he finished with had the Egyptian totally mystified. I can see him now, pushing his fez back and scratching his head with a look of total bewilderment as the Old Man just smiled and walked away.

Nor did the fun finish there. The Captain was also an accomplished ventriloquist who could project his voice and make it sound as though it were coming from somewhere else.

For that transit we had a French pilot, although there were very few left working for the Canal Authority by that time. I was on watch with the Third Officer and we, of course, were aware of the O M's skills. Several times after darkness had fallen, the Captain called the pilot who then rushed out to the bridge wing, 'Yes, Captain?' only to find that he was not there but had been standing almost next to him in the wheelhouse.

Eventually, the Old Man decided to let the pilot in on the joke. We all heard this faint voice calling for help.

'Is that someone calling?' the old man asked.

'I can't believe,' said our unsuspecting pilot, 'But it really sounds like its in that box.' He pointed at one of the binocular boxes on the forward bulkhead, under the wheelhouse windows.

'Really?' The Captain casually walked over and opened the lid. The voice changed completely, 'Can I come out now?' The lid was firmly closed again. Then, very faintly, pleading from inside, 'Please let me out. I promise to behave. I won't steal the pilot's supper again, I promise.'

When I made my last Suez transit, nearly fifty years later while bringing a new passenger ferry from Korea to Europe, I concluded little had changed. It still cost around fifty cartons of cigarettes (ten packets per carton) as 'presents' for all the 'official' visitors. Boatmen and barber, electrician and gilly-gilly man, they were all still there. All holding their hand out. Still prepared to steal whatever they couldn't scrounge.

Usually, the pilots were never satisfied and wanted more, pleading, 'But Captain, I am the *senior* pilot. For me you must have a special present?' They never gave up, 'Some Johnnie Walker Black Label you have? Only one bottle.' That they could demean themselves so, I always found somewhat distasteful. It was also a source of some puzzlement that there could be so many *senior* pilots.

There was one pilot on that last transit however, who was an exception. I had met him before. My talk with Farouq then, and an event which occurred not long afterwards when several hundred people lost their lives, including a mutual friend, influenced me in making up my mind to get on and retire.

But that's a story to tell much later in this narrative.

## CHAPTER 13
# STILL HEADING EAST

*Red Sea*

Within a few hours of leaving the Canal, we cleared the Gulf of Suez. Passing near the narrow entrance to the Gulf of Eilat (or Gulf of Jordan, depending on your point of view) we left the starkly foreboding Sinai Mountains behind us and entered the much wider Red Sea.

At 0700 hours, the Captain had, I was told, asked the watch officer on the bridge what the temperature was. The procedure in Brocklebank vessels was that if the temperature exceeded 70°F at 0700 hours, the Master would issue a written directive to all department heads which they had to sign. 'Rig of the day will be whites' after which all the officers turned out in white tropical uniforms. Anyone not properly attired was not permitted to use the officers' mess—dining room.

Chippie had warned me that the Red Sea can be one of the hottest places on earth but I could never have imagined just how hot it would be. Our situation was made worse by a following wind which seemed to be travelling at the same speed as the vessel. There was hardly a breath of air and we seemed to be carrying all our ambient heat and funnel gasses along with us.

One of the immediate tasks for us apprentices had been to rig canvas awnings on the boat deck and various other exposed decks. We even had an awning to rig over the top of our accommodation to stop the direct sunlight and reduce the heating affect.

Instead of the customary coffee or tea at the morning smoke ho everyone was served fresh lime juice. I don't think I had ever tasted lime juice before—certainly not fresh. The limes, purchased from the Chandler with other fresh provisions in Port Said, were squeezed, sweetened slightly and served with crushed ice. It was a delicious and very refreshing drink. In those days it was a legal requirement on all British ships that lime juice be made available whenever the vessel sailed in tropical waters. There was even a special lime juice concentrate, *Board of Trade fortified lime juice*, supplied in Winchester quart bottles and carried in the ship's medical stores for use when fresh limes were unavailable. That, too, was a pleasantly refreshing drink.

Clearly, the Americans didn't refer to British seamen as limeys without cause!

We entered the Red Sea, passing two landmarks important to the Navigator (officially, the Second Officer) as we did so. The landmarks were important as they provided the Navigator with an opportunity to calibrate the equipment used to measure distance travelled.

Apart from calculating distances steamed, in those days a towing-log was also used. It consisted of a torpedo-shaped spinner at the end of about forty fathoms of line towed behind the ship. The inboard end was connected to a clock which, as the line rotated, recorded the distance travelled through the water. The Brothers and Daedalus Reefs, conveniently, are exactly one hundred nautical miles apart. As I had never done the checking before, Ian had to accompany me and show me what to do. It was really very simple. I just had to stand by on the poop listening for the officer of the watch's pea whistle signalling that the reef was exactly abeam and then zero the log. One hundred miles later, it was John, I think, who stood by to read the log clock on a similar signal.

It is not always so, but on that first voyage the air in the Red Sea was particularly clear which gave rise in the extreme heat to some very abnormal refraction. Mr Roberts shouted at us to go to the bridge on one occasion where he pointed out a ship sailing towards us. It was well within our horizon and on closer inspection it appeared to be sailing upside down! Also, the humidity was very low and as in the Gulf of Suez, there were some stunning sunsets.

We were also told about the phenomenon of a green flash at sunset, occasionally visible just as the last sliver of sun disappears under the horizon. At first, I thought it was a tall story told to gullible first-trippers. Over the years, since then, I have seen it very many times. The word flash is slightly misleading. When the conditions are right, in the split second before the last crescent of sun is lost from view, the tips turn emerald green which quickly spreads over the remainder, then, pouf, brilliant green and the sun has gone. I believe this, too, has something to do with abnormal refraction such that the last visible part of the spectrum is green.

On down the Red Sea and through the bottle neck at its southern end, the Straits of Bab el Mandeb. Although the temperature was no lower, as often happens half way down the Red Sea the wind changed completely and a shift to the south gave us a head wind. The breeze through the open portholes made the ship seem much cooler and certainly more comfortable.

## Aden for Bunkers

Our next call was Aden where the vessel anchored to bunker fuel and freshwater but unfortunately, the latter was in short supply and *Manipur* did not receive all that she required for the next part of the voyage. There was also a small amount of cargo which was off-loaded into old wooden barges.

As with our Suez call just a week or so earlier, I had been hearing all about the shopping opportunities in Aden but was really unprepared for the reality. Barges for offloaded cargo and those containing our freshwater and fuel were secured along the starboard side of the ship. On the port side there was a scrum of 'bum boats' all clamouring to sell their wares, mostly electrical toys, cameras and binoculars manufactured in Japan. They were also selling a new type of radio which was only just becoming available in England and was much sought after. A transistor radio.

Unlike Port Said, the bum boatmen were never permitted on board but they could throw their heaving lines up to the ship's bulwarks with unerring accuracy. Goods were then hauled up in a basket by the prospective customer and the bartering process would commence. Ian had already warned me, 'Be careful when you first look over the bulwark that you don't get a monkey's fist in your face!' A monkey's fist was the ball-like knot tied in the end of the heaving line to act as a missile. It was advice I heeded and was thankful for it when I saw one of the quartermasters hit in the mouth. It loosened a tooth and he was so annoyed that he shortly returned with a bucket of galley slops which he emptied over the offending boat amid whoops and cheers from all around.

None of us apprentices had much money (I was only paid £7 per month, and £3 of that was remitted home as a 'Seaman's allotment'!) but we did manage to purchase a couple of pairs of rubber flip-flops each. They became our working footwear for most of the voyage—when we weren't barefoot. 'Indian sea boots,' Chippie called them. Safety footwear, hardhats and other such equipment simply wasn't available then, but I don't recall anyone ever coming to harm through lack of it.

For that matter, no-one had ever heard of sun cream and protection factors either. We spent most of our time when working on deck stripped to the waist but I don't remember that any of us got sunburned. When it got too hot, we simply went and found some shade or jumped into the small canvas plunging pool on the boat deck. It was one of our tasks to drain it each night, refilling it again in the morning using a fire hose.

After a little more than a day anchored off Crater City, Aden, we set off on the next leg of the voyage, bound for Gan Island in the Maldives.

## *High Days and Holidays*

Leaving Aden, our course down toward the Equator was set to pass between Cape Gardafui on the north east corner of Africa and the off lying island of Socotra.

Now, as I write, the waters off the Horn of Africa and the Gulf of Aden are, unbelievably in this day and age, beset with piracy.

The risks in 1958 were minimal, but of a very different sort.

One afternoon I was working on the bridge, varnishing the teak bulwark capping when Mr Milne called me to the wheelhouse door. 'Parks. Go and put on a shirt, then come in here,' he instructed. No-one would never dare enter the wheelhouse without a shirt! Then, 'Come and have a look at this. It's something to write home and tell your mother.' Our Second Officer was quite a family man, really.

Having put on a shirt as he had instructed, curiosity aroused, I followed him through into the chartroom. There he gestured towards the chart table where there was an open copy of the Admiralty Sailing Directions for North East Africa and the Gulf of Aden lying on the current chart. He placed a nicotine stained finger on the Island of Socotra, drawing my attention to an instruction: *See note.* I looked at the chart title and saw the caution:

*Vessels needing water are cautioned against approaching Socotra. Mariners should not land. The natives are unfriendly and are believed to still practice cannibalism.*

Then the Second Officer pointed to the Sailing Directions. Under the heading 'Horn of Africa, History' there was an historical entry advising that until the early part of the twentieth century, Italy had maintained a garrison at Gardafui whose task was to protect the lighthouse keepers. It went on to explain that there had previously been a number of occasions when the native Socotrans celebrated on their local festivals and holidays by getting into their canoes, paddling across the not inconsiderable distance to Cape Gardafui, and making a meal of the lighthouse keepers.

Yes, the area seems always to have been associated with risk, and in the past, especially so on high days and holidays.

## *Tragedy*

We had not long sailed away from the African coast and were headed out into the Arabian sea toward the Maldives, when the first tragedy of the voyage occurred.

During the night, in his sleep, the Engine Room Serang passed away. A senior rating and another 'lal dari' Hajji, much respected by the crew, I believe he was making his last voyage and had planned to retire when the vessel arrived back in Calcutta.

It saddened everyone, casting a gloom throughout the ship for the remaining days on passage to Gan Island where his body was landed ashore.

I remember the day after Serang died that Chippie remonstrated with the Chief Officer for allowing the engine room ratings to lay out his body on the boat deck immediately outside our accommodation. But it was too late and we stayed out of the way anyway, down in Wullie's mess room.

It was too soon, I was told, for the SW Monsoon, but the weather on passage was poor, overcast and raining with rough seas almost all the way to Gan. It was very unseasonable. Mr Roberts commented that it was almost as though the weather were empathising with the sombre mood prevailing on board.

I suppose that living close to the elements, so to speak, seamen generally are quite superstitious.

The weather also created some problems for the vessel's navigation.

## *About Celestial Navigation*

Before continuing my narrative and amplifying that last remark, a little about the navigation routines when the vessel was in deep waters.

In the days before global positioning systems, once out of sight of land position fixing was dependent on two pieces of equipment. A sextant to measure the altitude—angular height—of a heavenly body, and a chronometer to determine at what point the earth was in its daily rotation and thus its relationship to sun, planets and stars, and moon. Of course, a Nautical Almanac and other sets of tables were also needed.

The usual routine was that daily navigation took place in three phases, like the watches.

The Chief Officer, being on watch during the four till eight, morning and evening would take star sights. This could only be done at dusk, both sunrise and sunset, during the short period when both the stars and the horizon were visible. The more observations of different bodies he made and calculated, the more accurate the result—but it was still only within about one mile, depending on the skill of the observer with his sextant.

In the eight till twelve morning watch, as soon as the sun was high enough to be unaffected by abnormal refraction, the Third Officer would take two or three observations using his sextant. From these, the ship's longitude would be calculated. Usually around 0830 the Second Officer, as the officer with overall responsibility for navigation, would also come to the bridge and make some more longitude observations.

The next stage occurred at noon when the Third and Second Officers, Fourth Officer if there was one, and sometimes the Master, would all take observations as the sun reached its maximum altitude. Latitude could be then calculated. The star sight position and morning longitudes were then 'run up' and combined with the noon latitude.

I recall that it could be quite amusing at noon. A row of officers standing on the bridge wing looking though their sextants until someone would declare, 'It's gone!' meaning that the sun had reached maximum altitude and had started to set. Squinting through the magnifying lenses on their vernier sextants, altitudes were then compared amidst some good natured banter, often with remarks, 'Call that a sextant? More like a ham bone! About time you bought a new one!' and the like. The noon latitude was the one piece of celestial navigation for which accurate time was un-necessary.

Calculations were then all made independently and a 'noon position' was agreed by those participating.

Subsequently, the Navigator would calculate distance run, courses and speed since the previous noon, plus the requirements for the remainder of the passage. Working independently, all this was also calculated by the others as a cross-check on the Navigator.

(As I rose through the ranks, although I thoroughly enjoyed being Navigator, I think that taking star observations and calculating them was, perhaps, the most enjoyable and satisfying part of celestial navigation.)

## *Who got lost then?*

As we continued on our passage to the Maldives and Gan Island, the weather remained poor to the extent that for about two days it was not possible to 'fix' the ship's position. It was overcast and neither sun nor stars had been visible. The watchkeeping officers resorted to calculating the vessel's position using 'dead reckoning' which is probably most accurately described as a navigator's 'best guess' after using an estimated ship's speed and allowing for predicted ocean currents and wind drift.

Gan is one of the eleven islands in Addu Atoll, just fifty miles or so over the Equator, in south latitude. At that time, it was under lease to the British Government and in use as a Royal Air Force Station. Brocklebanks were contracted to the RAF and the NAAFI to take supplies out from UK and on that particular voyage we were also carrying a considerable amount of cargo for the civil engineering contractor Costain. They had a major project to rebuild the runway.

We had been expecting to make landfall on Gan in the early afternoon and the Captain and several others had all been standing on the port bridge wing in anticipation, armed with telescopes and binoculars, peering, on lookout for the first sighting.

Time passed and nothing was seen.

The truth was, no-one really knew *ss Manipur's* position but what was very clear was that the ship was not where dead reckoning had calculated it to be. So much for the navigator's best guess.

By late afternoon, we apprentices, too, had been co-opted onto the lookout team as well and had been sent aloft to increase the distance of our horizon and, thereby, the range we cold see. We were aware that the Captain was verging on making a decision to turn the ship round and start a search.

I think it was John Churchill who heard it first and shouted down from the mast, calling everyone's attention to a droning sound. It slowly became louder and we soon spotted an aircraft approaching from astern. It was a Shackleton and I think everyone instinctively ducked as it roared over us at deafeningly low altitude. A little way ahead of the ship, the aircraft rolled from side to side two or three times, wagging its wings, 'Follow me.' Then it turned and flew back again, still at such low altitude we could clearly see the pilot and the crewman in the gunner's bay down in the nose of the aircraft. The Captain had given the helm order and started to turn the ship while the Third Officer acknowledged, signalling an affirmative with the Aldis lamp.

It turned out that the RAF who had been given our eta, had seen the ship on their radar. When they realised what had happened, the Station Commander scrambled one of the two Shackletons based on the island to come and look for us. Guide us in. We had passed only twelve miles off but as the highest part of the island was a clump of palm trees at one end, it was no surprise that we saw nothing. At that distance, from the *Manipur's* bridge, the trees would have been below the horizon.

The ship eventually anchored within the lagoon a few hundred yards from the island and we apprentices had the not unpleasant job of running a boat service to and from shore for those wishing to enjoy some shore leave. We used one of the ship's lifeboats. All the ship's officers were made honorary members of the RAF Officers' Mess but I think there were more visits made *to* the ship and the officers' bar as RAF Gan was, if I recall correctly, a 'dry' posting. After the business with the Shackleton, not surprisingly, there was a lot of leg-pulling and our officers got a bit of stick. 'Call yourselves navigators?!'

## *Island in the sun*

We were in Gan for about two weeks.

Very soon after our arrival, arrangements were made to take the poor old engine room Serang ashore to another island in the atoll. The RAF arranged for a special boat to make the journey across the lagoon to Hitadu, his final resting place, and Serang was accompanied by several other members of our crew. It was a sad event and many of us stood outside, heads bowed, as the boat drew away and he finally left the ship.

Sad, but Serang's departure also marked a lightening of mood on board and the weather became very much better too.

As it was not a conventional port with dockers and stevedores, discharging was carried out using the ship's crew who off-loaded cargo into two landing craft which RAF personnel then used to ferry the goods a short distance to a small jetty or ran them onto the beach where they in turn off-loaded their craft.

There was a great deal of cargo, most of it for Costain. The consignment included a cement batching plant, other pieces of heavy machinery and a large quantity of bagged cement and aggregate. We apprentices were very much involved at first driving the winches but were soon taken off this task for a more important one. The *ss Manipur* was becoming desperately short of water. It was a consequence of the shortage when *Manipur* called at Aden and was unable to bunker all the water requested.

We were taken off cargo work to start bringing fresh water to the vessel.

The island didn't have a lot of water to spare either, and what they had, was rather brackish. Nevertheless, it was agreed we could have some—but then the problem arose over how we could get it on board. There was no water barge available.

The difficulty was overcome by using our other lifeboat. Unlike the port boat, this one had no engine, it was a rowing boat. We set to and virtually stripped it back to being a bare wooden hull, with all the extra buoyancy tanks, the provision lockers and every piece of loose equipment removed.

Using the motor lifeboat, we then took it in tow to the jetty ashore where we were met by a road tanker full of water. This was then gravitated into our boat. Because it was wooden and floating in salt water, the different densities allowed filling almost to the gunwale. This accomplished, our 'water boat' was towed back out to *Manipur* where we used a winch and derrick with a forty gallon drum to bale it out and discharge the water down an air pipe into the ship's freshwater tanks.

It was quite a lengthy process and we only managed two or three loads each day. Nevertheless, we were thoroughly enjoying ourselves and usually while waiting for the bowser to load our boat, we would step off the jetty onto the beach and go for a swim or snorkel out to the reef edge and back. No towels or bathing costumes. Just straight in wearing our working shorts. The sun would soon dry us off again. Who cared? Our working clothes became stiff with salt.

While we were anchored in the lagoon, a private yacht came and anchored nearby. I was fascinated to learn that it was a couple whose programmes I had enjoyed watching on television. Hans and Lotte Hass were very well known at that time for their underwater films, made in all sorts of locations. We were privileged that at the Captain's invitation they came on board for dinner one evening and afterwards talked to us about scuba diving and swimming on the reef. I was not alone in finding it particularly interesting and although I had always enjoyed swimming, it was probably that occasion which sparked a life-long interest in diving.

Meanwhile, despite all our work with the lifeboats, the ship remained seriously short of water. Fortunately, toilets used seawater, but for other purposes we all had to make a daily attendance at the forepeak with a bucket where we took our ration for the day, about ten litres per person, from a small hand pump. The situation eventually became so critical, that soft drinks were given freely in the dining room instead of the usual jugs of iced water.

Although the weather was hugely improved from that which we had experienced on passage down from Aden, often there would be a thunderstorm around dawn or in the late evening and personnel would run out on deck into the rain, using it to wash. At John Churchill's suggestion we had slackened off all the ropes on the boat deck awnings so that they collected rainwater. We then used this as a makeshift shower, pushing underneath with a broom to displace water causing it to cascade over the edge of the awning. It was very effective, but on more than one occasion when there was a tropical downpour, we had to hasten out and attend our 'reservoir'. If it overfilled, there was a real risk that the canvas awning would split under the weight of the collected water. What the Chief Officer's reaction might have been had we been the cause of such damage was better not tested!

Although our visit to Gan Island was not without hardship, it is a time I recall as having been really quite idyllic. The four of us thoroughly enjoyed ourselves working out in the sun, swimming in the sea, and generally 'mucking about in boats'. All this was in unspoilt surroundings of beaches, palms and turquoise coloured coral reefs that many are never fortunate enough to see. There wasn't an ice cream van in sight!

Ian, who played a guitar, made an adaptation of the calypso *Island in The Sun.* One evening after sunset while sitting on deck sipping a cold drink, he amused us strumming his guitar and singing:

This is my island that's called Gan
Willed to me by a Pakistan

All my days I will sing it's praise
Of its brackish water—those lazy days.

After the manner of our arrival at the island, and the ribbing he received, I recall Mr Milne showing me a quotation from a famous mariner who had compiled many of the navigational tables we then used.

Captain S T S Lecky:

*A good navigator is never lost, but he may occasionally be puzzled for an hour or two.*

At anchor off Colombo, Ian strums while I toot. I got into trouble later and was told to pull my socks up!

# CHAPTER 14
# CEYLON

## *Colombo*

Although we were sorry to be leaving Gan Island, the water shortage on board was causing so much inconvenience that we were all looking forward to docking in Colombo. We were tired of taking showers in rainwater under an awning and the engineers had been worse off than any us. The inability to maintain a high standard of personal hygiene had caused many to suffer severely from heat induced sweat rashes and dhobi itch.

The few days of sea passage quickly passed and we were soon rolling easily in the swell off Colombo waiting for the pilot to arrive on his boat.

In due course we were docked at the passenger terminal but our visit was brief and only of sufficient duration to replenish the *Manipur's* fresh water tanks. This accomplished, the pilot boarded again and the ship steamed back, outside the port, this time to anchor. We 'dropped the pick' about a mile from the harbour entrance along with a number of other vessels that were also delayed and waiting for a berth.

The delay to our docking in Colombo was a consequence of Ceylon (as it still was then) being subject to marshal law.

The country was in political turmoil and subject to a nightly curfew. Within two years, it would lead to the assassination of President Bandaranayake.

I cannot now remember exactly how long we remained at anchor, rolling gently in the swell off the Arabian Sea, but it was several weeks. Sufficiently long, anyway, that at least once the ship had to return to port briefly and bunker fresh water again. Every few days, we received a visit from the pilot vessel that delivered eagerly awaited mail which Brocklebanks' Agent had arranged to have sent out.

The phrase 'eagerly awaited mail' does not really convey how important letters from home were to the seafarer in those days. Lack of mail or a delay in getting it on board could have a noticeable effect on morale thus everyone was extremely grateful for the pilot boat's visits. Writing letters home was part of everyday life at sea and replies were always eagerly awaited. We all numbered out letters so than if any were missing it was readily apparent. When the mail came on board, swift distribution was a very high priority. Everyone who could, ceased work to go and read their mail. Postmarks would be compared to see how long it had been in transit. 'That's not bad—only six days from England!' Often, there was also friendly banter, 'Got that Dear John letter yet then?'

Now, we take satellites and global communications very much for granted—and are quickly losing the skills of letter writing as a consequence. An American friend once said to me 'All the time you are writing to someone, that person is occupying your thoughts to the exclusion of almost everything else. What could be a greater complement to them?' How true.

While the ship was at anchor, we apprentices split our time between working out on deck learning seamanship skills, and spending time with the officers on anchor watches and learning navigation. We were also sometimes given time off during the heat of the early afternoon to work on our correspondence courses. Distance learning was a requirement of our indentures and the Merchant Navy Training Board administered the programme on all British ships. Annual examinations were a measure of our progress.

Some of my watchkeeping time was on the four till eight morning watch. It was a time I especially enjoyed. The air at that time of day was often very clear after a thunderstorm and as the sun rose, the mountains of central Ceylon would be silhouetted. Sometimes, if the air was very clear, the mountain in the north of the island would be visible. 'Adam's Peak, that's where Buddha's footprint is. He stepped off there on his way to Heaven,' Mr Davis told me one morning. I was thankful he seemed to have mellowed a little since the snowball incident in Middlesbrough.

Working on deck, we did a lot of chipping and painting. I didn't mind the painting too much but I did find tapping away with a chipping hammer at flaking rust to be a somewhat mindless task. There seemed so little to show for one's efforts—unlike painting. Of the seamanship we were learning, probably the task I most enjoyed was being taught by one of the Quartermasters how to use a sailmaker's palm and needle, to wax the twine and how to sew canvas. I would happily sit for hours on the boat deck sewing canvas and roping the edges. It was, I felt, productive. Something to show for one's efforts. I enjoyed being taught to splice too.

On other occasions, we worked under Chippie's direction making wooden hatch boards. That was another task I enjoyed. There was an end product; also I was able to put into practise some of the skills I had learned when working on the building site.

After a couple of weeks or so, we were joined by another Brocklebank vessel which anchored nearby. The *ss Markhor*, strangely named after a member of the goat family, was a very elderly lady. She was powered by a quadruple expansion steam engine and had a tall 'woodbine' funnel, black with the blue and white bands of the Brocklebank livery. The four of us were standing at the bulwark admiring the ship when Mr Roberts, who had sailed on her, came and joined us.

'You know,' he said, 'That Brocks is the oldest shipping company in Britain—probably in the world.'

'Yes,' we agreed.

'Well, there you are. Look at that,' he said, pointing at the *Markhor*. 'They've got the ships to prove it, too!'

I have not remarked before but all Brocklebank ships' names began with the letters *Ma* and they were all named after places, people or other things associated with India. *Manipur* is an area.

The days at anchor off Colombo seemed to drift lazily on but eventually it was our turn to dock. There was a berth for *Manipur* and we hove anchor and proceeded into the harbour. During the weeks outside we had settled into such an easy routine, work during the day, relax out on deck in the balmy air of the evening making music or just talking. Ian had his guitar and I my clarinet; everyone knew the words to *Peggy Sue* and other pop music of the time, and would join in to Ian's strumming and my tooting. Someone also had a ukulele, which John sometimes plonked. Later in the voyage, we formed quite a group with a number of other instruments—but I'll come to that in due course.

When we were told to heave anchor, we almost resented the change. *Almost* resented, not quite. I was looking forward to visiting a new port. New things to see; new things to experience.

No-one could have even imagined then, that before the ship left Colombo, before she was at sea again, there was to be the most awful tragedy.

Arriving inside the harbour, this time the ship moored between buoys and, as in Aden, freight was discharged into barges. Cargo operations were supposed to carry on around the clock but the curfew was still in force ashore and it had a detrimental effect on the stevedoring operations, slowing things down. Also, quite often, shortly before dawn there would be a tropical thunderstorm and all six holds had to be quickly covered using special canvas tents. I knew all about those tents. I had spent enough time repairing them; sewing insets where the canvas had been torn, splicing and roping the edges! Once the rain started, it could go on for an hour or two and knowing this, all the stevedores would quickly find a sheltered spot, curl up on the deck and go to sleep. They seemed to be able to sleep anywhere—and at any time. We would then get no more work from them for the remainder of the shift. The ship would lie idle until after the curfew when the next shift arrived on board at 0800 hours.

## *Making the most of the curfew*

After just a few days, it was obvious that we were destined to be in Colombo for some time.

'Who'll volunteer to work nights, then?' the Second Officer was asking the four of us. There was silence for a moment; no-one seemed to want to do it. However, the more I thought about it, the more I realised that it would afford the best opportunity for shore leave. There seemed little point in working all day when the curfew prevented shore leave in the evening. There was too much to see and do for me to be content with spending every evening on board. Sitting on the boat deck after dinner was something best enjoyed at sea or at anchor when there was no alternative. Night work then, why not? I thought.

'I'll do it,' I told the Second.

'Right, Parks. You're on with me, 1900 tonight through to the end of the shift—but they usually finish early,' he affirmed. Then, 'By the way, can you cook?' I was puzzled at what this had to do with cargo work. It must have shown on my face.

'It's a long night. Can you cook a breakfast?' He amplified the question.

'Yes, I suppose so,' rather hesitantly. I could fry a simple breakfast but I wasn't too sure exactly what he expected.

'That'll be good then. I'll have the chef leave all the necessary goodies in the galley. You get together with the duty quartermaster, Charlie, around midnight and by 0100, we'll all enjoy a belt-buster. Black pudding, fried bread. The works. Full house.' Mr Milne was almost licking his lips in anticipation. 'It's the best thing about being on nights,' he concluded.

He was certainly right about our middle-of-the-night breakfast being a belt buster. It was an enjoyable meal, pleasant, too, stodged out and relaxing afterwards with fresh coffee and a cigarette. Perhaps because most of the rest of he ship's complement were asleep, there seemed to be a special camaraderie between the three of us and things were much more informal. 'There's no need to keep calling me Mr Milne. Second will be fine,' I was told.

The Second thought it was the meal, but for me, the best thing about working the night shift was the opportunity for shore leave in the afternoons.

By five o'clock most mornings, the rain would have started and stevedoring would be at a standstill. There would be sleeping bodies scattered on all areas of the decks not directly exposed to the rain. Once I had checked that the stevedores had rigged the hatch tents properly and that the portable cargo lamps had been unplugged and their cables tidily coiled, I would report all was secure to the Second. He knew it was unlikely there would be any more work that shift.

'Right. Thanks Parks. Off you go then. Have a good sleep.' I would head for our accommodation. A quick shower, then, my bunk.

## *Colombo Swimming Club*

I never bothered to get up for lunch, the extra hour or so of sleep was more important, but by around two o'clock I had my bathers and towel rolled ready to head off to Colombo Swimming Club. Because it was a popular venue and all ship's officers were automatically honorary members, there was always someone to accompany me. The rowing boat to the passenger terminal and taxi to the club cost only a few rupees anyway, but were shared.

There were many ex-patriots living in Colombo, and in other parts of Ceylon, and the Swimming Club was quite a social focus locally. Looking back on it, it was very British, very Colonial. The buildings were substantial and evidently old. There were wide verandas surrounding the pool. They had big arches and spacious recesses full of cane furniture. The clubhouse and restaurant had lofty ceilings with fans hanging from them which always seemed to be wobbling and in need of balancing as they quietly swished the warm air downwards. Often a gecko would dart swiftly across a wall or pause for a moment, perhaps looking for a tasty insect. There were numerous servants, bare feet padding quietly across marble flooring as they carried trays of drinks or snacks. They may have had no footwear but they were always immaculately attired in white trousers and tunic, stiff with starch, divided by a burgundy-coloured cummerbund. Drinks were cheap and the food was good but also inexpensive.

When visiting Colombo Swimming Club I was, I now see with hindsight, experiencing one of the last remnants of the British Empire. As an adjective for it all, for the total experience, the word *pukkah* seems apposite. I didn't fully appreciate it at the time, nor did I realise how very fortunate I was.

In the afternoons, the Club was a popular meeting place for other young people. There was no senior school for them in the heat of the afternoon and I made several friends of my own age, sixteen. Among them was an American girl, Linda. She had a younger brother Joey who was, to be as kind as possible to him, a rascal. He was one of those noisy small boys who always seemed to be in trouble. One afternoon it dawned on me that I had not seen him around for a day or two. Perhaps I eventually noticed his absence because it was just too quiet. Joey was mischief magnet.

'Haven't seen Joey lately,' I commented to his sister when a group of us were sitting under a veranda sipping fresh lemonade. Linda looked somewhat uncomfortable. She evidently didn't want to talk about him.

'He's okay, isn't he? Not got one of these stomach bugs?' I asked. I had heard that there was a gastro complaint doing the rounds ashore.

'Yeah, he's just fine thanks,' she replied.

'Not like Joey to miss the club,' one of the other then remarked.

'He's been banned. His membership has been suspended for a week,' Linda told us.

'Whatever for?' I asked. I knew he was mischievous, but banned! Hell, it must have been serious!

'He kinda did something in the pool he didn't have oughta have done.' Linda was really embarrassed.

Supposing that he had maybe taken a pee in the pool, I asked,

'Well unless he was daft enough to tell someone, how on earth did he get caught?' By now, Linda's face was bright red, but she had to respond.

'Well, gee, I guess like. Well, it was kinda left floatin' there.' The loud eruption of laughter even brought some of the parents out from the bar to see what was up.

## *Mount Lavinia*

The Swimming Club was only a little over a mile out of Colombo along the Galle road and was, thereby, easily accessible. Somewhat less accessible, six or seven miles further down the coast road towards Galle as I recall, was a very pleasant cove with palm trees overhanging a sandy beach. We knew it by the name of the hotel on the promontory above, Mount Lavinia. Nowadays, it's a significant holiday resort.

The beach and hotel feature briefly in the film *The Bridge Over the River Kwai*. I think it was as a venue for convalescing personnel. The entire film had been made on location in Ceylon and on another occasion I was fortunate to be taken to visit the valley and see the remains of the wooden bridge.

At weekends in Colombo there was no cargo work. Mount Lavinia was a favourite alternative to the Swimming Club when there were several of us to share to cost of getting there.

Later during our stay in Colombo, all four of us were on the beach along with some colleagues, apprentices from two other Brocklebank vessels, the *Markhor* and the *Marwarri* (named after merchants from Rajasthan), which had had also docked in Colombo.

The beach was quite busy and our group had been sitting under the palms at the back of the beach, swapping stories and enjoying fresh pineapples we had bought from a vendor traipsing back and forth along the sand. The lady selling them, and fresh coconuts, would prepare each pineapple by cutting off the top and paring down the sides. The fruit was left with the short stalk which was used like the stick on a lollipop to hold it while being eaten. The pineapples were very juicy and clad in a bathing costume with the sea nearby to bathe in afterwards was definitely the most practical way to eat them.

That afternoon, I was the unwitting cause of a panic on the beach and among other bathers. It wasn't my fault really. It was all down to John Churchill.

John was in the sea rinsing the pineapple juice off; I was still on the beach talking to our friends. For some reason which I cannot now remember, John decided he need me for something and proceeded to shout my name.

'Parks! Parks!'

Bathers came running from the sea and many people even started edging back towards the palm trees at the back of the beach. For a moment or two we didn't understand. John was still in the sea and called me again.

Then it dawned. What people were actually hearing sounded very much like something entirely different:

'Sharks! Sharks!'

When I told Chippie later, he thought it the funniest thing he had heard in many years—and afterwards often pulled Churchill's leg about it.

## *Toe hold but time to leave*

The Mount Lavinia event had been a Saturday. On Sunday mornings I and one or two others from the ship, several times went ashore to the Mission To Seamen. There was a quaint little stone chapel where we were made welcome for the Communion service. Although it was a facility for seamen, it was well supported by some of the ex patriots and there was almost a small crowd in attendance. Afterwards, some of the wives would serve coffee or fresh juice.

One of the things I particularly remember was a Singhalese gentleman. The first time I visited, as I walked into the pleasant gloom of the chapel, I noticed he was crouched in a corner just inside the door. He was slowly swaying one of his legs in time to the movement of a large carpet hanging high in the roof, between the trusses. The swinging carpet served instead of a fan and gently wafted air around the chapel, keeping us cool as the air outside heated up. It wasn't until we were leaving and my eyes were accustomed to the dim light that I saw what he was actually doing. There was a piece of string looped around his big toe. It wasn't that he was keeping time with the carpet. He was actually swinging it. Such a simple thing—but we were all very grateful to him.

Slowly, our cargo for Ceylon was being netted and winched out of the ship. Some of the holds were becoming empty and after several weeks, the time to sail was approaching.

With some sadness at parting, it was time to say goodbye to friends in Colombo Swimming Club. Time to make the last taxi journey back to the ship, riding along road at the back of the Galle Face beach where crowds of local people, Singhalese and Tamil together, were standing on the wide pavement with their families. It was evidently the thing to do in the early evening, the place to be. Many were flying large and colourful kites in the onshore breeze and some of the small children waved as we passed.

Norman, John and I make music on the boat deck

Relaxing on the Mount Lavinia beach, Ceylon, with Chris
the Second Radio Officer

## CHAPTER 15
# AS BAD AS IT GETS

*Norman*

In my narrative thus far, there is one name that has seldom been mentioned. Norman Segar—and I am struggling to find how best to write this.

Norman was from Merseyside, Liverpool I think, and about a year older than I. As had I, he had come to sea directly from school, which is to say without the benefit of a pre-sea training school. Both our other colleagues had gained a one year reduction in their apprenticeships by virtue of having attended Conway and Warsash and were somewhat elitist about it.

Norman was on his second or maybe third voyage and we had one other thing in common. Like me, he had a brother just a few years his junior. Norman was a quietly industrious apprentice who generally kept his head down and got on with things. Had he been less conscientious, things may have been very different.

We were in the final throes of our stay in Colombo. I had been taken off night shift after a spell of several weeks and was finding it rather difficult to adjust and to get back into normal sleep and work routines again. The four of us were on day work and involved mainly in clearing up and tidying the cargo decks, making *Manipur* ready to leave Ceylon for the final part of our outward voyage, the passage up to Calcutta.

The final day came, the last slings of cargo were going ashore and we were scheduled to sail later in the evening. It was the afternoon smoke-ho and the four of us were sitting on the after deck outside the entrance to the petty officers' accommodation drinking tea, coffee or perhaps sipping an iced drink. I think Wullie was also with us.

In the middle of this, the Third Officer, or it might have been the Second, came and told John, as the senior apprentice, to arrange to get number one lower hold inspected to ensure that there was no cargo remaining. To confirm that it was empty and no cargo would be over-carried.

We finished our smoke ho and then resumed our tasks around the decks which we had individually already been engaged in. Number one lower hold was completely forgotten about.

Somewhat later, all the holds had been battened down, the vessel was ready for sea and we were back in the accommodation getting cleaned up and showering in readiness for dinner.

We were sitting waiting when the dinner gong was sounded and it was at this stage that we realised there were only three of us. It was very unusual for Norman to miss a meal but at first we thought he may have been enjoying an illegal beer with one of the engineers and lost track of time. Illegal because apprentices drinking alcohol was a serious offence.

Thinking that Norman would not want to miss dinner, John had a quick tour around all the likely cabins but no-one had seen him. Then it dawned on us that because we had not been working as a group, none of us had realised that we had not seen him since our afternoon smoke-ho. Now we were beginning to be concerned, so much so that John went to the Chief Officer who was already in the dining room, interrupted his dinner, and reported that we were unable to find Segar.

Dinner was abandoned by everyone and emergency search teams were set up without delay.

Ian Verran and I had been detailed to start at the bow, searching first under the fo'castle in the various stores, working our way back checking other spaces. I think one of the quartermasters may also have been with us.

The fo'castle was searched and we moved back to number one hold. It was the only hatch on the ship that was not secured by wooden hatch boards and tarpaulins but had a steel lid as better protection against seas being shipped over the bow in heavy weather. In one corner of the steel lid, there was a manhole access which we quickly un-dogged and opened. The 'tween deck hatch boards normally covering the lower hold had been left off and as soon as Ian shone his flashlight down we could see Norman lying perhaps thirty feet below us on the steel deck. I was sent off immediately to fetch the Chief Officer and ran off down the foredeck hollering his name.

His search group arrived in double quick time at which point we apprentices were sent from the scene and told to stay away.

Norman was taken ashore to hospital. He was in a very poor way having fallen onto the steel deck, incurring severe head injuries.

Not surprisingly, everyone was shocked to the core and none more so than us three apprentices. I spent quite some time in his mess with Chippie that evening and it was his calm presence that helped me—helped the three of us remaining apprentices—to face the awfulness and reality of what had happened.

The ship sailed very much later that night than had been planned.

Late the next day, I think it was, the Old Man received the telegram we had all been dreading. Sadly, Norman had Crossed the Bar.

When we heard the news, Wullie said to me quietly, 'It's nae over wi' yet.' I said nothing, thinking that he was probably referring to the efforts that we had heard Brocklebanks were making to get Norman's parent flown out to Ceylon.

One never forgets such an event but without doubt, time softens bad memories. While writing this I have been remembering more the fun we shared and occasions we enjoyed. positive times, like working together in Gan loading water, pushing each other overboard from the lifeboat, mucking about in the plunging pool, sitting on deck learning to sew canvas, sitting on deck in the evening with a cold drink singing popular songs. Those are the powerful memories. But about two years ago, nearly fifty years after the tragedy, its awful reality was all brought back to me once again.

Ruth had been idly looking through the Numast Telegraph, a monthly newspaper published by what used to be called The Merchant Navy and Airline Officers' Association. She spotted a small paragraph asking if any readers knew about an accident that happened on the *ss Manipur* in 1958 when an apprentice, Norman Segar, lost his life.

'Wasn't that your ship?' she asked. She knew, too, that there had been an accident when I was an apprentice.

I responded to the request in the paper, sending an e-mail. Soon afterwards I spoke at some length on the telephone with David Segar, Norman's younger brother.

I think David was looking to blame Brocklebanks. He told me how his parents never really recovered from their loss, especially his mother, and how he had lost an older brother who having gone away to sea, was his hero. 'I was only a small boy at the time and thought a lot of my big brother,' he said.

Later, I found that even more poignant when my younger brother William said something rather similar to me. He was not much more than a toddler when I left home but, very much to my surprise, he and Steve had thought of me in a rather similar way. The big brother who had left home and gone away to sea.

'Why else,' said Will, 'Do you think we called that old rowing boat Steve had on Sheerwater *The Manipur*?' I had had no idea. Sheerwater was a lake on the Marques of Bath's estate where we used to go and play as children.

Perhaps we all shared a little of the blame for Norman's accident. If only we had realised when we finished our smoke-ho that day that Norman had conscientiously gone off to search number one hold. Had any of us realised, he would never have been permitted to do so unaccompanied. We all knew that going into such spaces alone was dangerous. Sadly, life has many 'if only's'.

## *In the Bay of Bengal*

So, we had sailed from Ceylon, around the south of the island past the Basses Reef and on up into the Bay of Bengal. I don't remember much of that part of the voyage. I think we were all too preoccupied with the recent tragedy. The morale on board was low, to say the least.

Then, only a day or two before we were due to embark our Calcutta Pilot at the entrance to the Hooghly River, there was another tragic event, this time while lunch was being served in the officers' mess.

The saloon was full and the stewards, 'boys' as they were always called, were busy, deftly waiting-on with full silver service. Quite suddenly, there was a commotion behind me and I looked round to see that the steward serving the top table had collapsed and was lying on the deck.

The Purser quickly went to his aid thinking, perhaps, that the steward had only fainted but it soon became apparent that that was not so. A nod from the Purser to the Captain and everyone was quietly told to leave.

Apparently, the steward had suffered a massive heart failure.

Once again, I was in my old friend's mess. 'That'll be the end of it. Three. There'll nae be mair.' So *that* is what he'd meant when he said last time it wasn't the end of it.

Chippie was correct. Three deaths. There were no more and morale slowly started to improve.

## *The real end of it*

Although I was writing home regularly, I never mentioned the two deaths and certainly not the tragedy to one of my fellow apprentices. I thought it would worry Mother too much; she wasn't very keen about me leaving home in the first place.

The story didn't come out until the ship had returned to Southampton many months later. Mother and Dad and my two brothers came to visit the ship. Not long after they came on board, Dad took me quietly to one side. He had spotted that something was amiss.

'Andrew, in all your letters telling us about your adventures and experiences,' he began, 'You have never mentioned the fourth lad. Where is he?' Dad had noticed that we were only three.

I told him the full story, concluding that I had said nothing before as I had not wanted to cause Mother any undue worry.

'Probably it was for the best. I know how you will have felt.' I said nothing, but wondered how earth he could possibly think he would know how I felt. I had yet to hear the story of how his pal had been killed falling down a mine shaft, Father hearing him screaming all the way to the pit bottom.

Before they left the ship, Mother and Dad met with Wullie Carroll again. This time there was no chipped teapot. We met down in Chippie's mess. Dad couldn't say too much in front of Mother but I do know that he nevertheless managed to convey his thanks for all the guidance I had received and particularly, his gratitude for the rock Chippie had been for all three of us when Norman met with his accident.

## CHAPTER 16
# CALCUTTA

*Trifling omission*

As I start to record something of my first visit to Calcutta I realise that before actually docking in that fine city we stopped a little way downriver at Gardenreach to discharge explosives. When writing of the *Manipur's* loading around the UK coast, I omitted to mention a call at Milford Haven.

While the vessel had been in Avonmouth we were attended by a gang of carpenters whose task was to construct a special wooden magazine in number four hold in preparation for loading explosives and detonators. After sailing from Avonmouth the vessel anchored at Milford Haven for a few days where a quantity of explosives was loaded from a coaster which moored alongside *Manipur*.

I later learned that Mother had thought the explosives were gelignite but had, to Dad's amusement, done a Mrs Malaprop when telling her cousin Margaret.

'Damn fond of trifle in Calcutta, are they then Molly?' had been Aunt Margaret's response.

'What do you mean? What's trifle got to do with it?'

'Well, you can make a one hell of a lot of jelly with two hundred tons of gelatine!'

## *India at Last!*

As we sailed further up the Bay of Bengal, the mood on the vessel was slowly improving and everyone was looking forward to reaching our final discharging port and to commencing loading for the voyage west. It would be a turning point; homeward bound.

There was much speculation as to whether the *Manipur* would head directly back to Europe or first visit the East Coast of the United States and if the latter, we should not really be homeward bound until after discharging cargo in America. Unlike most on board, I was really hoping that *Manipur* would not return directly to Europe but voyage via America. I was the inexperienced 'first tripper'.

In due course we arrived at the estuary of the River Hooghly, a branch of the Ganges delta, where the ship had to anchor for several days. *Manipur* was 'neaped'. There was insufficient depth of water to cross sand banks in the river's estuary and make passage upriver. In my eagerness—youthful enthusiasm—to see a little of India, the wait was frustrating.

During the previous months I had been regaled with many stories of Kolkata, as it has now reverted to being more generally known, many of which seemed to contradict each other. How could it be such a poverty-stricken, mal-odorous and filthy place and yet provide everyone with such good memories of time spent there?

'The River Hooghly,' I was told more than once, 'Is the arsehole of India—and Calcutta is one hundred miles up it!' Then, almost in the next breath, 'Make sure you go to Kidderpore Seamen's Club for the weekly Dingbat's Ball, Parksy. It's a fun night out and a walk along Chowringee is not to be missed. You've never seen so many cinemas!' Beggars and homeless children were never mentioned.

I was looking forward to finding out for myself what Calcutta was really like; impatient to draw my own conclusions.

We waited in the appropriately named anchorage, Sandheads, until the moon and sun came closer to syzygy and the tidal range started increasing. Eventually, from a rather decrepit pilot launch, we embarked a Sikh river pilot to guide the vessel up the notorious and treacherous River Hooghly. At last! We were on the final leg of our outbound voyage.

There was much to see on the river and I noticed that numerous small craft just seemed to be drifting. Many were carrying what looked like flax and were loaded to the extent that with the cargo brushing the water, overhanging the sides of the wooden boat, the actual hull was often invisible. Ian had already described these as 'floating haystacks'. As we passed them I could then see that far from drifting aimlessly, the craft were actually being rowed by two men, one standing on each side in the bow. They were tirelessly stepping backwards and forward, two paces at a time, to gain sufficient reach as they each put weight on their large oar. They were paddling the boat with the tide. The tidal flow in the river was considerable and the floating haystacks took advantage, moving only when the tide was running in the direction they wished to travel. When it turned against them, the boat would be secured at the river bank, waiting for the next favourable tide.

Several times, *Manipur*, too, had to drop anchor and await tides. Then, at night-time, the smell of burning wood as food was cooked on open fires pervaded the listlessly humid air. It seemed depleted of oxygen. Lights on the outside decks would soon become almost obscured by the insect they attracted. They then seemed to become alive, undulating, swarming with huge, often brilliantly coloured moths and other insects. Anchoring in *Manipur's* case was due to lack of water and we waited until the flood tide gave sufficient depth for safe passage over some of the many sand or mud banks we encountered. I say water, but it may more accurately have been described as fluid mud. It was also dotted with numerous floating trees, large clumps of vegetation and other debris. I was to find out more about this 'other' debris while we were in Calcutta, more than a little to my dismay!

## *The Hooghly Bore*

Eventually, after discharging our explosives, we continued up the river to Calcutta and moored at buoys a few yards off the riverbank. It was an unbelievably protracted and laborious process which took almost a full day. I watched from the fo'castle, in sweltering heat as both anchors were hung-off on wires and then unshackled from their chains. Two lengths of chain were then manhandled onto a barge before being taken to *Manipur's* stern. I was instructed then, to stand by on the poop to observe the rest of the mooring operation and record the times of each part of the process. One end of each chain was shackled to a buoy. The other ends were then heaved onto the poop and fastened to enormous four-fold rope tackles stretched the length of the afterdeck. The chains forward had been crossed and shackled directly to buoys under the bow. The process seemed to take for ever.

Within a day or two the need for such substantial moorings became apparent. The moon phase had reached the stage at which the river bores started. Their arrival time on the commencement of each flood tide had been carefully calculated by Mr Roberts, usually amid muttering and some pencil chewing. Some half hour or so before the predicted time, crew went to stand by fore and aft. The rope tackles, which acted as shock-absorbers on the after chains, were heaved bar tight; the gangway was lifted clear and engines were made ready in case the ship should break adrift. My station was on the bridge with Mr Roberts where we waited on the starboard bridge wing, looking as the last of the ebb tide trickled along the muddy river bank. Tugs and any craft moving in the river had come virtually to a standstill and all turned to face downriver, stemming the imminent flood tide. Watching. Waiting for the substantial wave of flood water to come surging around the bend from Gardenreach.

'Quick, Parks, Look!' Mr Roberts was pointing at the mud. At first I did not see what he was showing me. 'Look! Can't you see? The water's started rising!' Then I saw what he was meant. Although the level was noticeably rising up the mud, the tide was still running out. How was it possible, I asked.

'It's a surge ahead of the bore. It isn't far away now,' the Third predicted and almost as he spoke I heard a cacophony of whistles and horns as craft down river signalled the bore's passing, warning craft still waiting, of its arrival. Very soon the large wave swept into sight round the bend. It reached us and *Manipur* surged ahead with the chains screeching in protest as they held fast. The bore had slammed against *Manipur's* stern, vainly trying to take the ship with it. Compared with the swells and waves I had seen in bad weather at sea, it seemed rather insignificant. It was probably only about one metre high, but there could be no doubting the enormous energy it unleashed as we were buffeted and all the river craft bounced around in the bore's turbulent wake. The engines were not needed and our chains held fast.

The bore tides lasted for several days and whatever time of day or night, we had to be prepared and 'on stations'. It interfered with shore leave as the vessel needed to be properly manned and the bore times were even posted on the gangway board.

Mostly, officers complained bitterly at the nuisance and could hardly wait for the ship to move into Kidderpore Dock. Me? I never found it less than amazing and so many years later, well remember the feeling of excitement as the craft out of sight downriver heralded the bore's approach on their horns and whistles.

The Severn Bore? Pah!

## *Other Hooghly memories*

Earlier, I mentioned debris in the river.

Soon after the vessel had moored, Mr Milne gave John Churchill a printed notice that he had received indirectly from the harbourmaster. It caused a great deal of amusement. The notice was in the form of an open letter to our *Esteemed Captain* and urged him to draw *to the attention of all your smart young officers* the danger of sharks *lest they be tempted to swim in the cool, inviting waters of the River Hooghly.* That was the gist of it but the letter was interspersed with many very flowery phrases and was typical of what I later came to recognise as Victorian English, a carry-over from the days of 'The British Raj'. Above a large copper-plate signature, probably written using an old fashioned dipping-pen—possibly even a quill!—it concluded:

*I have the honour to remain, Sir,*
*Your most obedient servant,*

Our mooring was only a little downriver from the Howrah Bridge and the Shamshan Ghats where there were frequent funeral pyres on the riverbanks. As well as trees and vegetation, it was not unusual to see the bloated carcass of a cow floating past, often acting as host for numerous carrion crows. Occasionally, there would be a corpse, floating distended belly uppermost, also acting as a host to the ubiquitous crows. I think the birds were correctly called kite hawks but we always referred to them as something that rhymed with kite.

On a later voyage, despite being warned about the hawks attacking, I foolishly ventured out on deck eating an apple. As I stood leaning against the railings, one of the birds swooped and approaching from behind snatched the apple from my hand. I hadn't seen its approach and was just about to bite into the fruit. As the hawk swept past, one of its extended talons raked the side of my face leaving a scratch which, not surprisingly, soon showed signs of infection. Apart from frequent cleaning with iodine, the Purser was sufficiently concerned to supplement the cleaning with a course of penicillin injections. It was my task each morning for the duration of my anti-biotic course, to sterilise the equipment and prepare the injection. There were no such things as throwaway needles.

The River Hooghly was indescribably filthy and odorous. I thought the Harbourmaster's letter must be a joke. Young people in the idiom of today would probably have questioned if he were on the same planet. I could never have imagined anyone even remotely tempted to swim in the Hooghly—until John pointed out to me that many of the local people actually waded down the muddy banks at the ghats until they were waist-deep in water before proceeding to bathe in the river, even washing their hair with its noxious water!

Also on a later visit while moored in the river, I had a particularly gruesome experience. I had been tasked with re-painting the vessel's forward draught marks and was working from a bosun's chair suspended only two or three feet above the water—and I was making very sure my feet stayed clear of it! The ebb tide was gurgling through the anchor chains where they crossed ahead of the ship's bows. The current was so strong that the buoys were being pulled almost beneath the water. I had almost finished when there was a disturbance at the chains' intersection. It was accompanied by the most awful smell imaginable. The putrefying carcass of what appeared to be a cow had surfaced and had become lodged between the chains. It was very near and the odour was more than I could endure. Hastily, half retching, half choking, I signalled to be hoisted back on board.

Serang, who had operated the winch, was urging me look, pointing excitedly, 'Saab! Saab! Look Saab. Muchli,' (fish). I wished I hadn't. The carcass was alive, crawling with what I supposed were freshwater prawns.

It was some while before I could bring myself to eat curried prawns again—and I often wish I had kept a copy of the Harbourmaster's letter, too.

## *Kidderpore Dock*

Eventually we completed unloading into barges in the river and commenced the lengthy process of un-mooring and restoring the anchors and chains. This done, the ship locked out of the river and entered Kidderpore Dock.

What a place! I had thought the river dirty—but at least there was some movement of water to dissipate the filth.

Not so the dock. There were many barges all of which had crew living on board; cooking on the open decks, throwing their garbage overboard, directly into the dock. The stern of each barge had a sort of canvas curtain hung outboard of the rails that partly concealed a wooden frame. 'It's a Bengali Ensign,' Verran explained. I soon understood. The curtain provided but little privacy for barge crew as, squatting on the wooden frame, they defecated directly into the dock.

Then there were the wild baboons. Fortunately, they usually confined themselves to the roofs of the warehouses but Chippie had cautioned me that if I came across one on the quay, I should give it a wide berth. The roof of the warehouse was more or less on the same level as the ship's boat deck and we could observe the animals quite closely. When I saw the baboons bare their teeth, snarl and scream at each other in between cavorting along the along the apex of the warehouse roof, I was more than prepared to accept the advice!

It was during our visit to Kidderpore Dock that I felt the only real pangs of homesickness since we had left Europe.

I had been observing the cranes along the dockside, interested to note that they used chain in place of the wire usually used for lifting. Apart from the slight rattle of the chain, the cranes were almost silent in operation the consequence, I was told, of being hydraulically powered, literally by water. Then I noticed the builder's plate on the sides of the cabs. "Stothert and Pitt. Bath England".

The Third Officer, Chippie and I were standing on the boat deck. 'During my last term at school we went on a visit to their works,' I told them, 'It was really interesting.' I recounted the coach outing when we had spent a full day being shown around the fabrication shop, the foundry and the pattern shop.

'Remember that batching plant we carried to Gan Island? That was made by Stothert and Pitt, too,' said Mr Roberts. I hadn't realised it and stood in quiet reverie recalling the visit and thinking about home, family and schooldays. After a short while, the Third Officer surprised me. He seemed to sense my thoughts.

'Graham, if you're feeling a tad homesick don't feel in the least ashamed or embarrassed. It's a normal thing we have all felt at some time,' he said, standing with one foot in the railings and looking thoughtfully down at the dockside. 'At least, we do if we have any family and home to be proud of.' Mr Roberts had never used my Christian name before and I was surprised that he even knew what it was.

'Ay. The man who claims he's *never* been homesick is either a liar—or he has nae a home worth the name,' Chippie concluded.

It is a conversation that has stayed with me and on many occasions during later years when dealing with cadets and others making their first voyages to sea and clearly feeling homesick, I recounted how I had felt and how I had been reassured. It put things into perspective and I usually arranged for new cadets to telephone their parents soon after joining to confirm their safe arrival.

## *Port services*

While in Calcutta, tailors, cobblers and shoemakers frequently came on board seeking trade. Many of the officers had their white uniforms made to measure and at incredibly little cost. I didn't need any 'whites', having been so well outfitted at the start (not did I have much cash to spare!), but I did have a pair of suede slip-on shoes made to measure. The process was simple in the extreme: an outline of my bare feet was drawn on brown paper; measurements were made across the top of my feet; I was shown a selection of suede leathers in various colours and finally made my choice of style from a colour brochure. Some three or four days later, the shoemaker returned with my shoes. They were among the most comfortable I have ever worn and I had them for many years.

Daily, the ship was attended by 'runners' who took orders for items of shopping or messages to be carried between the several Brocklebank vessels in Calcutta. I found the language used for inter-ship messages rather quaint as in it the runner would be instructed to 'Present my complements to Mr . . . .'.

The two runners who always attended the Brocklebank ships seemed to know the names of all Brocklebank officers—and which ship they were currently serving on. They frequently provided officers with updates of where former shipmates were serving.

One runner known as The Ghost was probably really called Ghosh, the other, Verdigris was actually Verghese. Usually, within an hour or two of collecting orders, The Ghost or Verdigris would return to the vessel, laden with assorted packages. They were extremely reliable, being very well aware that this casual employment was entirely dependent upon their trustworthiness and honesty. The reward of a rupee or two from each person using their services plus odd change, was by local standards, very lucrative and not to be jeopardised.

## *Kidderpore Seamen's Club*

I cannot close the chapter about Calcutta without recounting an incident that occurred at the Seamen's Club during the weekly dance.

Earlier in the voyage, possibly during one of our evenings at anchor off Colombo when we sat out on deck with Ian Verran strumming his guitar and me playing the clarinet, I had stated that it is virtually impossible to continue playing a wind instrument if anyone nearby sucks a lemon. The tang or zest of lemon juice inevitably drawn in when breathing tends to cause one to salivate to the extent that continuing to blow into an instrument is difficult in the extreme. My assertion was met with a measure of disbelief, which was put to the test at the Seamen's Club.

The dance evening was a weekly event when a full band was engaged when a full dance band was engaged to provide music—no such thing as a disco! The attendance of a number of Anglo-Indian girls who were very attractive, graceful and lissome in their in their saris, ensured that the dance was well supported by ship's officers. All the girls, though, were entirely respectable and often chaperoned but, sadly, they were outcasts because of their mixed blood. They were not accepted by the Indians and most certainly not by the remaining British residents.

The evening was progressing well and apart from the dancing, we were enjoying renditions of Glenn Miller compositions. Although it was strictly forbidden for apprentices to drink alcohol, Churchill was enjoying a gin and tonic when he remembered my statement about the effect of citrus juice. He went to the bar and returned with half a lemon.

'Go on, then Parksy,' thrusting the lemon at me. 'Put your money where your mouth is—or rather, put the lemon where your mouth is.'

With some encouragement from the others in our party, I was dared to go and sit on the edge of the stage immediately in front of the three saxophonists. I did as I was bade and sat slurping the lemon. The musicians nearby carried on valiantly for a short while but eventually had to cease playing as their saliva levels became too high. When the point was reached at which only the more distant trumpet and trombone were playing to the accompaniment of drums and a piano, the music petered out.

It had only been a bit of fun and normal music soon resumed, but the Chaplain was evidently devoid of any sense of humour. He didn't see it that way and I was told to leave.

The next day, when my Scottish friend, Chippie, found out, he thought it hugely funny.

'Tis surely a claim to fame ye have there lad. Getting thrown out of the Dingbats Ball has got tae be a first!'

It had happened on the day of my birthday. I was seventeen years old.

CHAPTER 17
# WESTWARD BOUND

*Loading for America*

Eventually, we completed cargo operations in Calcutta and the *Manipur* sailed for what was then East Pakistan, now Bangladesh, where the ship called at Chalna and Chittagong. One was an anchor port where we loaded from river barges, the other, a normal berth at a key on the riverbank. The ship loaded a large quantity of rolls of hessian and jute products much of which, I was told, would go to the manufacture of carpets.

I recall little of my first visit to East Pakistan, but my final call was memorable. It was in late in 1960 and as we sailed up the Karnaphuli River our pilot pointed to a vessel which appeared to be several miles inland. It was, we were told, the British-flagged cargo liner *Clan Alpine* and was high and dry in the middle of a rice field.

In last two days of October 1960, Chittagong had been directly in the path of severe tropical storm with wind speeds in the cyclone reaching 210 km/hour. The *Clan Alpine* was only one of several vessels which had broken adrift in the extreme winds and there had been numerous collisions in the river. Despite having dropped anchors, the Clan boat was dragged and blown some eleven miles inland. The tidal surge was such that she left the river entirely and when the waters eventually subsided she was dumped, stranded, well inland. The vessel was declared by Lloyds of London to be a 'Constructive Total Loss' and remained something of a landmark for several years.

There was also another vessel similarly declared a loss. It was a smaller ship, which was fully laden with bags of cement. When she was in collision with other vessels adrift in the river, her hull was pierced. Capillary action between the tightly stowed bags of cement sucked the water up like a sponge and the entire cargo turned to concrete! When I saw the vessel, she had been run aground and abandoned on the river bank.

We were, I remember, amused at the fate of these two vessels, oblivious at the time to the severity and extent of the disaster. An estimated ten thousand people lost their lives, more that twice that number of cattle perished and over half a million homes were destroyed.

Back to my first voyage.

From East Pakistan, we sailed on down the Bay of Bengal, calling next at Visagapatnam to load a quantity of manganese ore. A series of platforms was erected one above the other on the ship's side. The ore, in wicker baskets, was actually passed up from person to person, one platform to the next, before being carried across the deck and tipped into the hold. It was an incredibly labour-intensive process and was carried out mostly by women who, on the ship's deck, lofted the baskets and carried them on their heads. Their ragged clothing and grimy appearance did not detract from the grace of the women's posture and the very elegant and fluid manner of their walking.

In our next two ports, Madras then Trincomalee, the ship loaded enormous quantities of tea. There were several varieties and consignments, all of which were carefully marked and separated for discharge in a number of different ports. The odour of tea permeated the accommodation and, even all these years later, I still find the smell of loose tea evocative of those days. When *Manipur* had completed loading Ceylon tea the Second Officer, who was responsible for arranging the separation and marking of the different consignments, was given a number of miniature tea chests each about the size of a shoebox. They contained a sample of Orange Pekoe tea, which, I was told, forms the basis of the best blends. It was my friend Wullie, I think, who made sure that I received one of these 'perks'. When I went on leave at the end of the voyage, Mother was thrilled with the small tea chest. That the tea was undoubtedly of high quality impressed her less than the fact that I had carried it home for her on such a long voyage.

On our arrival in Trincomalee, there was an incident with the harbour pilot when I learned that pilots are employed only as an advisor to the master and do not actually take responsibility for the vessel.

I had been sent to meet the pilot as he boarded our gangway. Because of the port's former naval significance (I had been told), the pilot was a Queen's Harbourmaster who, I suspect, felt that he should have been met and escorted to the bridge by an officer of rank, not a mere apprentice. A Midshipman. Anyway, as we ascended, I politely asked for his name, as I had been taught, so that on our arrival in the wheelhouse, I could formally introduce him to the Captain.

'The pilot, Sir, Mr . . .'

'*Commander* . . .' he rudely interrupted, and pompously introduced himself, while removing the white gloves he had been wearing. After shaking hands with Captain Cowling, he thrust them at me with a very curt and dismissive instruction.

'Your gangway's dirty. Get these rinsed.'

A very charged silence ensued but it was quite clear to me that Captain Cowling was affronted at an insult to his ship and may have been struggling not to lose his temper. Red in the face, he then held out an open hand towards me gesturing for me to give him the gloves. I did so. Calmly, the Captain walked across the wheelhouse and threw them in the trash bin before turning and glowering at the pilot. He gestured for me to leave the wheelhouse—but I could still hear what ensued.

'*Mister*,' Captain Cowling said with unmistakable emphasis and considerable dignity, 'You are a guest on this vessel and not a particularly welcome one. You would do well to remember it and I would also remind you that you have no authority here, not even over an apprentice.' The pilot started to splutter in rage.

'Yes?' the Captain invited, but our pilot quickly realised silence was a more prudent option after such a put-down.

'Close your mouth, Parks,' the Third hissed at me as he joined me outside on the bridge wing in case his laughter should be heard and possibly exacerbate a fraught situation—and I noted the quartermaster was struggling to keep a straight face, too.

Thereafter, *Ss Manipur* continued into Trincomalee harbour and anchored with barely a word spoken by either master or pilot. On the bridgewing the Third, his former laughter now well under control, pointed out to me the graceful lines and gleaming brass of the ex-admiralty steam tug that attended to act as a pinnace. It was waiting to tender the pilot ashore again.

'Damned sight more grace to her than her bloody passenger,' he observed.

It was my first experience of pilot rudeness. Over the years I would have many more experiences with pilots, some very humorous, others fraught—but I will come to them in due course.

## *The Voyage West*

From childhood days, India had been a name to conjure with and as a consequence I remember much of my first visit to the subcontinent. Our visit to the United States was the next thing to really look forward to and as we made our way towards Minicoy and the Lakshwadeep channel between the Maldives Islands, bound for Aden, I was already thinking about seeing New York, imagining my first sighting of the skyline with the Statue of Liberty, the Empire State Building and other skyscrapers.

After calling at Aden for bunkers the ship visited several Red Sea ports but the only one I have any real recollection of was Port Sudan and that was due to my friend Wullie.

The visit was brief as *Manipur* was only loading a small quantity of cargo; uncured hides which were shipped in wooden casks (and smelled foul), and sacks of groundnuts.

Chippie and I were standing outside the apprentices' accommodation, one foot in the boat deck railings and idly watching the cargo being loaded into hold number four, two decks below. I had commented on the wild appearance of one or two of the stevedores who had a huge bushy head of unkempt hair. I preferred not to think about what they may have been prodding on their scalps with the long-toothed wooden combs they wore like hat pins!

'They are Fuzzy Wuzzies,' Wullie explained, 'They're descendents of brave warriors of the Hadendoa tribe. It's the butter they smarm in their hair that make it look so fuzzy—and they never cut it—and that's camel dung on the tendrils around their neck.' Then followed a history lesson as he told me that they were the only force ever to smash a British infantry square. 'Occasionally you will see one of them wearing a Sam Brown belt which they proudly pass from one generation to he next.'

He finished off by reciting a piece of poetry by Rudyard Kipling commemorating the prowess of the Fuzzy Wuzzy warriors. A man of surprises, Chippie Wullie Carroll.

In much the same way as the officers had been given tea samples in Trincomalee, the Second Officer had been given a large sack of groundnuts. As apprentices, for several days, we were tasked with the boring job of removing some from their husks before passing them on to one of the bandaris—Indian cooks—for roasting. For sometime thereafter, when relaxing out on deck in the evenings we enjoyed freshly roasted and salted peanuts. Often, they were still warm and I have never enjoyed peanuts quite like them since.

Passage through the Suez Canal was uneventful and we set out on what seemed an incredibly long voyage to America. The Chief Officer urged us apprentices to use our time wisely, to try and catch up with correspondence course assignments which had been somewhat neglected during busy port visits. The three of us settled into routines of practical work on deck in the mornings, learning seamanship skills, and either keeping one four-hour watch daily or spending time in the afternoon studying.

The ship settled into other routines, one of which involved everyone on board. As *Manipur* sailed west, the ship's clocks had to be changed—put back—regularly, in order to maintain reasonable daylight hours. It happened that the change of longitude was fairly constant and in the region of seven degrees each twenty four hours. So, to avoid possible confusion, the navigator arranged with the Captain that clocks would be 'flogged' half an hour during each night. There was a blackboard in the wheelhouse where such announcements were chalked up and the Second Officer had duly noted, 'Clocks will be retarded half an hour each night until further notice.'

This was fine—until one of the quartermasters decided to make a small amendment. With a moistened finger and piece of chalk the notice was changed slightly.

'Clocks will be retarded half an hour each night until Father notices.'

It was like it for several days until Father *did* notice. Captain Cowling was not even slightly amused and the notice was hastily corrected.

## *Leisure Hours*

In an earlier chapter I recounted how we sometimes passed time out on deck in the evenings when the ship was anchored off Colombo. Ian would strum his guitar, accompanying me as I played the melody from popular ballads of the time on my clarinet. There was little provided on board in those pre-television and video days for seafarers' recreation and amusement and any form of self-made music was always welcome, often leading to a sing-song.

It was while on passage to the States, that the idea of something more than just strumming a guitar and tooting a clarinet developed. It turned out that the junior radio officer also played clarinet and one of the engineers was carrying a bagpipe chanter. When we also found out that one of the Indian Quartermasters who had joined in Calcutta played a saxophone and the Fourth Officer had a harmonica, there was sufficient to form a small band. Not surprisingly with the cargo we were carrying, it wasn't long before someone commandeered one of the spare tea chests supplied for spillages and a tea chest base was added to the group.

Although no musician, Chippie, too, became involved and showed me how to make a rumba box. For several evenings as we voyaged west through the Mediterranean, we adjourned to his workshop where we constructed a rectangular plywood box. It was about the size of a shoebox and had an elliptical hole cut though the face and a strip of wood mounted along the edge of the hole. Clamped to the wood and protruding across the hole was a series of steel strips (scrounged from the engine room workshop) of differing lengths. When plonked, these strips resonated in the box and, adjusted to length accordingly, were tuned to produce a scale of notes. It was a most unusual instrument but very effective as a rhythm backing.

Practising in the apprentices dayroom, we had a great deal of fun and the group had not been in existence long before the Assistant Purser asked if he could join.

'What instrument will you play?' he was asked.

'I haven't made it yet,' was the rather secretive response but a few days later, Charlie joined us carrying a six-stringed harp. It was made from a lavatory seat, using the tuning pegs from a broken guitar. Not a very versatile instrument—but it did add something uniquely special to the rhythm section!

It was while we were all in the apprentices' dayroom practising one afternoon that there was an incident which caused a great deal of amusement, and was often recounted later—but first I should explain the background.

In those days, even lowly apprentices had a steward to look after them. It was a part-time job usually undertaken by the deck Topas, the sweeper, a low caste Indian, an 'Untouchable', who, by tradition was always called Jacki.

Earlier in the voyage, I had asked Cassab (he of the 'bend to kiss' incident recounted earlier) if the word topas in Hindi translated to English. Cassab stood, with his head on one side for a moment or two, looking at me with some amusement before replying.

'Sarb, do you not think that the man who cleans and sweeps the decks and looks after Chota malim sarb is indeed a most precious jewel?' On our own, Cassab's English had been as impeccably correct as ever.

Back, then, to the occasion we were practising our instruments. While The Saints were somewhat discordantly Marching In, the door opened and Jacki entered. He stood seemingly enthralled, slowly rocking his head from side to side in the Indian manner of an affirmative, while we continued to the end of the number.

'What do you think of that, then, Jacki?' Ian asked proudly as the last strains died away down the alleyway.

'Sarb, Sarb,' Jacki replied with enthusiasm in his heavily accented English, 'That was totally first class number two!'

## CHAPTER 18
# THE UNITED STATES

*Tea, but too late for the party*

I had vague memories of history lessons and being taught of the rebellion against British Colonial rule late in the eighteenth century and found it somewhat ironic that our first port of call in America should be Boston, to discharge tea from Ceylon.

The voyage from Suez had seemed almost interminable and I think everyone on board was looking forward to being in port again and, most importantly, to receiving mail and news from home. The only news we had had for several weeks was from occasional snippets received by the radio officers, usually gossiping on the airwaves, in Morse, with their opposite numbers on other British vessels. Thus there was an air of excitement throughout the vessel as we approached land again.

We neared the boarding area for our Boston pilot and I had been sent down to the foredeck to meet and escort the him to the bridge. I recall it was slightly misty and as the pilot tender approached, looming through the damp haze, I was surprised to see that it was under sail. I didn't appreciate at the time what a feat of seamanship it had been to bring the cutter alongside, snuggling against *Manipur's* hull as the pilot stepped from the cutter's ratlines onto our boarding ladder. Furthermore, the cutter was flying an enormous blue and white flag from her masthead. It looked familiar—and then I realised it was the Brocklebank house flag. I was surprised.

Brocklebank's house flag was, and still is I suppose, a special flag and is the reason why the International Code flag to signal the letter 'A' has a swallow tail. When the flags already in common use were being rationalised internationally, a blue and white flag identical to the Brocklebank house flag was already generally being used to represent 'A'. Brocks were asked to change. They refused and the international flag was amended to differentiate it by making it a burgee.

Later, I was told that the Boston pilots always displayed the Brocklebank house flag when boarding a Brocklebank vessel in recognition of the port's special association with Daniel Brocklebank who had established an important ship-building company in Boston almost two hundred years earlier.

That call, on my first trip, was the only time I visited Boston by ship.

I met the pilot off the boarding ladder and, after politely asking his name, escorted him the wheelhouse and formally introduced him to Captain Cowling.

'Are we in time for a tea party?' the captain asked, mischievously. I suspected the pilot was well used to such humour from British ships as he replied, 'Gee thanks, Cap, but a *cup* of tea'll do just fine.'

'An American choosing tea?' asked the captain, 'I thought you Americans only drank coffee.'

'Cap,' our pilot replied, 'There are two things you never do as a pilot. You never drink tea on an American ship and sure as hell you never drink coffee on a British ship!'

It was my first experience of Pilot Humour and I soon came to realise that the American way of making tea is to toss a teabag into some tepid water. Also, in a country where so much coffee is drunk, their coffee is generally rather appalling stuff!

As Boston was our first American port of call, the ship was subject to a rigorous inspection by the Coastguard and Immigration authorities. The latter photographed the entire ship's company and we were issued with plastic identity cards which, in those pre-visa days, were essential when taking shore leave.

Terrorism and an almost hysterical attitude towards security were still things of the future but the Americans, then, seemed inordinately concerned with sexual health. They were almost paranoid about venereal diseases being brought into the country and all our Indian ratings were subjected to the indignity of what was referred to as a short-arm inspection.

Internationally, there was general outrage at ship's crews being so examined by the American authorities—especially as STD's were often conditions requiring treatment *after* visiting the United States—but the Americans remained obdurate and the practise continued until there was an incident several years later with the American flag-ship passenger liner, *SS United States*. On arrival in one of the French ports, the French authorities subjected not the crew, but all the American passengers to the same indignity. Not surprisingly, there was a huge outcry—and the American practise ceased forthwith.

## *New York*

Our next port after Boston was New York. As we sailed up the Hudson River, I stood out on deck with Chippie marvelling that I was actually passing the Statue of Liberty. I thought how very fortunate I was to be visiting such a city, thinking, too, of my old school friends. What they were missing!

We watched the double-ended Staten Island ferries, busy on the waterway, as the Manhattan skyline loomed larger ahead of us. It was incredible and all that I had imagined. 'Do ye realise the Hudson is named after an Englishman, a sailor, Henry Hudson?' My Scottish friend asked, giving me another of his little gems of information.

We docked at one of the piers on The Battery in lower Manhattan. I could scarcely wait to get off the ship and later, Wullie took me ashore in this incredible city.

We visited Times Square where I was impressed by all the neon advertising. In particular, I remember, there was one huge advertisement for Camel cigarettes where an animated figure regularly took a puff on a cigarette and then blew a smoke ring out across the street.

Just as I had seen on films, there were manhole covers on the pavements emitting puffs of steam. All the cabs—Americans didn't understand the term taxi, I was told—were yellow and the street noise was mainly a cacophony of their horns, sounding impatiently in the dense traffic and reverberating, echoing, from the sides of all the tall buildings towering above the streets.

We rode the subway. We visited Radio City Music Hall. There, at the Rockefeller Centre in midtown Manhattan, we saw a show featuring the Rockettes, reputedly the longest on-stage chorus line on the widest stage in the world. I watched in amazement after the stage show as the theatre was transformed into a movie cinema.

Then, Wullie took me to the Empire State Building. We rode the express lift non-stop to the 86$^{th}$ floor observation deck with Wullie urging me to hold my nose and blow to stop my ears popping with the pressure change caused by our very rapid ascent. It took less than one minute! After walking around the viewing area, we took another lift to the 102$^{nd}$ floor. Looking out over the parapets, everything below seemed so miniscule that it was like looking down on a model.

## *Coasting*

Our coastal voyaging was a busy time when the *Manipur* called at several ports. I don't now remember the details of those first visits and have since called at the same ports very many times but there were certain events which do stick in my mind.

From New York, we sailed down the coast, then up the Delaware Bay to call at Philadelphia where Wullie took me on another 'educational' tour ashore to see the Liberty Bell. He told me of its historical importance; that the original bell had been cast in London and he recounted how the bell had twice been recast after it developed the famous crack.

Then, it was back down the Delaware and a short voyage down the coast before entering the Chesapeake Bay and sailing the not inconsiderable distance back up to Baltimore. Shortly after entering the Bay, we sailed past the Chesapeake Bay Bridge Tunnel, a twenty three mile structure, mainly causeway, across the mouth of the Bay. Mr Roberts told me that the tunnel was a security measure as the alternative, another bridge to allow vessels to pass, could effectively block the entire Chesapeake Bay if anyone were minded to do so. I suppose that despite my remarks above, even then the Americans had some concerns over national security. I was later told that, like the twenty-odd mile causeway across Lake Ponchartrain near New Orleans, when in the middle, traffic using it actually lost sight of land.

While we were in Baltimore there were two memorable events.

The first occurred as I was going ashore from where the ship was docked at Locust point. A freight train was rattling over a level crossing on a nearby road. I waited patiently, listening to the clanging bell as the locomotive at the rear of the very long line of wagons signalled its approach. I recall that I was thinking about some new pieces of music our band had been learning. At the time skiffle had become very popular and we had been working on some compositions by Lonnie Donegan. As the locomotive passed, I was amazed to see the freight company's identity boldly painted along the side of the engine. *The Rock Island Line*. It wasn't just a name for a piece of music after all.

What a coincidence! I could scarcely believe it. I had never thought that the line actually existed and could barely wait to tell my friend Wullie.

The other memorable sight was that of a fire engine driving through the streets of downtown Baltimore. It was a very long vehicle due to the turntable ladder mounted on its back. It wasn't an articulated truck with tractor and trailer but a fixed chassis. The Americans evidently had an ingenious solution to improve the truck's manoeuvrability. I thought at first that it was some sort of hoax or joke when I spotted a second driver sitting high in the air in a sort of tractor seat at the rear of the fire engine, manipulating a very large steering wheel. He was actually steering the back end through the other traffic, swinging it around the corners quite independently from the front end. I had never seen anything like it before—nor quite like it since, for that matter.

After visiting Savannah, Georgia, where I was fascinated to see the French moss hanging from the trees in shrouds, we sailed south through the Florida Straits, passing very close inshore seeking a counter-current to avoid the strong northerly drift in the main axis of the Gulf Stream. Then, rounding Key West, we headed on into the Gulf of Mexico.

Passage up the mighty Mississippi to New Orleans was exciting and interesting. Swamps and alligators. Two or three river boats with their huge stern paddle wheels and ornate smoke stacks. So much to see and interspersed with stories of Mark Twain and how he took his name after hearing the seamen calling out the river depths from the marks on their hand lead-lines.

It was also the time I first heard about George Washington and his father's favourite cherry tree.

Wullie and I were standing on the starboard side of the boat-deck, watching the banks slip past as we journeyed up the Mississippi. He had been telling me about the Cajuns living in the area and of their origins in Nova Scotia and of their particular French dialect. Wullie had a keen sense of humour and went on to tell me a story.

There was once, he said, a Cajun family living close to the river and their outhouse was conveniently placed on the top of the levee. One day, it fell into the river and the father suspected that his small son may have had something to do with the incident. Later, he summoned the small boy and questioned him.

'Did you push ma privy into the Mississippi?' he drawled.

'No Pa,' his son replied but Pa was unconvinced.

'Son, let me remind you of the story of George Washington's father's favourite cherry tree. Think about it.' The boy did so and remembered that because George

Washington had owned up, stating that he could never tell a lie, his honesty had had been rewarded and he escaped punishment.

'Now, son, ah'll ask you once more. Did ya all push ma privy into the Mississippi?'

'Yeh, Pa,' was the somewhat sheepish reply, whereupon his father took his belt to him.

Surprised at the punishment, later, when Pa had calmed down the boy questioned his father.

'Pa, when George Washington owned up and told the truth his Pa didn't punish him. Why did you take your belt to me?'

'Well, son, you have to understand that when George Washington chopped down his father's favourite tree, George Washington's father wasn't sitting in the tree.'

## *Loading for Home!*

Leaving New Orleans, *SS Manipur* was empty of cargo and sailed in ballast to Houston where she commenced loading for the voyage back to Europe.

Thence to Galveston before voyaging on to our most westerly call at Brownsville, close to the Mexican border. We were in Brownsville for longer than any of the other American ports while shore labour constructed special wooden bulkheads, 'shifting boards', inside two of the holds. When these were completed, the holds were filled with grain and we sailed back across the Gulf of Mexico and up the Eastern Seaboard revisiting and loading cargo at several of the ports we had called at when discharging our cargo from the far east.

The final port of call before sailing across the Atlantic and back to Southampton was supposed to have been New York but it didn't quite work out as planned.

It was late in the year and the tail end of the hurricane season.

We were scheduled for only a brief docking in New York to top off one of the holds with ingots of aluminium, load some billets of silver in a special locker, the ship's specie room, and to load some deck cargo.

The billets of aluminium (I had learned that the American pronunciation dropped the second 'i', reducing the word to four syllables,) had been loaded and number two hatch battened down.

Carpenters had boarded and commenced constructing two special cradles on the after deck. One of them eventually carried a very handsome wooden pinnace with gleaming brass fittings, the *Ravahine*. The other cradle stood two decks high and we all watched as the yacht *Sceptre* was carefully lifted on board and secured. *Sceptre* was returning to England after an unsuccessful attempt to gain the American Cup.

Finally we loaded the silver, nearly two hundred billets—and what a performance it was! Armed guards swarmed all over the ship before a bullion truck arrived on the quayside with an escort of police cars; sirens blaring, lights flashing. Each piece of silver was manhandled up our gangway, passed from hand to hand by a chain of stevedores, along the deck and into the specie room. They were counted, tallied, at every turning and corner as they passed from one line of sight to another before being finally counted again by the tally clerk, then John Churchill and myself as the precious metal was stowed in the specie room. I took the opportunity to lift one. It was about the size of two house bricks end-to-end and I was really surprised at its weight.

Finally, the door of the specie room was locked—which seemed a bit pointless as two men standing by with arc welding equipment secured the door to its frame by welding several small pieces of steel plate across. Only when all was secure did the armed guards disembark.

*Manipur* was 'cleared' by Customs to sail for Europe, first call Southampton, next, London. The Docking and Sandy Hook Pilots boarded, the tugs made fast and the ship was eased gently, stern-first, from the piers at Weehawken and into the river.

## *Port of Refuge*

We were finally on our way home and after such a long voyage and a lengthy absence, I know that I was not the only one looking forward to reaching England and seeing loved ones, family and friends again.

Almost before we disembarked our Pilot and cleared Ambrose Light, despite being fully laden, *Manipur* was being tossed around in a severe storm. It was the tail end of a hurricane which had re-curved across the Bahamas and it had lost none of its ferocity as it hurtled up the East Coast.

We had experienced bad weather on other occasions during the voyage, not least of which was the Southwest Monsoon in the Arabian Sea, but it was as nothing compared to the fury of that which we experienced leaving New York.

The ship started pitching so heavily that her bow was lifting clear of the water as the swells passed beneath the hull, only to come down again, smashing into the next wave with a bone-shaking thud as it hit solid water. Alternately, the propeller would lift clear, vibrating and racing in air as the stern lifted. In the accommodation, the creaking of the ship could barely be heard as the wind was causing two big ventilator pipes outside to resonate like gigantic bass pipes on a cathedral organ as it roared across their apertures.

It was really severe and when Captain Cowling altered the ship's course to reduce the likelihood of damage to the hull being caused by pitching and pounding, *Manipur* started to roll heavily.

I think we apprentices were the first to be aware of the *Sceptre's* predicament. We heard a rending crash right outside the back of our accommodation and quickly ventured out onto the after end of the boat deck to investigate. The magnificent bow, which had been level with the rails two decks above the cargo deck, was no longer there. The side of the yacht's cradle had collapsed and *Sceptre* had fallen sideways across the after well-deck. It was only one of the big ventilator pipes that had stopped her going overboard and her bow was all smashed in where she had come to rest against it. The cradle had been well constructed to secure the yacht *down* onto the deck, but it had virtually no lateral strength against the ship's rolling and the side had been pushed out, collapsing the cradle.

Realising that the watch on the bridge could not see the after deck and were almost certainly unaware of what had happened, John quickly donned oilskins and made his way along the boat deck, grabbing and grasping railings to keep his footing as the ship continued to roll heavily, as he fought his way to the wheelhouse.

Soon, the ship was turned again, head to the seas, to reduce the rolling. Clad in oilskins, we then attended the after deck and under Chippie's instruction, helped him cut baulks of timber and secure *Sceptre* against further damage.

There is no doubt, looking back on the episode, that what we had to do was extremely dangerous but the yacht could not be left sliding a foot or two each time the ship rolled in case the ventilator sheared off and compromised the watertightness of the hold below. It had to be secured—but I was aware that Wullie, shouting instruction over the noise of the tempest, was doing his utmost to ensure that we stayed in as safe a location as possible while the task was nevertheless accomplished. It was he who, as the yacht started to slide, would step into its path, seemingly unconcerned for his own safety, confident he could arrest the movement as he dropped large pieces of timber into position. Then, as the yacht started to move away again, bracing the timber shorings by swiftly hammering in wooden wedges we had cut.

Afterwards, divested of wet gear and warming ourselves with mugs of tea in Chippie's mess room, Wullie complimented us on a job well done. Having absolute confidence in him, in a dangerous situation the three of us had followed his instructions unquestioningly and we were proud of ourselves.

'We'll make seamen of yous yet.' Then with a twinkle in his eye, 'But I'd still rather have ma wee dug!'

Thus we came to make one more call before returning to England and diverted to Halifax, Nova Scotia. Amidst much interest by press and TV crews, *Sceptre* was lifted ashore and her cradle re-built. The interest continued until she was finally lifted back onto our after deck and we sailed again for England.

It never occurred to me that the publicity would be anything other than local.

## CHAPTER 19
# BACK IN BLIGHTY

*The 'Channels'*

While *Manipur* was in sheltering in Halifax and the *Sceptre's* cradle was being reconstructed, the storm passed through and was well ahead and to the north of the ship by the time we sailed for England. As a consequence, what wind remained was behind us, creating a following sea and we had a good passage back across the Atlantic apart from the inevitable fog on the Grand Banks near Sable Island.

I noticed that as we progressed, there was an atmosphere of joviality developing on board among the officers and petty officers and the closer we got to landfall, Bishop's Rock and the Scilly Isles, the more pronounced it became.

The excitement of returning home after a long voyage was almost palpable. Everyone was in a good humour and even the Captain, who normally never demeaned himself by speaking to apprentices un-necessarily, cheerfully passed the time of day with us. Silly jokes were cracked and childish pranks played—and I was no exception. I just felt in a thoroughly good humour, looking forward to seeing Mother and Dad and my brothers again. I had seen so much of an exciting world! I had so much to tell them!

As had so often been the case, it was my mentor Wullie who explained what was going on.

A day or so before we were due to sight Bishop's Rock, I had been keeping the four till eight watch with the Chief Officer. That morning he had an errand for me.

'After you've had your breakfast, Parks, go and see the Second Engineer in the engine room and ask him for a long stand. Chippie needs it for his workshop.' It never occurred to me that an officer of such seniority would play a prank on a lowly apprentice and in due course, fortified by a good breakfast, off I went to the engine room and asked the Second for a long stand.

'What do you want it for, Parksy?'

'I don't know. The Mate told me to fetch it for Chippie,' I replied.

'Wait here, then. I'll see what I can do.'

Well, I waited. Waited some more. Waited a bit longer, then eventually I went off to seek the Second, thinking he may have forgotten. He was no longer in the engine room and I found him taking 'smoke ho', having coffee with Wullie. 'Did you forget my long stand?' I asked politely.

'I should think you stood for long enough!' was the response, 'How long a stand were you after?' amidst much laughter.

I realised that I had had my leg pulled and joined in, mainly in surprise that the Chief Officer, of all people, should have pulled such a prank.

'Ay, he's got the channels,' Chippie said and went on to explain that it was quite common. After being away from home for some time, as they approached the English Channel, seamen often behaved quite childishly in their excitement at returning home.

When still some three days or so from port, I had asked the Radio Officer to send a ship's letter telegram to Mother and Dad advising when the ship was due in Southampton. An SLT was a special arrangement for seafarers whereby a radio-telegram was transmitted to Portishead Radio Station who then forwarded the message via the normal land mail. It was far less costly than a full telegram and, with the reliability of the post in those days, usually only took one day. Although I would not disembark for leave until the second port, London, I was hopeful that with Southampton less than an hour by car from my home town of Warminster, they would come and visit the ship. Meet me.

## *Secret Assignment*

The morning before our landfall at the Scilly Islands, all three apprentices were called out at four o'clock and summoned to the bridge. John Churchill was concerned that we were in trouble for something but it was not the case. Chippie was there too, and somewhat to our surprise the Chief Officer required the four of us to take an oath of absolute secrecy before he would tell us the reason for our early call. Curious, and of course, more than a little relieved that we were evidently not in trouble and about to be castigated for some unwitting misdeed, we all agreed. We were threatened with dire consequences if we broke the Chief Officer's confidence. We were forbidden to even discuss the matter, and then he told us what was required of us.

The four of us made our way to the specie room where Wullie burnt off the steel tabs securing the door. Then, still in darkness, we manhandled all the bars of silver out to the nearby deck, opened number two hatch and re-stowed the silver just inside the hatch-coaming, near the pallets of zinc ingots.

As we sailed across Lyme Bay and on past Portland Bill, I was keen to recognise the landmarks and was telling anyone who would listen about my Dorset holidays and staying in Bridport. I was definitely suffering—although 'suffering' is perhaps not the right word—from The Channels !

Eventually, we reached the Isle of Wight, picking up our Southampton Pilot as we passed The Needles. I could scarcely wait to dock, hoping that I would be having visitors. The passage through the Solent and up Southampton Water seemed interminable and I really had little interest in the Saunders Roe Princess flying boat which was moored at Calshot on brief respite from the regular flight to Lisbon.

## *Southampton, First Port*

Eventually, with the help of tugs, *Manipur* edged towards the dock in Southampton. I was stationed on the bridge and as we got closer was anxiously, but surreptitiously, peering at the visitors on the quayside waiting for the ship to dock. I was looking for Mother, Dad, and my brothers, hoping against hope that they would be there to meet me. It was the Third Officer, Peter Roberts, who spotted them first.

'Isn't that your family down there waving?' he asked, pointing. Sure enough, there they were. Foolishly, I felt too emotional and too embarrassed in the presence of Captain Cowling to respond but it was he who pushed me toward the bridgewing.

'Aren't you pleased to see them lad? I'd be waving and yelling if I had my family waiting on the quay to meet me!' The Captain smiled as he lifted his uniform cap and waved it at them. I think even our captain had a touch of the channels!

None to soon, the arrival formalities were completed. The doctor from Port Health had boarded and, with our clean bill of health, granted pratique. The yellow quarantine flag was struck which was the signal for customs to board and give *Manipur* their clearance. A message was sent to the Quartermaster on duty at the gangway and visitors were allowed on board but I, of course, was too impatient and rushed ashore to greet my family.

Looking back, it seems so formal, but after a hug and kiss from Mother, I actually shook hands, first with Dad then my brothers. Men, at least men in our family, didn't hug one another in those days. I was in my fifties before I had the courage to put my arms round my father.

Back on board, I had to show Steve around the ship and while doing so noticed that number two hatch had been opened and the silver was being stacked onto pallets on the deck before offloaded directly onto the back of a flatbed lorry on the quay. It didn't take very long and when finished, a grubby tarpaulin was thrown over it and the lorry drove off.

I couldn't help thinking of the circus when the silver had been loaded in New York. If there *was* any security in Southampton, it was so discreet as to be entirely invisible! I understood, then, why we had all been sworn to total secrecy. Later, I was told the stevedores had been led to believe they were handling loose zinc ingots.

Meanwhile, Dad was keen to renew his acquaintance with Wullie Carroll. He was well aware from my letters home that Chippie had indeed, been as good as his word when they had met in London on my joining day some eight months or so earlier. He had kept an eye on me throughout the long voyage.

I have already recounted that in a quiet moment, it was Dad who took me to one side and asked where the fourth apprentice was.

Mother was told nothing of Norman's accident and death but she was already upset over our visit to Halifax. I noted earlier that I had never thought the press attention our visit received was anything other than local. Mother put me right. That the

'... *cargo liner SS Manipur diverted to Halifax seeking refuge following an accident in extreme weather when the Americas Cup contender, the yacht Sceptre, was severely damaged* . . .' had been reported in the ITV news. It had worried her, despite Dad's reassurance.

'Wouldn't it be nice to have a family lunch together, ashore, Bill?' Mother had suggested and I went off to ask permission for shore leave from the Chief Officer.

I was sitting with my brothers in the rear of Father's Austin as he drove out of Southampton's Western Docks when Steve rather dropped me in it. I am sure that what I said would have passed un-noticed had it not been for his reaction.

I was pleased to have completed my first voyage and commented that on my next trip, I should no longer be disparagingly referred to as a 'first-tripper'. I cannot now remember what had actually been said but it related to something that had happened during the voyage. I had made a response that it would be a dammed sight different next trip.

'Why do you say that, dear?' Mother asked.

'Well, I shan't be bloody first-tripper!' I replied.

There was a moment's silence before Steve's snigger could be suppressed no longer and he erupted into full-blown laughter. Had it not been for him, I don't think Mother would have noticed my brief lapse. She looked a little shocked as realisation dawned. Goodness me! Andrew swearing.

Actually as I write this, and think back to my embarrassment, let me be honest. Having spent months in male company, I had briefly and seriously forgotten my language. I said something far stronger than 'bloody'. There was even some alliteration with the word following it—first-tripper.

But then, even looking back to the days of his gas experiment and the subsequent explosion, Steve always could get me into trouble.

CHAPTER 20
# JUNIOR APPRENTICE

*Other Brocklebank Memories*

I have written at some length about my first voyage on *SS Manipur,* it is the ship I remember best, but during the remainder of my four-year apprenticeship to T and J Brocklebank, I served on six other vessels, all having names associated with India and in keeping with Brocklebank tradition, they all also began with the letters Ma.

They were all were steam turbine ships: *Makrana, Marwarri, Martand, Mahout, Matra and Macharda.* The newest vessel, *Makrana,* was less than one year old when I joined her; the oldest, *Mahout,* was built in 1928.

All were very traditional vessels, lines peculiar to Brocklebanks and at sea they were easily identifiable as one of 'Brocks crocks', even at considerable distance. Brocklebank cargo liners were all built in Clyde shipyards and it is a sad reflection that now, very little remains of that proud shipbuilding industry nor, for that matter, of the British Merchant Navy. There are very few 'red dusters' fluttering on vessels today.

Brocklebanks, Clan Line, City Lines, Ellermans, British India, to name but a few of the traditional cargo liner companies, have all been consigned to the annals and Britain's absolute dependence on her merchant fleet throughout World War Two is more or less forgotten. Forgotten, too, the merchant seamen lost in the wartime convoys. At the Remembrance Sunday Services each November it is never acknowledged that there were more British merchant seaman killed during that war than were lost in all the British armed forces put together.

Looking back, I count myself very fortunate to have been an apprentice during those years not too long after the war. Despite the residual austerity in Britain, world commerce was booming and the British Merchant Navy was still very much in its hey day. I was fortunate, too, to have been indentured to such a prestigious company. They were good days and although I will not write in detail of all the voyages, each ship holds special memories of events, adventures and experiences some of which I *will* recount.

## *Reunion*

I joined my second vessel, the Makrana, in Glasgow travelling overnight by train from Westbury. It was the first time I had been north of the border and I was keen to use the opportunity and see my friend Wullie again.

At the time, *Makrana* was completing a dry-docking and was moored at the John Brown shipyard, not too far from Wullie's home. We were able to meet up and, typically, he was keen to show me something of his home city. I spent several evenings in Wullie's company during one of which we went to see Billy Eckstine who was appearing at the Glasgow Empire.

On another occasion, I was taken as a guest to a party in the Scottish Television studios. There I had the pleasure of meeting Wullie's one other living relative, a niece, and on whom he clearly doted. She was one of the studio staff and our hostess at the party.

When we arrived, Wullie's niece came to meet us and after giving Wullie a hug turned to me and held out a welcoming hand.

'I'm me,' she said. Thinking she was, perhaps, gently chiding her uncle for not having introduced us first, I decided to get into the spirit of it.

'That's a coincidence,' I responded, shaking her hand. 'I'm me too.'

'No, you silly! May. M-a-y.' she laughed, spelling out her name, quickly realising that I hadn't recognised the Scottish pronunciation. What a prat I felt but May wasn't the in least upset—and certainly not as embarrassed as I! I think she thought *my* accent was somewhat broad too.

At the time, I hadn't realised it but Wullie, already close to retirement, was quite ill. I don't think he went back to sea again after our voyage on the *Manipur* and sadly I heard not long afterwards that he had passed away.

Now, I reminisce with fondness and count myself extremely lucky to have been mentored, guided, during my first voyage at sea by someone such as our ship's carpenter, William Carroll. Indeed, all us apprentices were fortunate.

## *Ship's pets*

One often hears references to 'the ship's cat'. In fact, the *Makrana* was the only ship I sailed on that had any pets. We had two cats, of a rather mangy variety, and for a while, one mongoose, of a definitely unfriendly variety. Nowadays, the carriage of pets is internationally absolutely forbidden.

Anyway, the mongoose was acquired in a Calcutta bazaar by the Third Officer, Mr Webster—and there is some doubt that he was sober at the time. The animal was a nuisance and it really did not enjoy being handled. It was only on the ship for a matter of weeks before being put ashore in Ceylon on the instructions of Captain Bain.

The cats, however, were already on board when I had joined the ship in Glasgow. They were an accepted part of the ship's complement as rats on ships were not uncommon. The care of our moggies was the responsibility of the Assistant Purser and it is probable that their presence was the reason *Makrana* had no rats.

Barry took his responsibilities very seriously. He always ensured that the cats were properly fed and never lacked for watered-down condensed milk (long-life milk had not then been invented). He also made sure that they had dirt boxes of shredded paper for their sanitary needs but we were all puzzled that the dirt boxes never seemed to be used. Where the cats 'performed' was the source of much speculation as they very seldom ventured outside the accommodation—although I did once see one of them being chased by a gull!

The Assistant Purser was also tasked with looking after a number of decorative plants in handsome teakwood troughs in the rather impressive entrance lobby to the officers' dining room. The plants were positioned beneath an imposing, guilt-framed photograph of the Queen and both plants and photograph had been a commemorative gift from the *Makrana's* Godmother at the ship's naming ceremony. (Traditionally, then, British ships *always* displayed a painting or photograph of the monarch.)

However, despite Barry's assurances of his best efforts in watering and administering plant food, over a period of several weeks the plants slowly became yellow, withered, and were obviously dying off.

Every Sunday morning it was routine, and a Board of Trade requirement, that British ships underwent the 'Master's Inspection'. The Captain, Chief Officer, Chief Engineer and Purser, all formally dressed and with uniform caps tucked beneath their arms, traipsed through the accommodation, mess rooms, galleys and provision stores inspecting the ship for cleanliness and supposedly checking the potability of the fresh water. This weekly event was often disparagingly referred to as 'the march of the unemployed'. Afterwards, the inspection party would invariably end up for 'pre-luncheon sippers' in the Captain's cabin. His butler, immaculately attired in black trousers, spotless white tunic and crimson sash, would be waiting with canapés, an ice bucket, lemon slices and Angostura Bitters. The drinks were referred to as 'chota pegs' but *chota,* the Hindi for small, was definitely a misnomer. Once the gin bottle was opened, it was usual to throw the top away. It was unlikely to be needed again.

On *Makrana* it was our Captain's routine to have one of the apprentices trail along behind the inspection party, similarly attired in full uniform, carrying a pump-up sprayer filled with insecticide. Should any cockroaches be discovered, and they often were, they could be dealt with forthwith.

There were two apprentices on *Makrana* and neither Brian Caxton nor I were keen to join the inspection party. It was a nuisance and it cut into our routine Sunday morning time-off for study. Also, we tired of being the butt of engineers' jokes. 'Joined the unemployed then, Parksy?'

One Sunday, the coin had been thrown but I had lost the toss and was unenthusiastically, disinterestedly trailing along, clutching the spray gun and probably idly wondering what was on the luncheon menu. The official party had come to a halt in the lobby outside the mess room when Captain Bain started berating the Purser, complaining about the deteriorating condition of the plants.

'Mister. These plants are a bloody disgrace. I thought your assistant was supposed to be looking after them,' he complained irritably, while the Purser looked on in dismay. He had already been taken to task for the untidy condition of some of the store rooms.

'Needs his arse kicking,' the Captain continued in full spate. 'May as well throw the damned things out. Look, he's obviously not watering them.' Whereupon he plunged his hands deep into a planter to grab a fistful of earth and illustrate his point.

Now we knew. It wasn't lack of care that was killing the plants. Our Captain had found out where the cats had been defecating. It wasn't a handful of compost he was holding—and the smell was dreadful! Even worse, the Captain was not wearing the white gloves he customarily donned when making his inspection!

We did have a pet of sorts for a short period on one other occasion and it was my introduction to mina birds, a name actually coming from Hindi. It was on the *Marwarri* (of which more later) and the vessel was proceeding up the Bay of Bengal towards her next port, Calcutta.

I was on afternoon watch with the Chief Officer, Mr Milne. It was his first voyage in the rank having been promoted since I sailed with him on the *Manipur*. We were idly watching two or three rather sleek, black birds that were walking around on the fo'castle head. I didn't know what they were, but after viewing them more closely with the bridge telescope, Mr Milne concluded they were mina birds.

Subsequently, I was despatched to the galley to fetch a soup plate with a generous portion of rice and told to collect a bottle of gin from the 'fog locker' in Mr Milne's accommodation on my way back up to the bridge. In due course, the plate of rice, having been very liberally soused with gin was placed on the fo'castle deck and some more, un-adulterated, rice, scattered around nearby. The birds had initially been frightened off but they soon returned. We watched from the bridge as one bird discovered first the scattered rice, then the plate of gin-soaked rice.

'Mina birds are as fond of gin as a P and O purser,' Mr Milne told me confidently, 'Just wait.'

He was right and it wasn't long before the bird was clearly inebriated and couldn't stand, let alone fly! One of the lascars was sent forward to pick the bird up. I don't know exactly where the cage came from, probably one of the crew, but the bird was kept by the quartermasters until arrival in Calcutta when it was sold and by which time, thanks to them, it had a very good knowledge of profane English. The bird was almost fluent and some of its vocabulary was delivered with a Geordie accent!

## *Maiden Call at New Orleans*

As *Makrana* was one of the newer vessels, it was not surprising that I should have been on board when she made her first call at the port of New Orleans. To honour the occasion the quartermasters were 'dressing' the ship with bunting as she made her way up the River Mississippi. This entailed taking the international code flags and stringing them together to make a streamer which was then stretched on a wire stay between the trucks of fore and main masts.

The result was very colourful but I don't think any of the visitors who attended the ship when she was docked really looked, or maybe no-one could read the alphabet code flags. *Makrana* was docked with her port side to the wharf and starting from the foremast truck, reading naturally from left to right, the flags read: SEEKNAYDENMAD.

I thought it lucky we weren't starboard side towards the jetty when the flags may have been read backwards and to this day, I don't believe the Old Man saw what his quartermasters had done!

At that time there was a thriving club of expatriate British in Nola (as we experienced salties abbreviated the port's name, from New Orleans LA). I think they enjoyed the rather grand name of Daughters of the Elizabethan Empire or something similar. The club had a special relationship with the Brocklebank ships based on several years of association and always extended hospitality to the officers. Our call was no exception and a number of us junior-rankers were taken ashore for an afternoon when we went off on a horse-drawn hayride, followed by a picnic. It was a terrific outing and one we talked of for the remainder of the voyage. Another afternoon, we were challenged to a cricket match and there is no doubt that it aroused quite some interest among passing Americans who didn't understand these crazy Limeys—especially as we were playing in the rain.

The Club also entertained the Captain and several of his senior officers at bridge parties in their homes.

We had all enjoyed their hospitality so much that Captain Bain wanted to thank our hosts and he instructed the Purser to arrange a dinner party on board. Invitations were issued but Purser Roberts soon realised he had a problem. Unfortunately, there were too many acceptances to accommodate in the officers' dining saloon. After some thought he solved the problem rather ingeniously and our visitors were entertained to a fish and chip supper, standing in the lounge bar.

Several of the officers had received copies of British newspapers in their mail. These old newspapers were collected, used as outer wrapping and all the portions of fish and chips were served in a genuine British newspaper! It was certainly a novel way of dining for the ship's officers, too, dressed formally in white number ten uniforms, eating fish and chips with their fingers. It was a very nostalgic occasion for everyone and our visiting Brits would not have been more delighted with a seven-course meal.

## *Precious metals*

Not quite in the same league as the silver we had carried on *Manipur*, but brass was a very negotiable metal with scrap dealers who invariably descended on the vessel in Port Said and other ports east of Suez. Furthermore, the many brass fittings on ships were always a desirable target for thieves and anything of brass not secured was likely to be stolen.

Whenever a ship was to be in a port for more than the briefest of visits, it was considered prudent to remove loose items like fire hose nozzles and brass deck plugs and keep them, under lock and key.

After a lengthy call in Calcutta on the *Marwarri*, we were proceeding down the River Hooghly in the late afternoon and the Serang and several others of the crew were busily engaged in replacing all the brass fittings that were being retrieved from storage.

Rather unusually, I was the only apprentice on the vessel. As a consequence, much of my time was spent watchkeeping, often on the four till eight watch with the Chief Officer Mr Milne.

Overlooking the foredeck from the wheelhouse, and watching the hose nozzles being replaced, Mr Milne was congratulating himself on his foresight and commented 'Bluidy thieves didnae get anything this time, Parks,' but his comment was a little premature.

As the ship neared the estuary and open water, *Marwarri* started to roll very gently in the swells. I was making some tea for our river pilot when there was an almighty crash from the deck above the wheelhouse. 'Away and see what that was, Parks,' Mr Milne instructed.

I ran up the ladder to the 'monkey island' and found the entire wooden binnacle housing the magnetic compass was only prevented from rolling across the deck by the speaking tube fixed to its side.

Apart from the soft iron correctors attached to the binnacle, ferrous metal is not permitted within several feet of a magnetic compass and the binnacle is normally secured to the deck (also non-ferrous) by large brass bolts.

The brass bolts had gone. *Marwarri's* compass had been visited!

## *Water sleighing*

On the same voyage, while we were anchored in Trincomalee Harbour loading tea, one of our lifeboats was being used as a liberty boat ferrying ship's staff for evening shore leave to the nearby town. During the afternoons, we were having fun using it for water skiing.

It wasn't that the boat was particularly fast but chippie had provided a piece of marine plywood about three feet long by one foot wide which we fastened to a line astern of the boat. We took turns holding a short bridle attached to the front of the board to stand up and ski behind the boat. It was great fun and no-one was the least concerned about some of the undesirable creatures in those tropical waters.

When the *Marwarri* had called at Aden on the outward voyage several of us had each purchased a swimming mask, snorkel and fins from the boatmen. During our visit to Trincomalee these were put to good use observing the marine life in the shallow water in the vicinity of the small jetty ashore. One particularly venomous species of fish, lionfish, were quite prolific and we enjoyed seeing their strikingly defined brown and white fronds at very close quarters. Thinking back, it is fortunate that no-one was stung!

I remember asking if anyone had seen the film 'Underwater' which starred Jane Russell. In the film, she had been towed slowly along behind a boat, lying on a sort of underwater sled. It had a hand-operated flap on each side, like those on a submarine, by means of which the sled could be steered, dived or brought to the surface. After some comments and discussion, much of it relating to how the buxom Jane Russell looked in a swimming costume, I was in luck. The Third Engineer had seen the film too and with his skill in fabricating a simple metal frame and cranks for the control flaps, we soon had our own version of Jane Russell's underwater sled. We had enormous fun, lying on our bellies, riding it in Trincomalee harbour, diving and planing from side to side in the water behind a very slowly moving lifeboat!

## Barberyn Lighthouse

It was while *Marwarri* was in Colombo on our way west that voyage that I had a very memorable trip to a lighthouse a few miles down the coast from Colombo.

When the ship had been outward bound, we had called at the port for the usual two weeks or so and during visits to Colombo swimming club I had made friends with a brother and sister of a similar age to myself. Their father was employed by Trinity House, on secondment to the Imperial Lighthouse Service and responsible for the maintenance and operation of a number of lighthouses around the Ceylon coast.

As was often the case with many expatriate families living in quite a small community, they were very hospitable to visitors from 'back home' and when *Marwarri* called at Colombo again on the voyage west, I was once again invited to dinner. That evening after a very enjoyable biryani, John, his sister and I were sitting on the veranda of their bungalow on the outskirts of Colombo and playing some popular music on a record player. Mr Stott came and sat with us and asked if I would like to join him and Mrs Stott with John and his sister on a family weekend trip to one of the lighthouses. Mr Stott had offered to relieve one of the keepers for a two-day break while making a routine inspection trip to the lighthouse.

What a wonderful opportunity—and John, with the prospect of company his own age, was probably as enthusiastic as I!

Now, it all depended on the Chief Officer agreeing but I expressed my doubts as it would mean my being absent ashore for a relatively extended period.

Nevertheless, Mr Stott solved the problem and came on board to ask the Chief Officer's permission, explaining what the programme would be. As Mr Milne was going 'up-country' himself on a shooting trip to Nuwara Eliya with Peter Boggon, the Purser, he could hardly refuse and I was duly granted leave of absence.

In due course, Mr Stott, with the family, collected me from the ship and drove us thirty miles or so down the coast towards Bentota. We all assembled on a sandy beach where, soon after, we were met by the assistant light keeper to make the half mile or so trip out to Barberyn Island. The means of transport was a catamaran and by that I mean a *real* one—a hand-hewn, dugout canoe with a pointed log for the outrigger.

There was quite an amount of kit and provisions to take with us in addition to which the light keeper had purchased a milk cow he wanted to take back to the island. Not surprisingly, in the strange surroundings of a sandy beach and with the not inconsiderable noise of the breaking surf nearby, the poor animal was frightened and very reluctant to co-operate.

Only after a great deal of heaving at one end, shoving and pushing at the other, was the stubborn animal finally manoeuvred between the canoe and the outrigger where she was lashed to the spars by hindquarters and horns, facing backwards. Mistakenly, the keeper had thought that if the cow couldn't see where she was going, she was less likely to struggle.

Wet through, we set off through the heavy surf with all but Mrs Stott paddling furiously for the island. The poor cow, meanwhile, was bellowing frantically and swimming hard in the opposite direction trying to reach the beach behind us. Eventually, but only after going round in a circle more than once, we made it and the canoe was safely beached on Barberyn. We went on to spend a very enjoyable weekend barbecuing on the beach, swimming and snorkelling.

But, all things have a price and it was John and I who every four hours during each night had to get up and attend the lantern.

It was an old lighthouse. The mechanism to rotate the lantern in its trough of mercury was clockwork and illumination was provided by a mantle, burning paraffin under pressure, like a Tilley lamp. Each time it took us both several minutes of hard work as we took turns; one wound the heavy weights back to the top of the tower while the other pumped up the pressure vessel supplying the paraffin to the mantle up in the lantern.

'Teach you lads some responsibility,' Mr Stott had said—but it was well worth it and an expedition which I have never forgotten. The days of manned lighthouses have mainly long gone but I still recognise the importance of those unseen light keepers. They were vital to mariners' safety.

And as a mariner, it gave me a valuable insight into the operation of a lighthouse. It afforded an experience that not many seafarers have been lucky enough enjoy.

'Educational,' had been Mr Milne's reason for permitting me to go. I don't think he realised how much fun we would have—and few seafarers will have had the opportunity to serve, albeit very briefly, as an Assistant Lighthouse Keeper!

## *Plague*

It wasn't bubonic but it was quite biblical!

One other memorable event while I was on *Marwarri* was a plague of locusts. We were off the coast of Africa nearing the Gulf of Aden when it occurred.

It was late afternoon and it appeared that there was a dark cloud ahead of us. I was on watch with Mr Milne and it wasn't until the swarm was almost upon us that the realisation dawned—at least, it did to the Chief. I had no idea what was about to happen.

Unexpectedly, Mr Milne suddenly started shouting at me to help him close the wheelhouse doors and windows. By the time it was accomplished, the insects were upon us.

'Locusts, Locusts!' The Chief was having to raise his voice to overcome the noise as they smacked against the wheelhouse windows. 'Be quick,' he urged. 'Run down into the accommodation and keep shouting out 'Locusts.' Don't be coy about it lad. Everyone needs to know.'

I did as he instructed and was more than a little surprised at the reaction as cabin doors opened, slamming back against the bulkheads, and people ran around closing windows and external doors. Nevertheless, a large number of the insects managed to get into the accommodation and were buzzing everywhere. I found it quite scary, having them land on me and in my hair but the mess-boys were soon chasing them with rolled paper, swatting the locusts, knocking them to the deck where they could be collected. It was all quite frenetic!

By the time I returned to the bridge, I had begun to understand the urgency. Although the ship soon cleared through the swarm, the decks outside were carpeted with the insects.

The Radio Officers were called out to transmit special messages, in Morse, reporting the migration and its location. It wasn't until the Senior R/O showed me the International Code of Radio Signals and explained that I understood the devastation locusts can cause. When the conditions are ripe, the normally unsociable insects swarm into a cloud often covering many square miles as they migrate. I began to appreciate the drama of what I had experienced.

In all my time at sea, I only ever saw it once again. It was very many years later and in a similar location. We were still required to make a detailed report by radio.

On the *Marwarri*, for days afterwards we continued to pick up dead locusts in odd corners and crevices around the ship, occasionally finding one as it crunched underfoot.

SS Makrana

In the veranda cafe on the boat deck looking pleased with myself as I had just come from using a sextant to take a sun-sight

Going on leave, summer 1959.

It was such good weather that we had docked in Tilbury wearing full white tropical uniforms! Mother and Dad had come to meet me and I was learning to drive.

SS Marwarri

SS Marwarri, sitting on the compass deck railings

At the helm, waterskiing with a ship's lifeboat in Trincomalee Harbour.

The engineers had disconnected the engine's speed governor!

## CHAPTER 21
# SENIOR APPRENTICE

*Moving up the ladder!*

When I was appointed to the *Martand* and found I was the senior of two apprentices, I thought that I was beginning to make some progress at last. I was looking forward to getting away from the Continental loading ports and settling down into the deep-sea routines when I should be the apprentice who had to report on the bridge to Mr Grayson, the Chief Officer, at 0645 each morning, report our progress on the previous day's tasks and collect our new work assignments. I was actually responsible for allocating work to a subordinate!

The Junior Apprentice was on his second trip but he already had extensive knowledge of the marine world as his father was a Thames Waterman. I was fascinated with some of the stories he told of his father's life and we both held hopes during the voyage ahead that the *Martand* would dock in London at the end of the voyage. Unfortunately, it didn't and we both eventually left the vessel in Liverpool.

## *Working on deck*

I was now at the stage when it had become important for my training to spend at least half my time on watch, learning from hands-on navigation. The remainder of the time, I continued to gain practical knowledge in matters of seamanship and whilst the watchkeeping was interesting, I cannot deny that I enjoyed 'working on deck' especially if the tasks were really practical and involved using my hands, preferably with something to show for my efforts and not just chipping and painting.

One of the most satisfying tasks was sewing canvas and while on the *Martand* I spent quite some time sat on a trestle, in the sunshine on the boat deck, with either superior grade white duck canvas or green tarpaulin canvas stretched across my knees. There were always canvas covers to be repaired or renewed and when I was asked if I could make four sea-anchors to replace the old, damaged ones in the lifeboats, I was well pleased and didn't hesitate in cutting one up for use as a pattern!

Each sea-anchor was about eight feet long, three feet across the mouth and tapered, rather like a square-sectioned windsock. At the mouth, the upper edge had a piece of wood sewn in and the lower edge, a piece of iron both of which were designed to hold the anchor open when streamed from the boat. All the seams had to be roped for extra strength and the roping was extended to form a bridle.

I had been taught the rudiments of sewing canvas during my first trip, when on the *Manipur*, and I made myself a holdall. Then I just needed practice and making sea-anchors was an excellent opportunity. I thoroughly enjoyed learning and to this day, more than fifty years later, I still have my sail-maker's palm and a set of needles. The palm is quite a personal tool as with use, it shapes to one's hand, the leather becomes softer and more comfortable.

It was while I was working on the boat deck sewing canvas that my cabin mate had a rather spectacular mishap.

Ted had been given the task of painting one of the lockers where spare equipment for the lifeboats was stowed. The locker, also on the boat deck, was about the size of a toilet cubicle and had a series of shelves fitted opposite the door. In order to reach the upper parts, Ted had commandeered small wooden crate, originally intended for ginger beer bottles, on which to stand.

While he had been standing on it, Ted had placed a nearly-full, one gallon tin of eau-de-nil paint at eye level on a nearby shelf, for ease of reach.

The first I knew of his accident was when a green apparition appeared around the corner of the boat deck. Little more than his eyes were visible through the green paint as Ted stood there in a slowly accumulating pool.

'What shall I do?' he wailed, spitting paint from the corners of his mouth and trying to squeegee it clear of his eyes with his thumbs.

I must admit that at first I was rather more concerned at what the Chief Officer would say about the mess on the deck and recall telling Ted to get the hell off the teakwood deck, bundling him back into the locker. That done, he waited dejectedly while I fetched the Serang to come and help when Ted was eventually taken off and cleaned down using linseed oil.

Fortunately, there was no real harm, either to Ted or to the deck—but he did have green highlights in his hair for quite some time. I just wished I had had a camera!

Apparently, the accident had happened when Ted went to step down from his wooden box. He stumbled and in reaching to grab the edge of a shelf to steady himself, caught his fingers in the handle of the paint tin. The tin toppled and was literally upended over Ted's head, pouring nearly a gallon of green paint over him in the process.

## *Gone to the dogs*

Much later in the voyage, Ted had another accident with paint after he had been painting the outside of our accommodation.

As with many of the Brocklebank vessels, we apprentices had our own quarters at the after end of the boat deck. It was rather like a small, self-contained apartment.

*Martand* was returning directly to UK and Europe from the East and not crossing to The United States. She was fully laden with tea and jute. The tea was for discharge in various ports around England but the jute was consigned to the mills in Dundee, which would be the first port of call. As always when returning to the home ports, the ship had to be immaculate and a programme of painting had been underway almost since the ship was in the Red Sea.

At the time of Ted's later misfortune, the ship was in the Mediterranean. The weather was fair and the crew had been painting the white mainmast and its surrounding derricks. The accommodation on the poop had already been coated and was gleaming. Ted had painted the outside of our accommodation, also white, and was at the stage of 'cutting-in' the stringer plate with black paint. This is the plate, rather like a skirting board, where the accommodation was attached to the steel underneath the teak planking of the boat deck.

When it was time to 'knock-off' that day, the stringer plate was only partly painted. As the weather was good and he expected to resume the task in the morning, rather than return the one-gallon tin of paint to the store, Ted dropped his brush right down into the nearly-full tin to prevent the bristles hardening and left the pot standing outside the door to our day room.

I was working part day, part watchkeeping, and was on watch at four in the morning with the Chief Officer.

That morning, it was just getting light and at that critical time of the day when the stars are still just discernable as the horizon starts to harden and become well enough defined to use a sextant. Mr Grayson was outside with his 'ham bone'; I was inside, pencil poised, writing down the chronometer times as the Chief called out the star's names and their altitudes.

All was going well and I had recorded some six or seven observations. Suddenly, there was an explosion of anger from the bridgewing.

'Parks! Parks! Get your arse out here!' Mr Grayson shouted. I did so.

'Look at it! Look at it!' he bellowed, gesturing hysterically in the general direction of the after deck. He was almost incandescent. I had never seen him so angry.

'Your bloody mate. He's done it again!' still gesturing aft angrily.

'It's like a f***ing Dalmatian dog!'

I looked aft and privately admired Mr Grayson's turn of phrase. During the night, the wind had increased sufficiently to overturn the paint pot Ted had left outside out accommodation. The spilled paint had then been caught by the wind and big splashes had been blown all over the mainmast, the derricks, ventilator cowls and the after accommodation housing.

Dalmatian dog was a perfect description: large, black splotches all over the new, white paint.

Ted and I received some gratuitous extra training as we spent most of the next few days working from a bosun's chair as we re-painted most of the mast and derricks.

## *Quarter bell*

I have already written of watchkeeping. It is a definite advantage if one is able to waken and get up easily and in that respect I count myself fortunate. It may well have had something to do with Father not permitting Steve or me to laze in bed at weekends or during school holidays.

Ship's timekeeping was regulated by the watch bells which were always sounded, accumulating one extra strike each half hour until the end of each watch at eight bells. Those on watch were always called fifteen minutes before eight bells at what was known as the 'quarter bell'.

While I was on the *Mahout* (named after the man in charge of an elephant), it became apparent that my cabin mate had a very unfortunate inability to wake from sleeping. There were many occasions during the voyage when we were both on watches, when the quartermaster came to call him for the twelve till four night watch but was unable to rouse him.

I had the luck of keeping the more sociable four till eight watch and would be fast asleep when the QM came to call my cabin-mate shortly before midnight. The quartermaster would tap quietly on his pillow in an endeavour to awaken him without disturbing me. It seldom worked and several times ended up with my being called to assist. The two us would then physically drag my cabin mate from his bunk, lever him upright and still have difficulty in making him wake up!

It wasn't that he was lazy, far from it; it was more as though someone had pulled his fuses. Yes, an ability to waken easily and quickly *is* rather essential for a watchkeeper.

I recall the first time I experienced a reluctant riser. I was on the eight till twelve and had been tasked with calling the Second Officer at quarter before midnight to relieve the Third Officer.

When I knocked on the Second's door, I had received and irritable response, 'Yes. Alright. I'm awake!' whereupon he evidently turned over and went straight back to sleep.

I was sent to call him again at five minutes to, again at midnight and yet again at five past. By this time, the Third was getting rather angry and his ire was directed at me for failing to arouse his relief.

As I was going down to call the Second for the fifth time, the Quartermaster coming off watch evidently took pity on me.

'Come on, lad. I'll show you how it's done. A little trick,' he promised, leading the way to the Second's cabin.

Frank rattled on the door then leaned around the jamb and hissed at the sleeping officer. 'Second. Second. Quick—your chronometer's stopped!' A total lie, but the Second was taking no chances. He almost caught us up on the companionway. He came up those stairs with his feet moving so fast I swear he was stepping on his own hands.

Heaven help the Second Officer, the navigator, who forgot to wind the ship's chronometers!

## *'Rules of the Road'*

From the commencement of my apprenticeship, I had often been told that that it was essential to study the 'International Regulations for the Prevention of Collisions at Sea'—the Rules of the Road as they were more usually known. It was impressed upon me that while I should at least become very familiar with content and application of all thirty-two rules, it would be worthwhile to become 'word perfect' before the time I should undertake examination for my first Certificate of Competency, that of Second Officer.

Until the voyage when I joined *ss Martand,* my learning of The Rules had been somewhat desultory. Now, when the Chief Officer told me at the commencement of the voyage that when the ship was on ocean passages, the Captain required the Apprentices to learn and recite one rule each day, it came as something of a shock and was greeted with dismay. Some of the longer rules ran to several pages.

'You, Parks, as the senior, will go first and you are to attend the Captain's accommodation each evening as soon as you have showered and are in uniform ready for dinner. When you have recited your Rule, your mate will attend and do the same.'

That was task enough, but he continued 'And don't think of getting away with it. The Old Man is word perfect and if he is not satisfied with your effort you will have to repeat it again the next day *as well as* the one for that day.'

At first, I found it very difficult as I always struggled to learn poetry and Shakespeare when I was at school, but Captain Owen Pritchard was relentless. We recited our daily Rule each evening before dinner, then, around eight o' clock, we again attended his dayroom. This time we were also joined by the Fourth Officer, Tony Laidlaw, who was a promoted apprentice making his last voyage before attending college to study for his Second Mate's Certificate. The next hour or so, among other items of seamanship, Captain Pritchard taught us to recognise the different buoys, their shapes and colours, and to and understand their significance. He had gone to considerable trouble, having made a set of small models each about the size of a cotton reel and these were set out on a coffee table to show deep water, shoal patches and wrecks.

Although it was difficult learning the Rules at the outset, it soon became easier and the three of us recognised that Captain Pritchard was giving us a very good grounding in some of the topics in which we would later face The Examiner of Masters and Mates. He was a good teacher and we were grateful—especially so on the occasions when we had done well and were each rewarded with a can of cold beer! Brocklebanks were very strict over apprentices drinking and we felt very privileged to be treated in this way.

Another memory I have of the *Martand* is that Captain Pritchard seemed to have a birthday every few weeks—at least, that was his excuse when inviting people he met ashore to visit the ship.

On one occasion, while in Trincomalee, the Captain had been ashore for the evening and enjoying dinner at a local hotel. He met a troupe of Indian dancers accompanied by two South Indian film stars.

'Come on board for lunch tomorrow. We'll have a party. It's my birthday.' The following lunchtime, smartly attired in white tropical uniform, we apprentices attended the gangway to meet his guests and escort them to the boat deck where everything was ready for a party.

Captain Pritchard always entertained in style; teakwood decks well-scrubbed, trestle tables covered in white linen almost groaning with the weight of food, brightly coloured flags decorating the area which later would be illuminated by coloured lanterns. All the officers attended but in public, we apprentices were constrained to soft drinks.

'You know you lads are not allowed alcohol,' he said. 'And what the engineers don't know won't hurt them,' he said, winking as he did so. He was concerned that no-one should tell Head Office that he allowed us an occasional can of beer and only permitted it when in the privacy of his cabin.

Yes, I had a great deal to be grateful to Captain Owen Pritchard for. It later became very evident when it was my turn to meet The Examiner and I could unhesitatingly quote every one of the International Regulations for the Prevention of Collisions. Each time I started quoting from a Rule, he would accept that I understood, was well prepared, and usually move on to another question.

In 1964, just a few years after I enjoyed my time on the vessel, the *Martand* came to a sad end. Outward bound from Calcutta with a cargo of iron ore and with a complement of fifty, she grounded in the River Hooghly, flooded and was lost. Fortunately, *Martand* was aground for some time before foundering and all were able to leave safely.

SS Martand

SS Martand

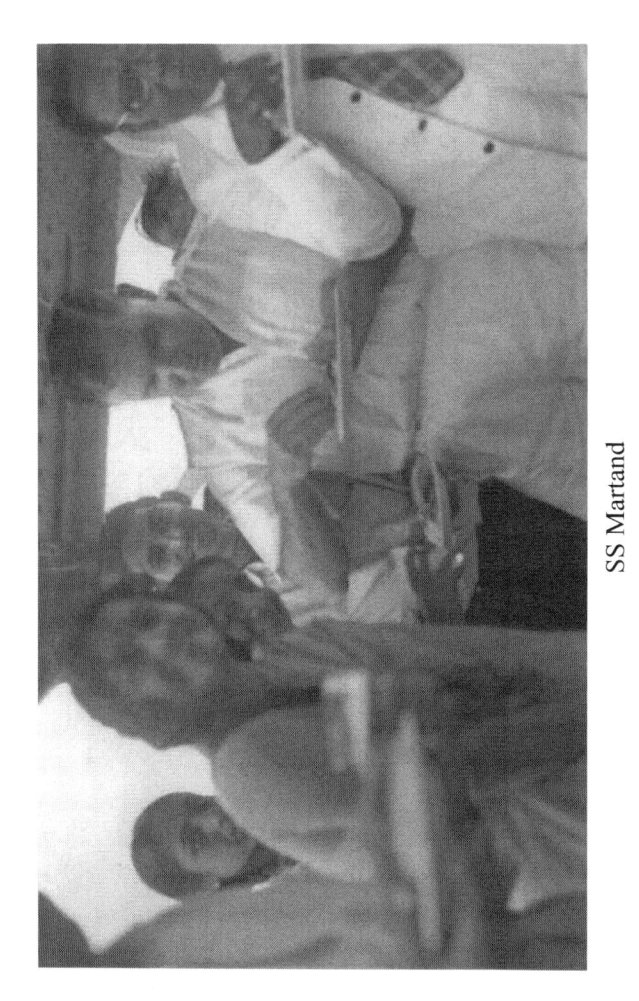

Captain Pritchard loved to party and enjoyed Indian food!

SS Martand in Trincomalee

One of Captain Pritchard's many 'birthday parties'! He had met two Indian film stars and a dance troupe in a hotel ashore. 'Come and have lunch on board. It's my birthday.'

The stern of the 8,000-ton British cargo ship s.s. Martand, awash in the Hooghly on Wednesday after the vessel had run aground on Monday at Achipurghat (Budge Budge), 17 miles downstream from Calcutta.—Statesman

## MARTAND BEYOND SALVAGE: MASTER ABANDONS SHIP

By a Staff Reporter

AFTER spending three nights of suspense on board the 8,000-ton British cargo ship, Martand, which ran aground on Monday near Achipurghat, about 17 miles from Calcutta, the Master of the vessel, Mr E. Watkins, the Chief Officer and the Chief Engineer left the sinking vessel on Wednesday morning, when it was finally declared beyond salvage.

Loss of the Martand

SS Mahout

SS Mahout

Returning to the ship, the lifeboat had been used as a 'jolly boat' taking ship's personnel for shore leave in Trincomalee.

Gus van Ludwig the chippie and I had been repairing wooden hatchboards.

## CHAPTER 22
# PROMOTION IN ALL BUT NAME

### *SS Matra*

I have already referred to the Brocklebank policy where apprentices in their final year were usually appointed as Fourth Officer. The reason for this was twofold. Firstly, it would ensure that at that stage of training, the apprentice would spend significant time watchkeeping and honing navigational skills. Secondly, it was a gesture by Brocklebanks to ensure that during the final year before completing his indenture and starting college studies, the apprentice's pay was significantly enhanced. It was generously altruistic by today's standards—my total pay for the third year only amounted to £186!

In February 1961, Brocklebanks appointed me to their vessel *ss Matra,* named after a place in Gujarat. I was just completing the third year of my four-year apprenticeship and had hoped that the appointment would be as Fourth Officer. I was bitterly disappointed when a promotion was not forthcoming—and worse, I thought, was that I was the only apprentice.

As it turned out, being the lone apprentice was very much to my advantage. Nearly all of the four months I was on *Matra* were spent with the Chief Officer, keeping the four-till-eight watch. As well as really learning how to handle a sextant, take and calculate celestial observations, I spent considerable time with my correspondence course and book learning.

Towards the end of that voyage, the Chief Officer, Mr Grayson, had sufficient confidence in my abilities that he often left me alone on the bridge, while he attended to other tasks. At these times, I became sole watchkeeping officer and to all intents was carrying out the duties of a Fourth Officer.

The Chief Officer's teaching on the bridge had been painstaking and comprehensive and late in the voyage he confided in me that both he and the Master, with access to my confidential reports and training records, had been very surprised that I had not been promoted to Fourth Officer. While this confidence was surely well meant, intending to be encouraging, it served mainly to make me feel somewhat bitter towards Brocklebanks.

Nevertheless, despite my disappointment, I look back on the time I spent on *Matra* with some very good memories.

## *Wives on board*

In those days, the early sixties, on cargo liners it was almost unheard of for wives to be permitted to sail. It was a privilege more usually associated with vessels tramping which were often away for up to two years. However, the winds of change were beginning to blow through the

Merchant Navy and there were three wives on *Matra:* the Captain's, the Chief Officer's and the Chief Engineer's.

We saw very little of the former and the rumour was that she had a full-time job keeping the Captain sober. The other two were pleasant and would always pass the time of day. In the tropics, they seemed to spend much of their time on deck chairs, sunbathing on the boat deck.

Audrey, the Chief Engineer's wife (I cannot remember his surname) was a keen card player and in the evenings, after dinner, was often invited by the quartermasters to join them in their messroom for a game of cribbage. It was Audrey who finally settled a small dispute that had been ongoing for some time. There was an idea that one of the QM's was gay. There was nothing overt, just a suspicion.

I should explain that some of the vessels carried Indian QM's—Sukunnis—while others were manned with six British Quartermasters. As the vessels then had no auto-pilots, their primary function was that of helmsmen. Whenever there were British QM's, as petty officers they enjoyed, if not actually the status of officers, certainly something close to it. They had their own alleyway of accommodation and usually had a special relationship with the ship's officers. Thus it was not unusual for an invitation to join them in their mess and on this occasion, the Chief Engineer's wife would be no exception.

On the evening in question, as she passed along the alleyway toward the mess at the far end, the Chief's wife walked past the QM's bathroom and showers. Not surprisingly in an environment which would normally be entirely male, people tended to be somewhat casual about closing doors and I suppose it was a perfectly natural reaction for Audrey to glance in as she passed and heard the noise of a shower.

'Well, as walked I past, I heard this shower running,' Audrey later told the Second Engineer. 'I couldn't help myself and glanced in,' she continued. 'Peter was in the shower and he hadn't pulled the curtain.' By this time, apparently, she could scarcely continue for laughing.

'When he saw me, he shrieked and crossed his arms over his chest!'

Now we knew—and the Second Engineer won a wager he had made with the Purser, which he took great delight in telling everyone.

## *Crossing the Line*

When *Matra* was outward bound, she called at Gan Island and thereby crossed some sixty miles into the southern hemisphere. Probably because there were wives on board, crossing the equator was treated with more than usual importance and a Crossing the Line ceremony was planned.

The ceremony has a traditional format that has, apparently, remained little changed for over two centuries. It is fun and a ceremony of initiation where crew who have not previously crossed into the other hemisphere, irrespective of rank or position, are summoned before Neptune's Court and after due process become 'shellbacks'.

On *Matra*, the Third Officer, Derek Hammond, was dressed as Neptune and, amid a fanfare blown through brass fire-hose nozzles, arrived on the foredeck carrying his trident and with seaweed in his beard, having supposedly ascended through the hawse pipe. He was accompanied by Davy Jones and Queen Amphitrite, two of our Quartermasters. Other crew, suitably dressed for their parts, comprised the rest of Neptune's Court: the barber, the doctor and the two bears. The latter preceded Neptune and his entourage along the foredeck, continuing to blow noisily through the fire nozzles, announcing the Court's arrival.

Several crewmembers who had not been across the line previously were summoned. It was all very relaxed. I recall there was a mixture of officers and Indian ratings and, of course, two wives.

The pantomime commenced as all initiates were given a 'medical' followed by some foul concoction of medicine. On this occasion, I think it may have been a mixture of rhubarb and prune juices. The barber, wearing an apron well stained with fake blood, played his part as all the initiates were lathered with shaving foam made from flour and water before being 'shaved' with a huge cardboard razor. I was already a 'shellback' (from my first voyage, on *Manipur)* and was tasked with assisting the barber.

The ceremony ended with each initiate being dunked into the plunging pool from a chair secured to one side above the pool.

Throughout, there was much hilarity and everyone entered into the spirit of the ceremony. The biggest laugh, though, came at the end—much to the good-natured embarrassment of the Chief Officer's wife. When she was unceremoniously dumped into the swimming pool, she was wearing a white sunsuit. It was never intended for use in water and realising this too late she was unable to clamber out without revealing all. Amid much laughter, eventually a large towel was thrown and she exited the pool, her modesty intact.

The afternoon ended when certificates made up by the Purser, were presented to the new Shellbacks.

*Be it known . . . given this day under my seal, without let or hindrance, be permitted freedom of my oceans . . .*

## *Final Voyage as Apprentice*

When I signed off the *Matra* I had completed almost half of my fourth and final year and when, after little more than two week's leave, I was appointed to *ss Macharda* I had really expected to gain my promotion. After all, I had been carrying out all the Fourth Officer's tasks while I was on *Matra*.

Once again, I was disappointed and when I learned that some fourth-year apprentices, who would have been my junior, were sailing on other vessels as Fourth Officers, I felt very bitter towards Brocklebanks. What, I wondered, had I done? Generally, I had worked reasonably diligently at my correspondence course, apart from one trip when I had joined the ship without the necessary books, and as far as I had been led to believe, confidential reports submitted by the Masters had all been of an acceptable standard.

I could only remember once having been in serious trouble—but I'll come to that in due course.

So, when I joined *Macharda* I was not in the best frame of mind. Once again, I was the only apprentice so I decided to keep my head down and get on with my studies. It didn't help that the Chief Officer kept me on day work, carrying out mundane tasks on deck and I felt rather as though I was being used solely as additional labour.

I had always been interested in calligraphy and when the Chief found this out, I was tasked with painting many of the ship's notices: *No Smoking, No Admittance, Officers Only* and the like. I felt I was being taken advantage of and was being treated like an underpaid sign writer. I resented it. I was fed up with *Macharda* and everyone on her.

Apart from my own circumstances, it was not a happy ship and the problem evidently stemmed from the very top.

The captain was the senior master in Brocklebanks and was making his last voyage before retirement. He kept very much to himself, possibly with a gin bottle for company. He was seldom seen except when in the dining mess and was disliked by all his senior officers. They had no respect for him. For the remainder of the ship's company, as he never spoke to them, they were little concerned either way. In short, morale was extremely poor.

We were returning directly to the United Kingdom (thank goodness!), omitting to cross the Atlantic and visit America, and were mid-Arabian Sea, bound for Aden, when I was summoned to the Captain's accommodation. What, I wondered had I done now, fully expecting to be in some sort of trouble. That was the level of morale on *Macharda*.

With some trepidation, I knocked on the dayroom door.

'Come!' Nervously, I entered.

'I heard from Captain Scurr that you were keeping the four-till-eight when you were on his ship.' It wasn't a question but I answered anyway.

'Yes, sir. Mr Grayson kept me on watch with him and later I was left alone on the bridge for much of the time.'

'Right, lad. You're on full watches, starting at four tomorrow morning. You'll be on your own but if you have a problem, I'll be around. Just call me.' I probably stood with my mouth open I was so surprised.

'Right,' he continued, 'That's all,' and I was dismissed.

I had been on his vessel for about three months and it was the first time the Captain had spoken to me.

The following morning I was on the bridge in good time to relieve the Second Officer at 0400 hours. I heard the Old Man about in his office backing onto the chartroom and felt reassured that he was there to help me, should I need it. He never attended on the bridge and after the first two or three mornings, I heard him no more. I suppose he never bothered to get up. I ceased reporting to the Chief Officer for a work list each day and just carried out the duties of a Fourth Officer, navigating the vessel and taking star sights when appropriate.

Later, I learned from 'galley radio' (ship's gossip) that my new situation had been brought about by the Captain and the Chief Officer falling out. Word had gone around that with morale on board being so low, concerned for his staff, the Chief Engineer had had a discussion with the Captain in an endeavour to improve the situation. Apparently, their discussion became heated and acrimonious when the Chief told the Captain that it was a good job he was retiring as his officers would refuse to sail with him again.

Perhaps somewhat foolishly, the Captain was stung into asking each officer if, were this not his last voyage, would he be prepared to sail with him again. Not surprisingly, knowing that the question would not arise and being anxious to ensure a good end-of-voyage report, all said they would.

All except one, that is.

The Chief Officer, being many years in the rank, was expecting promotion on his next voyage and was senior enough not to care what the Old Man thought of him.

'Sail on another voyage? I wouldn't sail across a bloody dock with you!' was his alleged response

'Mister, until you apologise for that you will not set foot on my bridge again.'

An apology was never forthcoming. The Captain's mood became blacker than ever. The Chief Officer never came on the bridge again and morale on board hit an all-time low. I was probably the only person who gained anything from the entire unfortunate incident and I have to admit that I actually felt quite sorry for the Old Man. Whatever his shortcomings, what a sad way, I mused, to retire from his final command and a lifetime spent at sea.

Also, there was an incident while I was on watch after which he gave me some advice which I have never forgotten and years later, when in senior rank myself, have often repeated.

*Macharda* had called at Aden for bunkers and was bound for one of the Red Sea ports, Port Sudan if I recall correctly. The incident occurred during my afternoon watch when I was navigating the vessel in deep water between the coast and some off-lying reefs. Radar propagation was very poor and I was using a sextant to measure vertical angles and calculate distances off mountain peaks. In short, they were not accurate position fixes and I was continually crosschecking when to my dismay I saw, some distance ahead of the ship, what appeared to be breaking reef water. It didn't agree with where I thought the vessel to be and I was more than a little puzzled, thinking that maybe our magnetic compass was in serious error.

Alarmed, I went through into the chartroom and called the Old Man but he was not in his accommodation and seemingly nowhere to be found. Returning to the wheelhouse, I telephoned the Chief Officer's cabin but there was no response there either.

By now, I was becoming really worried, watching the slowly approaching white water, feeling quite sick. With no assistance forthcoming, I felt I had to take some action and telephoned the engine room to advise them I would be putting the telegraph to 'stop'. I think the Second Engineer thought I was joking. It is something only done in an emergency on a vessel powered by steam turbines. To protect the turbines, power is normally reduced only over a much-extended period as the rotor blade clearances are increased and some of the heat is dissipated from the turbines.

It is to the Second's credit that when I actually swung the telegraph he responded and immediately started to take the power off the turbines. With all the excess superheated steam, the safety valves in the funnel started to lift, fluttering with a noise like machinegun fire.

The noise of the safety valves brought the Captain to the bridge very quickly and he was closely followed by the Chief Officer but, from the stairs, as soon as the Chief saw the Captain he immediately turned away.

Captain Lyle looked far from pleased. I pointed ahead and started to explain my action.

'Sir, it looks like reef water. You weren't here and I didn't know what else to do,' I told him, nervously.

He took the telescope from its bracket under the windows, extended the tubes, braced himself with one arm on the doorframe, steadied the telescope over his arm and viewed ahead.

He took a good look for a moment or two then, replacing the telescope, walked to the telegraph and rang 'full ahead'.

'But Sir . . .,' I started to ask but was interrupted.

'You'll be alright. It's not a reef, then he walked off the bridge, leaving me.

Not long afterwards, we were approaching the white water and I was standing with my heart in my mouth not entirely convinced that there was no reef but the Old Man had been correct. It was just a patch of foam and we passed quickly through it.

My action was subsequently the butt of a great deal of leg pulling and chiding by the engineers, much of it in the messroom with comments like 'Panicky-Parks.' It became rather wearing but I determined to take no notice, thinking that if I responded—rose to the bait—it would likely make the situation worse.

Several days after the event, I was on watch in the afternoon and we were in the Gulf of Suez. The Captain came through the chartroom and into the wheelhouse. It as so unusual to see him that I wondered what was coming.

'When you started to stop the ship the other day, Parks, you realise that you could have caused considerable damage to the turbines?'

'Yessir, but . . .' I was interrupted.

'I have heard what has been going on in the mess and I suppose you think I'm going to give you a bollocking,'

'Well . . .' I was interrupted again.

'Think for a moment. Just suppose you had been correct. Suppose it was a reef, that you had done nothing and run the ship over it. Imagine the trouble would have been in then!'

I was thinking about this when he continued, giving advice I have never forgotten.

'The point is, lad, if you're going to get in trouble make sure you are in trouble for *doing* something. It is far better than being in trouble for doing *nothing*.'

After that, whenever the engineers started chiding me, it was much easier to smile and ignore them and they soon tired of trying to bait me.

My last voyage as an apprentice was not a particularly happy one. Morale on the *Macharda* remained low and I had felt quite isolated. Nevertheless, there had still been valuable lessons to learn and experience to gain.

One of them I didn't fully appreciate until I was somewhat older, more mature. That is, however low opinion we may have of someone and whatever their faults, if one is unable to find something good or something to admire in the person, then the fault is more likely with the observer.

Despite what others on board thought of their Captain, it was very sound advice that he had given me.

SS Matra

SS Matra

Relaxing on the boat deck after a 'swim' in the ship's plunging pool

SS Macharda

## CHAPTER 23
# MOVING ON

*End Days*

In November 1961, the *Macharda* arrived back in the United Kingdom and docked at the Royal Docks in London where I signed off the ship's Articles to go on leave. At that time, my next step was a little uncertain and would depend upon the Examiner of Masters and Mates.

During the latter part of the voyage, the Third Officer, who had some sympathy with my predicament, had been quizzing me about the actual time I had spent signed on ships' Articles since commencing my apprenticeship. We sat down and started totting up the months and days at the end of which the Third concluded that it could well be that when I signed off *Macharda*, I would have sufficient time to apply to commence studying at college and eventually sit the examination for a Second Mate's Certificate of Competence. It would all depend on the Examiner's assessment of my sea-time.

Consequently, a week or so before leaving the vessel I had approached Captain Lyle and told him what I thought to be the situation concerning my period of service. He evidently relayed this on to the office in Liverpool by radio telegram and by the time I arrived home, there was a letter waiting for me officially detailing my time on each of the vessels.

The letter was duly submitted to The Examiner who soon confirmed that yes, I was indeed eligible. For all practical purposes, my apprenticeship was now finished.

When I had arrived home, there was also another letter from Liverpool waiting for me. I read it with very mixed emotions.

When the *Macharda* had called at Colombo on the homeward voyage, the Captain had received mail from the Merchant Navy Training Board. It contained a specially sealed package within which were my third year examination papers. Suitable arrangements were made for me to undertake the examinations while on passage to Aden.

This second letter was from Captain Cadwallader, the gentleman who had interviewed me in Cunard Building nearly six years earlier. The letter was one of congratulations for 'achieving a most praiseworthy result'. I had evidently done better in the examination than had been expected.

I felt very gratified at his comments—and Dad, too, was generous in his praise, which meant far more to me.

Captain Cadwallader's letter concluded that the writer had given instructions any further services I performed would be in the rank of Fourth Officer. I felt very bitter about that because I thought it was long overdue and I had been doing the job anyway without being properly remunerated.

The sweetener was that, although the letter concluded stating the promotion would be effective until I was finally released to commence studying, they had little choice but to release me study immediately. Brocklebanks, however, would be obliged to continue paying me as Fourth Officer at least until the Indenture was completed on February 18$^{th}$, 1962. In fact, it was beyond that date as they were also obligated under the Merchant Navy Training Board agreements to pay me for 12 week's study leave.

The letter did nothing to quell my feeling of resentment at the way in which I had been treated during the final year of my training.

## *Arranging College*

Soon after I had arrived home, I visited the Marine Department of Brunel Technical College on Ashley Down in Bristol. My objective was to enrol on the next course to study for Second Mate. When I enquired what books and materials I would need for the course, I was directed to one of the lecture rooms. After some wandering, I arrived outside the door marked 'Second Mates' just as the lecturer was leaving.

I apologised for detaining him and asked for help. I explained that I hoped to enrol on the next course and would be grateful if he could advise what textbooks I should need.

'Have you been doing a correspondence course during your apprenticeship?' he asked in a heavy Welsh accent.

'Yes,' I replied.

'What books do you have then already?' was the response. I told him, adding that I had also ordered a number of books from our local library, including one which had been particularly recommended, 'Principles for Second Mates, by someone called T G Jones,' I added.

'Yes, I've heard of it. I expect you'll find it quite useful.'

Later, when I actually attended my first lecture, I met the same lecturer once more. He evidently remembered me and formally introduced himself.

'I'm Captain T G Jones,' he said with a twinkle, 'Did you get that book in the end?'

## *Reunions*

During the last four years, I had spent so little time at home that I had more or less lost contact with most of my school friends and, to be honest, what limited contact I had had with some of them left me feeling that we no longer had much in common. Although I would certainly not have said so, lest it sounded conceited, they had remained at home while I had been travelling the world. I had sailed up the Mississippi River when it was snowing hard; I had been in Port Said when there was a frost; experienced monsoon storms and water spouts, seen flying fish in the Arabian Sea, watched pelicans skim close above the water in the Mexican Gulf, swum in tropical waters from beaches shaded by palm trees and seen whales and dolphins at play.

My horizons were wider and I thought I should have little left in common with many old friends.

One old friendship was, though, renewed and strengthened. When only six or seven years of age, while attending St John's primary school Michael Le Marche and I were firm friends but we later lost contact when he went on to a different Middle School. Mike's mother Joan and his stepfather Eric, were friends of my parents and I learned that Mike had also gone to sea in the Merchant Navy and trained as a Radio Officer.

Mike, too, was on leave at this time and was very friendly with my parent's next-door neighbour's daughter. In fact, Mike went on to marry Sandra and they had a very tragic life. Mike lost his life when a vessel he was sailing on exploded and went down before even an SOS could be transmitted, leaving Sandra to raise their handicapped son.

Meanwhile, I *had* kept in touch with my old pal Malcolm Davies who had gone on to study at Oxford University. Although we had been friends from being small boys, Malcolm was slightly younger than I and when at the Grammar School, was in the year below.

On January 6th, 1962, Malcolm and my brother Steve, who was by then also an Old Pupil, persuaded me to attend a grammar school reunion dance and party at the school that evening.

I really had not wanted to go but attended solely because I had nothing better to do. If there were any old classmates there I thought it unlikely that we should have any common interests and that it would probably be a boring evening.

The reunion turned out to be a pleasant surprise. We had fun and when the interval arrived, as the school could offer only soft drinks, several of us even adjourned to a nearby pub. The Vine Tree was a hostelry that had been no stranger to students from Frome Grammar School over the years!

## *Change a foot*

My course of studies commenced in January when I started attending in Bristol, travelling daily by train from Warminster.

Over the next few months, the studying went well and I soon appreciated what a tremendous advantage it was, having learned all the Rules parrot fashion when on the *Martand* with Captain Pritchard. Few, if any, of the other students initially had much knowledge of the Regulations for the Prevention of Collisions and the International Buoyage System too, caused some head scratching. This freed up some of my lectures and I was able to use the time consolidating other subjects.

College was also a melting pot for information because there were former apprentices studying for the Second Mate's Certificates who had been indentured to a number of different shipping companies. I found it interesting to hear of adventures in South and Central America and even Africa had its attractions. All of this served to harden my resolve to change employer after completing my studies.

Despite that, while I was attending college it became very evident that the training I had received from Brocks was definitely better than that given by many companies, I still felt resentment over my final year and was actively looking for a change. Furthermore, although I had enjoyed visiting the ports on Brocklebank's routes, there were still so many other places and things to see.

During the period, Mike Le Marche came on leave a couple of times and on several occasions, we went out for a few beers to 'shoot the breeze' and compare experiences. His employment as a radio officer was with Marconi who contracted their services to most of the British shipping companies. At the time, Mike was assigned to work with Fyffes Line and was undertaking four-week voyages either to the Caribbean and back or to West Africa.

Both were areas I had never visited and the notion of serving on sleek, fast vessels carrying passengers and bringing bananas back to the United Kingdom and near Continental ports sounded attractive.

I made up my mind and wrote to Fyffes, explaining that I was studying and hoped to be the holder of a Second Mate's Certificate of Competency by the summer of that year. I was not too optimistic as Mike had told me that because of their short voyages, positions with Elders and Fyffes were much sought after.

Nevertheless, they sent me application papers and somewhat to my surprise, I was soon invited to attend for an interview at their head office adjacent to the Dorchester Hotel in London's West End.

I remember the occasion rather well, as it was a somewhat unusual interview carried out solely by no lesser person than the Managing Director. Also, it was not so much an interview as an explanation of Fyffes, their ships and their history. I was asked very few question and mostly sat listening to my interviewer. What is this all about, I was beginning to wonder, when Captain Foster concluded the interview.

He wished me success in my studies then made a statement, effectively offering me employment, which was so surprising I remember it well:

'At this time, Parks, Fyffes Line operate eighteen ships. You will be our thirty-third Third Officer—but you will be the first one to be employed who has not already obtained a Master Mariner's Certificate.'

I was not naïve enough to think this was recognition of my merits; clearly, the winds of change were beginning to blow through Fyffes as elsewhere in the Merchant Navy.

With my future employment secured, subject to examination success, I wrote to Thos and Jno Brocklebank, thanked them for all my training but advised that I should not be returning after my studies, as I wished to see other parts of the world.

By reply, I received a telegram from Captain Cadwallader asking me to telephone him, urgently, transferring charges, and in the evening if necessary.

Wondering at the urgency, I did so and was complimented once again on my third year examination results. He asked me to reconsider, even offered me a position on one of the vessels belonging to a company that Brocklebanks had recently acquired who served West Africa, Guinea Gulf Lines.

During our telephone conversation, I also politely aired my grievance at not having been promoted in my turn in accordance with the company's usual policy. Captain Cad sidestepped this and requested that I travel up to Liverpool and see him.

'There's not a lot of point, Sir,' I told him. 'I have really made up my mind—and I should like to have shorter voyages, too.'

'Well, come and see us anyway. You haven't set foot in the office for some time and we like to see our apprentices regularly. I'll have a rail warrant sent to you.'

I agreed, thinking that the notion of 'seeing our apprentices regularly' was somewhat empty; as to 'some time', I hadn't set foot in the office since my interview when I was fourteen years old.

In due course, I went back to visit Cunard Building and was once again interviewed by Captain Charles Cadwallader. I was twenty years of age.

It was very relaxed; he tried to persuade me to change my mind and openly perused all the confidential reports the ships' Master had written about me which were on his desk. I had never seen them nor until then, had I been made aware of their content.

'Really, Parks, you have had excellent reports throughout. One, here though, that we never understood and when we asked him, Captain Pembridge was quite vague.'

Remembering an incident when I was on the *Mahout*, I began to feel a tad uneasy.

'He has written that you should "take a more aggressive attitude towards life". Seemed strange.' Then continued, using the diminutive we had all used for a very popular Master, 'Pem refused to enlarge on the comment. Strange,' he mused.

When Captain Cadwallader realised that I really was not going to change my mind, the interview concluded with pleasantries. I thanked him again for my training and he wished me well in my career.

'Being a ship's master is not a bad job, you know. Good luck,' he said, as we shook hands on parting.

On the train travelling south, I wondered at the confidential reports he had been quoting. Captain Pembridge's remark puzzled me too.

While I was on the *Mahout*, I had been the constant butt of snide remarks from one of the junior engineers. He was course, rough and rude and had served an apprenticeship in a Birkenhead shipyard.

Frequent profane remarks about my accent and being 'lah-de-dah' when we were seated at table I could ignore without too much difficulty although it was wearying. It eventually culminated when his remarks became personal and about my family.

Now, I don't recall exactly what he said, but I was incensed and invited him to stand up and repeat the remark. I am sure he really didn't understand the reason for my request but somewhat to my surprise he did so, whereupon I leaned quickly over the table and punched him. Off balance, he fell back and grabbed at the table to stop himself. He succeeded only in grasping the tablecloth—which, with most of the contents of the table, followed him as he tipped over the chair and landed on his back.

I politely apologised to the Second Officer at the head of our table, then turned and apologised to Captain Pembridge before walking from a silent dining room.

Pem stopped my shore leave for four weeks. Why he thought I should take a more aggressive attitude towards life was puzzling—unless he thought I ought not have waited so long before taking action! He was surely aware of the baiting that had been going on.

## *Milestone*

Earlier, I recounted how I was virtually cajoled into attending the Old Pupils' re-union party at Frome Grammar School; how a group of us adjourned to the Vine Tree pub. It turned out to be a momentous evening as well as an enjoyable one.

On leaving the Vine Tree, we were making our way back to the school and a number of us were crammed into a car driven by Peter Brightman, one of the students who had been in Malcolm's year. There were four of my year crammed into the back and one, Josie Wingrove, was sitting on my lap. Squashed into the middle was another former classmate, Ruth Barrington.

On the journey back to school, I put my arm around Ruth and kissed her.

My apprenticeship may have finished, but that was the beginning of a completely new part of my life!

A sequel to this book?

\* \* \*

THOS. & JNO. BROCKLEBANK LTD.

CUNARD BUILDING
LIVERPOOL 3

MARINE OC/BEL

9th November, 1961.

G.A. Parks, Esq.,
Apprentice,
s.s. "Macharda",
c/o Messrs. Alexr. Howden & Co. Ltd.,
107/112 Leadenhall Street, LONDON, E.C.3.

Dear Sir,

We have received from the Merchant Navy Training Board your 3rd Year examination papers, and we note with great pleasure that your average marks for this examination are 83.8%. We consider this a most praiseworthy result and we offer you our congratulations.

The individual results work out as follows:-

| Seamanship | 94% |
| Mathematics | 93% |
| Navigation | 91% |
| General Science | 63% |
| Ship Construction | 78% |

It is always a great pleasure to see results such as these, and we hope that when you take your 2nd Mate's examination, your results there will be of the same high standard. About two years ago, one of our Apprentices passed his 2nd Mate's examination with the highest marks in that grade for the year.

The writer has given instructions that any further services you perform will be in the rank of 4th Officer, until you are finally released to commence studying for your Certificate.

Yours faithfully,
THOS. & JNO. BROCKLEBANK LTD.

*C. Cadwallader*

Marine Superintendent.

Letter of promotion

THOS. & JNO. BROCKLEBANK LTD.

Steamers Services
U.K. and Europe to and from India, Pakistan and Ceylon
India, Pakistan and Ceylon to U.S.A.
India, Pakistan and Ceylon to U.S.A. (Gulf)
U.S.A. to U.K.

TELEGRAMS "BROCKLEBANK, LIVERPOOL 3"
TELEPHONE: CENTRAL 9232

CUNARD BUILDING
P.O. Box No. 26

LIVERPOOL 3

In Reply Please Quote Our Ref
CREW WAGES
GH/EP

15th November 1961

TO WHOM IT MAY CONCERN

This is to certify that Graham Andrew Parks joined our service 19.2.58 as an Indentured Seagoing Apprentice on a 4 year Agreement since when he has completed the following voyages:-

| Ship | From | | To | M | D |
|---|---|---|---|---|---|
| S.S."MANIPUR" | 21.2.58 | to | 27.10.58 | 8. | 7 |
| S.S."MAKRANA" | 13.11.58 | " | 19. 3. 59 | 4. | 7 |
| - " - | 17.4.59 | " | 23. 7. 59 | 3. | 7 |
| S.S."MAHANADI" | 12.8.59 | " | 4. 3. 60. | 6. | 22 |
| S.S."MARTAND" | 18.3.60 | " | 24. 8. 60 | 5. | 7 |
| S.S."MAHOUT" | 15.9.60 | " | 1. 2. 61. | 4. | 18 |
| S.S."MATRA" | 17.2.61 | " | 20. 6. 61. | 4. | 4. |
| S.S."MACHARDA" | 6.7.61. | " | 17.11. 61. | 4. | 12 |
| | | | Total Sea Service = | 40. | 24 |

During the whole of the above period Mr.Parks conducted himself to our complete satisfaction, being at all times strictly and attentive to his duties.

THOS. & JNO. BROCKLEBANK LTD.

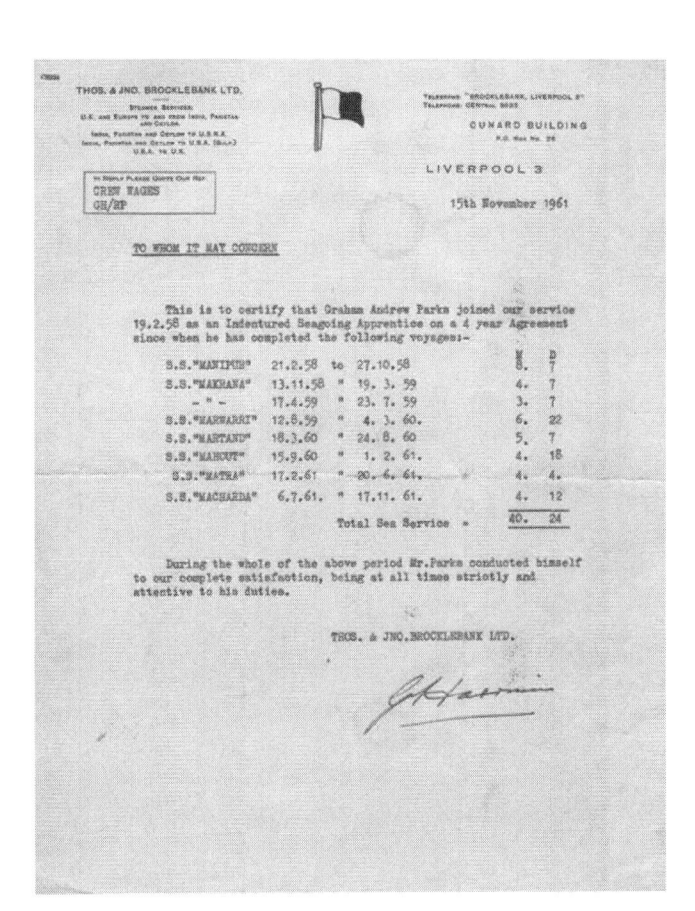

Sea time completed!

Ruth, Frome Grammar School 1957

Ruth, 1962

Andy, 1962